Aging *and the* Meaning of Time

A Multidisciplinary Exploration

Aging *and the* Meaning of Time

A Multidisciplinary Exploration

Susan H. McFadden, PhD

Robert C. Atchley, PhD

Editors

Springer Publishing Company, Inc.
11 West 42nd Street
New York, NY 10036

Acquisitions Editor: Helvi Gold
Production Editor: J. Hurkin-Torres
Cover design by Mimi Flow

06 07 08 09 / 5 4 3 2 1

New ISBN 0-8261-0265-4 © 2006 by Springer Publishing Company, Inc.

Library of Congress Cataloging-in-Publication Data

Aging and the meaning of time : a multidisciplinary exploration / Susan H. McFadden and
    Robert C. Atchley, editors.
                    p.   cm.
        Includes bibliographical references and index.
        ISBN 0-8261-1404-0
        1. Aged.   2. Aging.   3. Time—Social aspects.   4. Time—Psychological aspects.
I. McFadden, Susan H.   II. Atchley, Robert C.
HQ1061.A42443 2001
304.23—dc21   00-52656
                                                                                      CIP

Printed in the United States of America by Bang Printing.

Contents

Contributors

W. ANDREW ACHENBAUM is Dean of the College of Humanities, Fine Arts, and Communication at the University of Houston. He spent much of his career at the University of Michigan where he became widely known for working at the intersection of history and gerontology. He has reconstructed the social and cultural histories of elderly persons in the U.S., and he has studied the evolution of old-age policymaking in this country. His most recent work is on wisdom.

ANNE DAVIS BASTING is a playwright and scholar whose extensive writing about performance and aging includes *The Stages of Age: Performing Age in Contemporary American Culture*. She is currently the director of the Time Slips project and is writing a book about her experiences with the creative storytelling workshops with people with dementia.

JAMES E. BIRREN is Associate Director of the UCLA Center on Aging, Adjunct Professor of Medicine/Gerontology, UCLA, and Professor Emeritus of Gerontology and Psychology at the University of Southern California. He was the founding Executive Director and Dean of the Ethel Percy Andrus Gerontology Center at USC. He is series editor of the *Handbooks on Aging* and has over 250 publications in academic journals and books.

LAURA L. CARSTENSEN is Professor and Vice Chair of the Department of Psychology at Stanford University. She also serves as the Barbara D. Finberg Director of Stanford's Institute for Research on Women and Gender. Her specialties include socioemotional selectivity theory, emotional development through the life-span, the influence of social behavior and emotional well-being on health in later life, psychopathology among the elderly, and gender differences in old age.

HELENE H. FUNG is Assistant Professor of Psychology at the University of Alberta. She received the 1999 Behavioral and Social Sciences Student Research Award (predissertation) from the Gerontological Society of America and the 1998 Margaret Clark Research Award from the Association of Anthropology and Gerontology.

ARMIN GRAMS is Professor Emeritus of Human Development at the University of Vermont where he also served as Codirector, Center for the Study of Aging. He was President of the Association for Gerontology in Higher Education (AGHE). His chapter in this book was developed from a speech given when he received the Clark Tibbitts Award from AGHE, which recognizes outstanding contributions to the advancement of gerontology as a field of study in higher education.

MARITA GRUDZEN is Assistant Director of the Stanford Geriatric Education Center and a Lecturer and Academic Officer of the Division of Family and Community Medicine, Stanford University School of Medicine. She is also an adjunct faculty member of the Pacific Lutheran School of Theology. She is past chair of the Institute of Spirituality and Aging, Berkeley, CA.

JON HENDRICKS is Dean, University Honors College and Professor of Sociology, Oregon State University. He is past-president of the Association for Gerontology in Higher Education. He also has served as chair of both the Sociology of Aging & the Life Course section, and the Behavioral and Social Sciences section of the Gerontological Society of America. He is editor of the *Society and Aging* Series and has published extensively in gerontology.

QUINN KENNEDY is a graduate student in Psychology at Stanford University. Her research interests include aging and emotion regulation and the relationship between age, emotion, and autobiographical memory.

MELVIN A. KIMBLE is Professor Emeritus of Pastoral Care at Luther Seminary where he established the concentration in Ministry with the Aging and the Center for Aging, Religion, and Spirituality. An ordained Lutheran pastor in the Evangelical Lutheran Church in America, his ministry has included mental hospital chaplaincy as well as serving as pastor of the American Protestant Church in Bonn, Germany. He studied with Dr. Viktor Frankl at the University of Vienna and the Poliklinik Hospital.

JAMES P. OBERLE is Vice President of St. Patrick's Seminary, Menlo Park, CA. He received his Ph.D. from the University of Maryland and his Licentiate in Sacred Theology from the Pontifical Institute of Spirituality, Rome, Italy. He serves on the Governing Council of the Forum on Religion, Spirituality, and Aging, of the American Society on Aging.

ELIZABETH OATES SCHUSTER is Associate Professor of Gerontology and is director of the Gerontology Program at Eastern Michigan University. She is the cofounder of two award-winning community programs: The Traveling Young at Art Program (intergenerational) and Elderwise: An Institute for Learning and Retirement (lifelong learning).

PAUL R. SPONHEIM is Professor Emeritus of Systematic Theology at Luther Seminary, St. Paul, MN. Throughout his teaching and writing career, he has been concerned with the relationship of theology to other disciplines, including philosophy and the sciences. His major publication in Whiteheadian studies is *Faith and Process.*

JANE M. THIBAULT is Associate Professor of Family and Community Medicine at the University of Louisville School of Medicine where her area of expertise is Clinical Gerontology. She is author of *A Deepening Love Affair: The Gift of God in Later Life.* She has patented a restraint-free chair for frail elderly and is president of Eld-Arondak, Inc., the company that manufactures them.

L. EUGENE THOMAS was professor Emeritus of Human Development and Family Relations at the University of Connecticut. He edited *Research on Adulthood and Aging: The Human Science Approach* and with Susan Eisenhandler, he edited *Aging and the Religious Dimension* and *Religion, Belief and Spirituality in Late Life.*

CARTER CATLETT WILLIAMS is a licensed social worker and is Primary Consultant to the research project in Rochester, NY, entitled "Systematically Changing the Culture of Nursing Homes."

Foreword

Aging and the Meaning of Time is a book that provides an unusual window on contemporary culture, and the view is challenging to the reader. The scholars who have written the chapters of this book have many different vantage points from which to make wise comments about time and life.

We have produced a society that is marvelously efficient. Machines, computers, robots, and e-mail have made many things easier, yet a paradox emerges out of this marvelous efficiency. We are saving almost immeasurable amounts of time, yet the more we save, the more we feel the need for more time. We are breathless. People complain about the lack of time, and daily conversations revolve about the pressures of time to get work done, meet family needs, exercise, and relax with friends. It seems as though the twenty-first century is demanding more of us, and our minds have clocks with guilt-provoking hands pointing at us to remind us of our overflowing agendas.

The pressures of a high-tech society seem to create a bottom-line principle that we must continually seek to get more out of less time. This book suggests to me that we should take guilt-free breaks to reflect on who we are and the meaning of our time-stressed lives. It also arouses in me an interest in the lives of our ancestors. Did they experience time pressures in their lives in past centuries? Perhaps like them, we need a Sabbath on which to reflect on the meaning of time and the meaning of what we do. But would we even know what to do with a Sabbath?

This book explores many aspects of our growing up and growing old surrounded by clocks that distract us from considering the meaning of what we do with the time we have. As we read the chapters, our thoughts move from the guilty immediate to considering the philosophical and spiritual aspects of growing up and growing old. The chapters have much to say about experiencing time and spirituality. The reader is encouraged to explore the question of the relationship between time and spirituality as part of the basic quest of life.

An important perspective is provided by Mel Kimble (see chapter 8), who defines the spiritual dimension as the energy within that strives for meaning and purpose. This gives rise to the thought that our contemporary restlessness comes from wanting to consider the meaning of what we do in life. While we are doing more each day with the aid of electronic hardware and expanding software, there may be a building pressure to relate to something transcendent.

The fact that we are mortal may be masked in daily life by our full agendas until something halts the guilt-provoking hands of our clocks. An illness may do it, the death of a loved one or friend, or the collapse of a major enterprise. Such events can stop our clocks and turn our attention inward to the meaning of our doing, our existence.

Kimble tells us that "As I age, I have become more fully aware of a centripetal spiritual energy that centers and grounds my life and prevails over the centrifugal diverse forces that are ever present, working to spin out and scatter the fragments of my life."

As we mature we seem to look more to the meaning of what we do rather than just the completing of what we are doing. The chapters of this book and Mel Kimble's view encourage us to address the mysteries of life that are "at once overwhelming and fascinating." The chapters of this book encourage us to be both quiet and open to becoming more aware of what goes on in the time of our lives and its meaning. Our thoughts move from a guilty, immediate moment of presumed underproductive time to a greater sense of the meaning of what we do. We are led toward considering the philosophical and spiritual aspects of growing up, growing old, and perhaps growing wise.

James E. Birren

Preface

One of the strengths and delights of gerontology is its broadly interdisciplinary approach to aging persons and the study of later life. No one discipline is adequate to describe or explain the myriad of complex, interacting biological, psychological, social, and existential/spiritual experiences of human lives unfolding in time. All gerontologists must take time seriously, and yet this difficult construct is rarely addressed by those who would understand age and aging.

In this book, authors representing many diverse disciplines in gerontology act as guides in the exploration of the realms of time in later life and its meanings. They consider not only how the study of aging gives new meanings to time, but they also examine how the study of time can give new meanings to aging.

Throughout, like a motif in a musical piece, a theme weaves in and out of these chapters. In some, it is the focal point around which the ideas are organized, but in others, it subtly murmurs just beneath the surface. This theme concerns the religious and spiritual questions raised when human beings consider the temporal boundaries of life and consciousness.

Though long ignored in gerontology, research and scholarship on topics such as the effects of religion on well-being and the possibilities for spiritual growth in later life proliferated in the 1990s. We believe that this book on aging and time represents a new direction in the study of religion, spirituality, and aging. It witnesses to the ways that the encounter with temporality shifts our gaze toward the horizon of mystery—a horizon religious faiths have historically sought to portray in stories, symbols, and actions. It is a horizon approached through prayer, meditation, contemplation, and other spiritual disciplines. The question raised by some of the chapters presented here concerns whether as we age we see that horizon more clearly and whether religious faith and spiritual practice can provide "lenses" by which to do so. Other chapters, which do not directly address issues of religiousness and spirituality, nevertheless demonstrate that serious consideration of aging and time forces us to think about meaning in our lives.

This book honors Melvin Kimble's contributions to gerontology. Mel taught for over 30 years at Luther Seminary in St. Paul, Minnesota, where he founded the nation's first program on aging in a seminary. Mel's gentle acceptance of persons from many different religious and spiritual traditions influenced not only clergy but also professionals in health and social services. He taught them to think about aging holistically and to meet older people's spiritual needs for a sense of meaning and purpose in their lives. Nearly all the authors of the chapters included in this book had an opportunity to read a short essay he wrote several years ago (reprinted as chapter 8). In that paper, Mel offered personal reflections on how his own experiences of aging shaped his thoughts about the meaning of time. As a lifelong student of Viktor Frankl, Mel showed the applications of Frankl's writings on meaning to gerontological research and practice. Mel always insisted that Frankl's logotherapy "takes time seriously. . . . [It] stresses the temporal nature of human existence and the irreversible quality of human life" (Kimble, 1990, p. 120).

We organized this book into three parts, beginning with chapters that review scholarship on aging and time from the perspectives of history, sociology, psychology, and theology. Part II is shaped by our conviction that the academic domain, while important and necessary for our understanding of aging and time, cannot fully contain the topic. This subject cuts to the very core of human experience, and thus we created the second part of the book to reveal how older people—even those with dementia—discover meaning in time. The final part of the book shows how religious beliefs and spiritual practices point some aging persons toward meanings of time that may differ from those held earlier in life.

We sincerely hope that our readers will "take" time and "find" time to savor and study these chapters, for they were written by scholars who enthusiastically embraced the challenge of writing about time and aging and in so doing, risked revealing something of themselves in wrestling with this complex subject. We thank all of the persons who contributed to this undertaking, including Susanna Thomas who graciously allowed us to include one of the last papers written by her late husband, Gene Thomas. Our gratitude extends also to Helvi Gold of Springer Publishing Company whose support for this project has sustained it throughout, and to Connie Bowman, of the University of Wisconsin Oshkosh, who had the unenviable task of making sure the papers produced by all these talented writers conformed to the same formatting style.

Susan H. McFadden
Robert C. Atchley

REFERENCE

Kimble, M. A. (1990). Aging and the search for meaning. In J. J. Seeber (Ed.), *Spiritual maturity in the later years* (pp. 111–130). New York: Haworth.

PART **I**

Understanding Time and Aging

CHAPTER 1

The Flow of Spiritual Time Amid the Tides of Life

W. Andrew Achenbaum

> Time is what keeps the light from reaching us. There is no greater obstacle to God than time: and not only time but temporal affections, not only temporal affections but the very taint and smell of time.
>
> —Meister Eckhart

The words of Meister Johann Eckhart (1260–1327) challenge my sense of time. Clocks have long shaped my days. As a schoolboy I counted the minutes before recess; now that I am a dean, a staff sets my calendar. In moments of solitude I frame my daily meditations around the *Liturgy of Hours.* I like the semblance of order that regulates the flow of time as each day unfolds. I take comfort in the illusion that I seem to have some control over the tides of my life. In the autumn of my life, I delude myself with predictions about the severity and duration of my wintertide. Whereas I once crammed hours to get more done, now I leave gaps in the schedule for unanticipated crises or to relax. I exult in quiet times during which I can focus on Life's exquisite mysteries.

That is why the message of the Dominican mystic shakes my confidence in the human capacity for efficacy. If time is an "obstacle," as Eckhart claims, then my prayers might not be reaching God in a timely manner. Eckhart's epigram undercuts assumptions that I hold about the connection between aging and time. Not surprisingly, my self-perceptions of aging have changed. Fifty is not as "old" as it appeared when I was twenty. More importantly, I am becoming secure enough in who I am to re-present myself freely in the here and now to friends and to strangers. Increasingly I consider it my bounden duty and privilege to give thanks to—and gratitude for—that eternal Light that shines around and within my transitory being.

No wonder those "temporal affections" named by Eckhart soil and smell my world. Resigned to the fact that most of my life is past me, I treasure whatever time remains. I resist the notion that time is an obstacle to becoming the person I wish to be.

The gift of "Time" affords the passage of sufficient moments to make spiritual development possible. I cherish children's innocence, but I share Paul's conviction (I Corinthians 13:11–12) that young ones rarely see the Light, even dimly. I hasten to add that the search for Wisdom takes time and effort. Pilgrimages require thoughtful, actuating responses to both predictable and unexpected bends along the way. People must ripen before they can embrace the blessings and wounds that fortify them as they seek and experience God again and again in the tides of life, both high and low. With the flow of time unfold opportunities to perceive the cosmic in the particular.

Spiritual time, I will argue, is a key factor in any scenario that transports pilgrims to sacred space. The notion of "spiritual time" is not new. Medieval monks observed it. But with the extra years of living that come with societal aging, "spiritual time" may become as essential as biological, psychological, and social time in mapping the interior pathways of spiritual development. With maturity often evolves an appreciation that the mere flow of time affords hitherto undiscovered possibilities for celebrating the glories of Nature. We become more and more predisposed to seek happiness in intimate friendships and loving relations. We manage to cope as we suffer through the vicissitudes that come with being human.

Through personal experiences, an unending fascination with human bondings, and much soul searching, I have constructed a view of "spiritual time" that differs greatly from Meister Eckhart. It complements (at least in part) perspectives articulated by other contemporary writers, including elders whom I admire. In *The Presence of Absence* (1998), for instance, Doris Grumbach recounts an unexpected epiphany—an encounter with God at the age of 27. For the next five decades Grumbach prayed for another mystical moment. Neither church attendance nor private prayer provided what she wanted. So Grumbach sought solace from writers such as Thomas Merton, Kathleen Norris, and Meister Eckhart. At the end of *The Presence of Absence* she chose words from the Talmud to illuminate her journey through spiritual time:

> Look ahead.
> You are not expected to complete the task.
> Neither are you permitted to lay it down. (in Grumbach, 1998, p. 122)

With the passage of years, Grumbach discerned what impeded her spiritual development. Time per se was not a great obstacle, but she derived little solace from religious practices. Grumbach shed liturgies and rituals so that she could love God in her own way. She created her own niche within spiritual time.

Mel Kimble's story differs from Grumbach's. A health crisis in late life made this distinguished theologian eager to celebrate living. In his "postmortem life," Kimble (1993, p. 27; see also chapter 8, this volume) declares, "every day was now a bonus, and every person in my life more precious and valued. . . . Life, faith, and grace seemed to break into my life with greater intensity and sharper focus than ever before." Life has fresh meaning as Kimble helps "persons keep the door open between immanence and transcendence" (1996, p. 7). Yet Kimble remains characteristically humble in the face of his discovery, which he describes as a "mystery . . . unmeasurable, unprovable, and [which] lacks universal definition" (Kimble, 1993, p. 27).

Mel Kimble's example of humility is worth following. We are not the only pilgrims who have wondered about the impact of time on spiritual aging. What have others in various places and different periods of history gleaned about the "mystery" of time? Do their discoveries help us to elucidate the temporal dimensions of spiritual aging? Do they point to developmental triggers for embracing spiritual time? To answer these questions, let me survey some of the shapes of time that affect aging and spiritual development along the tides of life. How does the flow of time adumbrate inevitable, universal dimensions of human aging? Are the critical factors that define, animate, and contextualize spiritual time similar from one era to another?

THE FLOW OF TIME: A CROSS DISCIPLINARY OVERVIEW

Definitions of "*time*" fill more lines in most dictionaries than notions of "*god*" or "*thing*." The noun gets more space than "*space*." And "time" is often linked with a contradictory set of verbs and adjectives. We *waste* time as we *keep* it. We all experience *good* times and *bad* times; a few of us have *hot* times, not to be confused with *cool* times. "Time" is derived from the same Anglo-Saxon root as "tide" (hence the inspiration for the title of this essay), meaning "season" or "hour" (Aveni, 1989). Different languages differentiate the significance and shape of time. Students of Biblical Greek, for example, are taught to translate *chronos* as "measured time," and to interpret *kairos* as a time of opportunity (Barr, 1962, p. 20). Scripture differentiates between time's linear and circular qualities. Such dualisms persist today: we record birthdays and experience them subjectively. Certain anniversaries fuel expectations while sustaining memories.

The various levels of meaning embedded in the word "time" clash. Since time is irreversible, we never truly "repeat" mistakes, yet still can forget what made us err. Except on playing fields, in courtrooms, and through other contested events, we cannot "stop" the clock. "Conscious time," observed the distinguished anthropologist Robert MacIver, "has a different reckoning from that of the clock, but the experience it reckons moves on unceasingly" (1962, pp. 48–49). Finally, however human time is measured, we mortal creatures sooner or later must die. Some deny death. Others assess and reevaluate past, present, and future conditions in light of what remains to be done or how much might be accomplished.

Perhaps the most impressive scientific analysis of the relationship between aging and time appeared nearly four decades ago. For his landmark *Handbook of Aging and the Individual* (1959), James Birren commissioned Maria Reichenbach and Ruth Anna Mathers (1959) to write about "the place of time and aging in the natural sciences and scientific philosophy." Reichenbach and Mathers stressed that subjective psychological reactions toward time often manifested themselves quite independently of age: "Our personal estimates of time tend to be unreliable because in certain situations they are relative to our physical states or emotional attitudes" (p. 44). Because subjective experience is not reliable empirically, the pair distinguished between the physical and psychological aspects of time.

Drawing this theoretical distinction enabled Reichenbach and Mathers to analyze objective properties of time—which they characterized as time metric (stressing its uniformity), time order (contrasting its qualitative and quantitative properties), and time direction (invoking laws of physics, ranging from the Second Law of Thermodynamics to Einstein's theory of relativity, to bolster causal sequences). Turning to the thermodynamics of senescence, the pair distinguished between organic and inorganic systems. "This distinction determines the choice between causal and teleological explanation," concluded Reichenbach and Mathers (1961, p. 80). "The subjectively experienced time direction of aging is found to be identical with the direction of increasing entropy due to the fact that man's brain functions like a registered instrument."

Gerontologists have continued to ponder the relevance of time and temporality to their studies of human development and aging. Jon Hendricks (1995, p. 937) offers a different taxonomy than Reichenbach and Mathers to describe senescence and time: (a) time as an index of age-related changes; (b) temporal experience as a function of biological and social changes; (c) temporal perspective as a correlate of personality and social involvements or awareness of aging; and the (d) sense of futurity. Results from scientific investigations to date, Hendricks concludes, corroborate that time provides a basic index for mapping out continuities and changes in behavior. Several biological phenomena (such as RNA synthesis or oxidative metabolism) and social processes (such as emotional swings or proleptic imagery) presuppose time-dependent operations. But time itself, hypothesizes Hendricks, has little explanatory value. Temporal orientation, like memory, seems highly personal. Contemporary researchers on aging are not inclined (as were their predecessors) to presume that older people are less future oriented than younger ones. "Time, in its fullest sense, is lived; it can be partitioned only for purposes of analysis," Hendricks argues. "Past, present, and future commingle in the here and now, though the focal length of time perspective may be long or short, depending on momentary concerns" (1995, p. 939).

Biological and psychological factors are not the only influences on individuals' sense of time over their life courses. Contemporary Americans have inherited a mixture of antithetical notions about time. Some nostalgic images—like prints of decade-segmented pyramids marking the stages of life from birth to death at age 100—are obsolescent. Other images capture our imagination insofar as they resonate with our impressions of how the world operates. Social correlates do indeed affect temporal orientations, as Matilda White Riley and her associates demonstrate in *Age and Structural Lag* (1994). The age criteria that we build into expectations and organizations, Riley claims, have restricted opportunities for future growth in various domains. This is because contemporary cultures rely more and more on "age" as a way to designate specific norms, entitlements, and options at successive stages of life. Demographic, socioeconomic, and values shifts associated with population aging, however, have outrun dynamic changes in most other societal domains and structures. "The major responsibilities for work and family are still crowded into what are now the middle years of a long life, while education is primarily reserved for the young, and leisure and free time are disproportionately allocated to the later years," Riley points out (1994, p. 2). "Our failure to match in social structures the rapid gains in longevity, health, and style of life has had the unintended consequence of creating a poor fit between social institutions and people's capabilities and responsibilities at every age."

The current mismatch between individual aging and societal structures is not unprecedented. Such asynchronicity has ample historical precedent. To wit: Life was different, but surely not simpler, in Puritan New England. Collective survival required everybody regardless of age to contribute their talents and energy to the commonweal. Muscles, brains, common sense, and experiences were all valuable. The Bible gave meaning to people's lives; they saw their mission on earth in terms of a Divine calling. Even so, the Puritan worldview was riddled with inconsistencies. Cotton Mather, one of the colonial era's most venerable divines, urged the faithful elders in his congregations to withdraw voluntarily from significant positions when they no longer were fit to serve, but he chafed when he found himself, phased out of the pulpit in his ninth decade, excluded from centers of power. God ultimately provided all the essentials, the faithful fervently believed, but the Good Book also taught them that mortals could not rely on Good Will alone. Attaining old age without meaningful activities, sufficient income, or the guarantee of support from family and friends usually meant that one's life would end in a period of desuetude, poverty, and sadness (Haber, 1983).

Biographies of illustrious nineteenth-century Americans illustrate the variety of late-life spiritual pathways in which elders responded to changing environments. Ralph Waldo Emerson, who extolled the virtues of solitude in his prime, became more gregarious after the age of seventy. He delighted in the congenial company of Oliver Wendell Holmes, James Russell Lowell, Louis Agassiz, and Henry Wadsworth Longfellow among others at the Saturday Club or at Parker House (Russell, 1929, p. 272). Emerson in conversations with peers "did not wish to direct, but to instigate" ideas in later years; "his power lay in the novel face, the fresh turn, that he gave to very ancient wisdom" (p. 303).

Frederick Douglass, on the other hand, persisted in writing autobiographical accounts about his path from servitude to freedom. Critics dismiss his last volume, *Life and Times of Frederick Douglass* (1881, rev. 1892), by turns as tired and vain, full of resentments over slights. Despite the volume's poor sales, historians praise the author as a man reaching out "with his intellect, with an unswerving commitment to human dignity and equality" (McFeely, 1991, p. 384).

The evolution of Walt Whitman's spirituality attests to the effects of time as he came to terms with national tragedy (the Civil War) and coped with a personal trauma (increasing physical debility). Early in his writings Whitman acquiesced to the truth of an idea that seemed quite opposite to something to which he had assented only moments before. The first version of *Leaves of Grass* (1856) sang paeans to polymorphous tastes, universalistic convictions. Spiritualism and realism soared together in his verse. The bard's moral and artistic strength surged with his capacity to wonder. Nonetheless, he grounded his hopes for the betterment of humankind through "years of quarrying in the darker and less frequented ranges of human experience" (Smuts, 1894/1973, p. 126). Whitman's mysticism in advancing age influenced his tone in subsequent editions of the *Leaves of Grass*. The poet's spirituality was made authentic in the gritty realism of individual suffering, in Whitman's intimations of inchoate desire, and in his genius for conveying unconscious purposiveness.

To such historical layers of temporal imagery (besides those I pass over) have been added three additional ingredients that affect "modern" conceptions of time. The *media* is an important temporal force. Creative artists can use technology in ways that transport us "back to the future" or transfix the poignancy of spiritual encounters in the faces of youth and age. *Medicine,* through heroic interventions and more especially through the pharmacological revolution, has altered our understanding of acute and chronic illness. In some situations changes in doctor-nurse-patient relationships have encouraged greater spiritual awareness at the bedside; in other cases the care of the dying occurs in barren spaces, devoid of much sympathy and compassion. Finally, ours is an era of *megadeath* (Boyle & Morriss, 1987, p. 172). The twentieth century will be remembered for its genocides, for the capacity of political regimes to harness technologies and bureaucracies so that they could systematically murder more of their own citizens than were killed in civil insurrections or world wars. And, despite the official end of the Cold War, we all still live under the threat of a nuclear holocaust. Cursed with the power to extinguish human existence in a flash, we now are afforded the opportunity to bless life and respect human dignity in all its diverse forms.

It remains to be seen, as we enter what many critics and commentators characterize as the "postmodern" period, whether a new genre will arise to embody shifting sensibilities concerning the connection between societal aging and spiritual time. We may expect more and more spiritual biographies to be written, given demographic increases. Yet it is not clear whether tomorrow's elders will use conventional vehicles to tell their stories. Scholars tell us that "biographies" have not always existed through written history. Precedents were essayed in classical times, but biographical forms did not arise until most readers and writers believed that life imitated art. Here is how the famous nineteenth-century critic John Ruskin put it:

> In our whole life the music is broken off here and there by rests, and we foolishly think we have come to the end of time. God sends a time of forced leisure, a time of sickness and disappointed plans, and makes a sudden pause in the hymns of our lives, and we lament that our

voice must be silent and our part missing in the music which ever goes up to the ear of our Creator. Not without design does God write the music of our lives. Be it ours to learn the time and not be dismayed at the rests. If we look up, God will beat the time for us. (Quoted in Cooper-Goldenberg, 2000)

In Ruskin's cosmology, good and bad have measures in the Divine score.

Since the nineteenth century, the best biographical narratives have sought to represent significant events in everyday life in metaphorical terms. Motifs are prefigured in aesthetic inventions, in archetypes, and in the conventions of storytelling. "In 'making sense' of the world," Frank Kermode points out, "we feel a need to experience that concordance of beginning, middle and end which is the essence of our explanatory fictions" (1968, pp. 35–36). Gerontologists' interest in life review conforms to this biographical model. Life review is seen as a vehicle for enabling older writers to capture the essence of their lives, to share their voices and their messages with others. Some of the most prominent researchers and practitioners in the field of aging, such as James Birren and Connie Goldman, have encouraged elderly men and women to retrace their spiritual pathways through the medium of autobiography.

Current exercises in late-life biography may give way to new forms for making connections between social time and spiritual aging. Critics sense, after all, that existing models have grown inadequate. "To be a human individual is to instantiate a special sort of relationship to time," writes David Carr (1986).

At bottom it is, to be sure, always 'located' in an ever-changing now and thus to be subjected, like everything else, to temporal sequence. . . . But it is much more than this. It is not merely to undergo or endure or suffer this sequence as it comes, one thing at a time. . . . Nor is the individual merely a temporally persisting, underlying substance which supports the changing effects of time as subject to its predicates or properties, like a thing. (pp. 94–95)

Those who embrace postmodern sensibilities are more likely than earlier cohorts to accentuate the discontinuities between life and art. Rejecting visions of organic unity, they are inclined to challenge sequential narratives. Detractors charge that narratives tend to human agency. Worse, formulaic constructions objectify human capacities for the sake of artifice.

Will elderly men and women, who wish to capitalize on added years for pursuing Selfhood, create new ways for thinking about "time"? Will their efforts to articulate their ideas, to express their feelings, and to reconstruct their actions result in new narrative forms? If so, how are their endeavors likely to manifest themselves? The balance of this paper highlights a few efforts. The survey does not pretend to be exhaustive, but it does illustrate three ways in which people are writing spiritual guides or (auto)biographies that address the relationship between aging and time.

REFURBISHING TRADITIONAL APPROACHES

Memoirs sell, especially if composed by fascinating people who write in an engaging manner or who (readers expect) might have some juicy gossip to share. Many commercially successful authors like this genre. Some reach an age in which they want to probe the meanings of aging.

M. F. K. Fisher's *Sister Age* (1983) fits this genre. Fisher (1908–1998) made her reputation in journalism. Her sketchbooks dealing with travels to exotic places reveal a keen appreciation of the extent to which contingency touches character development. In *The Art of Eating* (1954), Mary Frances Kennedy Fisher showed millions of readers that there was more to the feast of breaking bread than preparing complex meals. In *Sister Age,* Fisher describes the art of aging in a subtle but firm manner—as if she were teaching at the Culinary Institute of America. "I know, for instance, that I like old people, when they have aged well. And old houses with an accumulation of sweet honest living in them are good," Fisher relates. "And the timelessness that only the passing of Time itself can give to objects both inside and outside the spirit is a continuing reassurance" (1983, p. 234).

Fisher acknowledges the losses that accumulate with passing years. She does not gloss over the hindrances caused by disabilities. But Fisher challenges the notion that the vicissitudes of life make healthy, happy adolescents grow into Nasty Old Men or Aged Crones. People resent and fight aging, she claims, because it comes on them unaware. They are repelled and frightened by the marks of time. Understanding the processes is necessary. Fisher recommends "dispassionate acceptance of attrition . . . to use the experience, both great and evil, so that physical annoyances are surmountable in an alert and even mirthful appreciation of life itself" (1983, p. 237). Fisher's recipe for well-being has deep roots in the national psyche: like Jeffersonian Americans (Achenbaum, 1978), she blends stoic detachment with inner faith in her menu for spiritual aging.

Jimmy Carter also has had a notable writing career since he left the White House. He has published a dozen books, including a volume of poetry and (with his daughter Amy) a collection of children stories. The former President is probably best known for his analyses of Middle East policies and for his candor in discussing the importance of religion in the public domain and in his private life. In his latest book, President Carter discusses *The Virtues of Aging* (1998). The book borrows anecdotes and themes from his earlier books such as *Living Faith, Keeping Faith,* and *Everything to Gain: Making the Most of the Rest of Your Life,* which he wrote with his wife Rosalyn. Nonetheless, *The Virtues of Aging* builds on some ideas he attributes to his friend Ken Dychtwald. The book extends the President's beliefs about lively religious sensibilities in late-life.

> Retirement years are a time to define, or redefine, a successful life, both in retrospect and for our remaining years—a definition likely to be quite different from that of our younger years. . . . It is a sign of maturity when we can accept honestly and courageously that frustrated dreams, illness, disability, and eventual death are all normal facets of a person's existence—and that despite these, we can still continue to learn, grow, and adopt challenging goals. (Carter, 1998, p. 122)

The President's observations are heartfelt. His words sound familiar, almost hackneyed, yet they have considerable credibility because of the author's reputation for integrity. Everyone knows that Jimmy Carter learned that he was bankrupt when he left the Oval Office in 1981. Rather than indulge in bitterness or wallow in self-pity, Jimmy got his house in order (fiscally and otherwise) and then became an international and domestic ambassador without portfolio. He works for peace and harmony. Such old-fashioned righteousness is terribly rare. But it remains an exemplary model for spiritual aging.

EXTENDING CONVENTIONAL WISDOM

Erik and Joan Erikson spent most of their working careers refining their epigenetic model of human development that they first set forth in *Childhood and Society* (1950). Taking a cue from Shakespeare, they originally conceived of seven stages of life. They then added an eighth stage—"generativity"—to embrace their own middle-aged commitments to raising a family while they pursued their intellectual and creative interests. As decades passed, the couple focused less and less on infancy and childhood. They chose instead to grapple with late-life development; their fullest treatment of senescence appeared in *Vital Involvement in Old Age* (1986), coauthored with Helen Q. Kivnick. In an almost Whitmanesque phrase, the pair characterized Wisdom as

> truly involved disinvolvement . . . for vital involvements, we believe, result, subjectively speaking, in a heightened awareness that can be no means necessarily claimed by the usual ego. This is all the more important to us since in old age a human being must not only confront nonbeing but also face the final maturation of what we may call an existential identity. (1986, p. 51)

The desire to nurture, to love mutually, and to be generative continues in old age, the Eriksons claim, but mounting losses, which culminate in the face of death, force aged persons to give up their ego. Paradoxically, in surrendering their protective masks, older people gain the wisdom necessary to accept with tranquility the finitude of life.

At several critical junctures in *Vital Involvement in Old Age* the authors focus on religious sensibilities in later years. They note, for example, that "the tension between identity and identity confusion is tied to a sense of abiding faith, perhaps more closely than is any other psychosocial theme in old age" (1986, p. 234). The observation takes on particular salience when one remembers that Erikson's two major biographies, *Young Man Luther* and *Gandhi's Truth*, both dealt primarily with how their respective protagonists resolved crises of faith. Yet references to spirituality are strikingly absent in their text, as they are in the Rileys' work.

It is hard at first to recognize the revolutionary paradigm shift in thinking about spiritual aging that occurred between the first and second versions of one of Erik Erikson's last books. When originally published in 1982, *The Life Cycle Completed* seemed mainly to rehearse themes and motifs that had made its senior author one of the most distinguished psychologists in this century. But Erikson became dissatisfied with what he had written. He began to underline key sentences in *The Life Cycle Completed* in green (to save them), in red (to modify them), and in black (to delete them). Because he died before he completed the task, his wife and collaborator took up the revisions.

Not merely extrapolating from her late husband's work, Joan Erikson added her own inimitable acumen and insights. In the process she invoked her own experiences, reorienting the thesis of the work, which was issued under the same title in 1997. Having now reached an advanced age, Mrs. Erikson saw the need to divide the last stage of life into two parts. The landscape in old age was more complex, physically and psychologically, than she had previously imagined. Vitally engaged in her remaining years, she nonetheless stressed the "retrospective despair" (1997, p. 113) in this new ninth stage. Echoing the notion that society does not know what to do with its aged, Joan Erikson worried that "the difficulties of the ninth stage both contribute to and are exacerbated by society's disregard" (1997, p. 114).

The portrait of *The Life Cycle Completed* certainly is not all bleak. Mrs. Erikson points to many ways in which older people can be connected into communities of their own making while they remain in touch with younger kin and friends. And she makes a great deal of the fact that the roots of the words "wisdom" and "integrity" (key terms in the Eriksonian lexicon) derive from the *veda* term "to know, to see." Here her Christian roots (she was the daughter of an Anglican minister) and late-life fascination with Eastern religions bear fruit. Spiritual consciousness animates Mrs. Erikson's theoretical reconstruction of late-life development. Acknowledging that "wisdom belongs to the actuality to which our senses give us access" (1997, p. 7), she nonetheless envisions aged persons making positive contributions of a transcendent nature that go beyond the purely intellectual. "It is also the role of wisdom to guide our investment in sight and sound and to focus our capacities on what is relevant, enduring, and nourishing, both for us individually and for the society in which we live" (p. 7).

Significantly, Joan Erikson entitles the last chapter of her extended version of *The Life Cycle Completed* "Gerotranscendence," a term she attributes to Lars Tornstam, a Swedish social scientist (see chapter 12). She proposes a slight alteration—"gerotranscendance," to reflect her own contributions to the performing arts. Joan Erikson believes that remaining physically engaged is essential to vital involvements in old age. The reference to gerotranscendence is critical on another level. Just as Mrs. Erikson has challenged us to rethink our conceptions of the impact of time on the life course by adding a new stage of life, so too Prof. Tornstam has combined religious terminology and Jungian theory to craft a paradigm to describe and explain older people's new attitudes about their place in the world. "Gerotranscendence," Tornstam argues, "is the final stage in a natural process moving toward maturation and wisdom. . . . The gerotranscendent individual experiences a new feeling of cosmic communion with the spirit of the universe, a redefinition of time, space, life, and death, and a redefinition of self" (2000, p. 11).

IN THE COUNTRY OF THE OLD ONES

Can the "gerotranscendent" motif set forth by Joan Erikson and Lars Tornstam be extended from the individual level to a communal context? Not only is it possible, but it has already been done innovatively. In 1984, a prominent Philadelphia rabbi, Zalman Schachter-Shalomi, spent 40 days at an ecumenical retreat in New Mexico. His "vision quest" resulted in a radical change in his priorities and relationships. Three years later, Schacter-Shalomi established the Spiritual Eldering Institute for older people who wished emotional support in a nondenominational setting as they prepared themselves, psychologically and spiritually, for their journeys. The rationale for the Spiritual Eldering Institute is set forth in *From Age-ing to Sage-ing* (1995), which offers a bold vision for growing older independently and together. Schacter-Shalomi reports:

> I have witnessed firsthand how people are searching for a new approach to aging. Most of us have grown up with a deep-seated fear and loathing of old age. . . . In the popular imagination, old age means wrinkled skin and chronic disease, rather than the wisdom, serenity,

balanced judgment, and self-knowledge that represent the fruit of long life experience. Fortunately, our culture's limited, one-sided view of aging is undergoing a profound reconceptualization in our time. We are the first generation to apply the insights of humanistic and transpersonal psychology and contemplative techniques from our spiritual traditions to the aging process itself, giving birth to what some people call the conscious aging movement. (1995, p. 3)

From Age-ing to Sage-ing is inclusive: it acknowledges and incorporates faith traditions from around the world and taps into psychological paradigms that are themselves nontheistic, even a-religious. Schachter-Shalomi is concerned with individuals cultivating their spiritual development in personal terms: his Spiritual Eldering Institute offers lectures and workshops on forgiveness, spiritual exercises, and meditations. At the same time the rabbi urges a *communal* movement: his program stresses service-leadership and mentoring, "to heal a fractured world in need of elder wisdom" (Leder, 2000, p. 39). In this way the inner work of spiritual growth animates an ecumenical program of outward service. Spiritual aging is socially conscientious as it probes its inward roots.

Such media-savvy, psychologically rooted, ecumenically spirited calls for elder wisdom (through conscious aging and other ventures) are not simply a new spin on an hoary notion. Yes, Schacter-Shalomi's spiritual elders resemble the patriarchs of old, and the good witches who adorn medieval fairy tales. What is novel here is the notion of a "movement," which builds on the political activism of the 1960s as it demands a new understanding of Self (not ego) in the Cosmos (not simply the workplace, the nation state). Spiritual eldering invites us to view the journey of life in its fullest dimensions. Those of us who have not gone very far on our pathways are expected to respect the perspectives of older pilgrims: only they understand firsthand the chemistry of aging and spiritual growth. Our elders are in a position to convey the power that the interaction has on their relationships with other people, with nature, and with the world beyond. Spiritual aging, rightly understood, "can be defined in terms of movement toward ultimate possibilities, and the highest regions of spiritual development occur in the development of a capacity that allows consciousness to transcend the boundaries of body, language, reason, and culture" (Atchley, 2000, p. 331).

Ironically, spiritual aging is so radical in vision that it might have appealed to Meister Eckhart. To invite others to participate intimately in one's personal journey is to violate ordinary conventions about the value of spatial lines. To recognize that our fractured present can only be healed by applying the balm of an ever-renewable past for a sake of a future in which we are unlikely to participate—surely that violates most people's sense of how to allocate time. Breaking through temporal boundaries so as to reach out to the Transcendent in the most of ordinary of places, however, is what this movement is all about.

REFERENCES

Achenbaum, W. A. (1978). *Old age in the new land: The American experience since 1790.* Baltimore: Johns Hopkins University Press.

Atchley, R. C. (2000). Spirituality. In T. R. Cole, R. Kastenbaum, & R. E. Ray (Eds.), *Handbook of the humanities and aging* (2nd ed., pp. 324–341). New York: Springer.

Aveni, A. F. (1989). *Empires of time: Calendars, clocks, and cultures.* New York: Basic Books.

Barr, J. (1962). *Biblical words for time.* Naperville, IL: A. R. Allenson.

Birren, J. E. (1959). *Handbook of aging and the individual: Psychological and biological aspects.* Chicago: University of Chicago Press.

Boyle, J. M., & Morriss, J. E. (1987). *The mirror of time: Images of aging and death.* Westport, CT: Greenwood Press.

Carr, D. (1986). *Time, narrative, and history.* Bloomington: Indiana University Press.

Carter, J. (1998). *The virtues of aging.* New York: Ballantine.

Cooper-Goldenberg, J. (2000). Private correspondence.

Eckhart, M. in Eknath Easwaran (1990). *Words to live by.* Petaluma, CA: Nilgiri Press.

Erikson, E. (1982). *The life cycle completed.* New York: Norton.

Erikson, E. H. (1950). *Childhood and society.* New York: Norton.

Erikson, E., & Erikson, J. M. (1997). *The life cycle completed* (rev. ed.). New York: Norton.

Erikson, E., Erikson, J. M., & Kivinick, H. Q. (1986). *Vital involvement in old age.* New York: Norton.

Fisher, M. F. K. (1954). *The art of waiting.* New York: Knopf.

Fisher, M. F. K. (1983). *Sister age.* New York: Knopf.

Grumbach, D. (1998). *The presence of absence: On prayers and an epiphany.* Boston: Beacon.

Haber, C. (1983). *Beyond sixty-five: The dilemma of old age in America's past.* New York: Cambridge University Press.

Hendricks, J. (1995). Time. In G. L. Maddox (Ed.), *The encyclopedia of aging* (2nd ed., pp. 937–939). New York: Springer.

Kermode, F. (1968). *The sense of an ending.* New York: Oxford University Press.

Kimble, M. (1993). A personal journey of aging: The spiritual dimension. *Generations, 17*(2), 27–28.

Kimble, M. (1996). A pastoral theologian responds. *News about Aging and Religion, 1*(2), 6–8.

Leder, D. (2000). Aging into spirit. From traditional wisdom to innovative programs and communities. *Generations, 23*(4), 36–41.

MacIver, R. M. (1962). *The challenge of the passing years: My encounter with time.* New York: Simon and Schuster.

McFeely, W. S. (1991). *Frederick Douglass.* New York: Norton.

Reichenbach, M., & Mathers, R. A. (1959). The place of time and aging in the natural sciences and scientific philosophy. In J. E. Birren (Ed.), *Handbook aging and the individual* (pp. 43–80). Chicago: University of Chicago Press.

Riley, M. W., Kahn, R. L., & Foner, A. (Eds.). (1994). *Age and structural lag.* New York: Wiley.

Russell, P. (1929). *Emerson: The wisest American.* New York: Brentano's.

Schacter-Shalomi, Z., & Miller, R. S. (1995). *From age-ing to sage-ing: A profound new vision of growing older.* New York: Warner.

Smuts, J. C. (1973). *Walt Whitman: A study in the evolution of personality.* Detroit: Wayne State University. (Original work published 1894)

Tornstam, L. (2000). Transcendence in late life. *Generations, 23*(4), 10–14.

CHAPTER 2

It's About Time

Jon Hendricks

WHAT TIME IS IT?

Those who travel outside their homeland quickly realize time and its marking are beset with ambiguity. What seemed unquestionably natural meets a curious time, peculiarly stippled and seemingly distorted. The customary inclination may be to wonder why strangers do it so differently, yet a moment's pause is all it takes to begin to recognize that time is highly nuanced. A bit more reflection brings appreciation that there are many faces to time and each makes sense in its context. The savvy traveler also recognizes an array of commonalties and comparable issues despite the overlay of diverse cultures. Gradually the traveler realizes time is indeed an enigma, the resolution more recondite than meets the eye. Engaging in another kind of journey, life's journey, also yields a changing cognizance of time. As people grow older they think differently about themselves, time's tensc, and the meaning of life. In either case, the process is comparable—if the platform from which we observe the world changes in any noteworthy way, so, too, will our perceptions.

When most scholars speak of time, their definitions are tacit or reflect the specifics of their paradigm (Hendricks & Hendricks,

1976). Be that as it may, over the course of the twentieth century influential commentators on things temporal have referred to levels of time, ranging from exogenous dimensions grounded in cosmological evolution to endogenous processes within systems—whether the latter are organismic, individual, or cultural. Within this seemingly straightforward matrix is a great deal of scholarly debate. From Einstein's relativity to Eddington's arrow, the passage of time remains a puzzle. In his *Brief History of Time,* Stephen Hawking (1988) provided an interesting framework. He spoke of thermodynamic time, with attendant energy loss, psychological time wherein no energy is lost through the process of remembering events, and cosmological time defined in terms of directionality implicit in the expansion of the universe. J. T. Fraser (1996), renowned commentator on time, has a slightly different cataloging, yet generally speaking their views encapsulate recognized opinion on time and temporality (Pixten, 1995). The purpose of this essay is to bring their taxonomies home to roost in terms of how you and I experience and think about time. The goal is to provide an overview and some insight into how aging is implicated. The bottom line is that the relationship between time and aging is symbiotic, cutting both ways. If we are to understand how time and aging interrelate, we need a better grasp of each; the results can only be salutatory.

Like many abiding conundrums, the way we conceive of time has tracings back to the ancients. In his *Physics* Aristotle noted that time exists to the extent motion (change) exists and is perceived by an observer. He was clear that time is not the same as motion but one is necessary to ascertain the other. Paradoxically, only the present can be said to exist; yet it can only be known as part of an emergent sequence. Though not all commentators align with Aristotle, the permutations of his pronouncements boggle the mind and continue to focus the discussion at the dawn of the twenty-first century. One of the conspicuous riddles revolves around the distinction between the sensation/perception of time as an anthropocentric construct and time cast as an ontological entity ticking away regardless of attention or observation. This duality is enduring and seemingly indelible, a fact of life as far as time is concerned. But what factors are involved?

THE CAVALCADE OF TIME

The Chronological Universe

To a great extent time is about clocks. Clocks are emblematic, unrivaled, virtually ubiquitous. Other means of telling time, calendars for instance, can be substituted for clocks, but generally the way people feel about time is based on the timepieces in their lives. It has not always been that way. It might be surprising to learn clocks came along centuries after people started keeping track of time. The advent of mechanical clocks prompted heated debates in which the wrath of one deity or another was importuned as an injunction for anyone tinkering with time. The position of the sun, the stars, the seasons, the ebb and flow of nature undergirded early time reckoning, and each worked perfectly well under the circumstances. Time was relational, not absolute, geared to the flux of proximal circumstances and widely regarded as natural or God given.

In the beginning, the length of an hour was contingent on the season, planetary orbits, and by where an observer was on the face of the earth—shorter or longer, depending. As inventors mulled how to keep track, the chore was to build a mechanism that could mark hours in flexible intervals. The resolution came not from the works but from altering the definition of an hour to something that was neither fluctuating nor dependent on relative position. What we now call mean solar time (based on averages) was adopted to equalize oscillations in planetary orbits, and the measure of an hour was fixed. However, a battle royal erupted over the move away from solar time, seen by many as God's time, to mean time as invented by humans and kept by clocks. Even though clock time carried the day, early models were supplied with convoluted conversion tables so those not yet convinced that clock time was the way to keep track—farm animals, tides, or deities do not tell time—might reconcile their clocks with "true solar time" (Lundmark, 1996). Though the debate subsided two centuries ago, from our vantage point today it is hard to imagine life without linear time or time without standardization.

Before time became standardized, locations only a few miles apart may have kept separate solar times—as well they might, given the circumference of the earth. It was not until the last quarter of the nineteenth century that what is labeled "standard time" took over to accommodate commerce and travel. In practical terms it meant that zones were created with time simply proclaimed to be the same throughout the zone. In the United States, Cincinnati, the last major city to adopt standardized time, did so in the late 1890s, and with it the movement to an abstracted, linear, mechanical time was complete. However, even a cursory glance at a time-zone map is all it takes to suggest something more than pure science was involved in drawing the boundaries.

The advent of universally recognized time schema was a long time coming. The Egyptians had invented sundials and waterclocks to mark time's measure by 1500 BCE. By the eighth century water-turned escapements were running balance wheels in China, denoting intervals, though the latter were not summed into larger units. By the fourteenth century sandfilled hourglasses had replaced waterclocks in the Western world though sundials remained in practical service for many years. To support liturgies and in keeping with the regularity of monastic life these "clocks" were utilized to ring bells at periodic intervals, signaling those outside the monastery that one activity was ending and another about to begin. By the fifteenth century mechanical clockworks had become reasonably accurate after the pendulum (originally conceived as a way to delineate the earth's rotation by recording the number of swings of the pendulum) had been adapted as a way to regulate clock mechanisms. In short order clocks spread across Europe, changing the way life and history were conceived. Time gradually became universal, synchronized around the world, divisible into infinitely smaller units, exemplifying the quantification and rationalization of the modern world.

Over the course of the twentieth century instrumentation was invented that could track time or distance to within a scintilla of a unit of measurement. Cesium clocks (pulsing at 9 billion vibrations a second) made possible a new International Atomic Time that is broadcast continuously while celestial positioning locators, accurate to within a nanosecond, exemplified the kind of precision that settled over many aspects of life—at least within the postindustrialized world.

THE CASCADE OF BIO-TIME

Time also springs from within. There is no doubt that at the micro-as well as at the macrolevel, life's rhythms have distinct periodicities embedded in the text of genetic materials. We are aware of sleep-wake cycles and the endogenous rhythms of breathing, heartbeats, and pulses. Plus, we have all seen sine waves of EEGs (alpha brain waves/second) or EKGs (heartbeats/minute) depicted on oscilloscopes, if only on TV, so we are not unfamiliar with bodily rhythms. Diagnosticians are trained to examine sine waves for both period and amplitude as signs of departures from normal patterns and for cues to disruptions and dysrhthmias. Estimates are that there are over two dozen semiautonomous rhythms ranging from metabolic, hormonal, and neurological activity to composite processes like eating and sleeping. To a certain extent, each helps shape our sense of time. In the argot of science it would be more appropriate to talk about periodicities, cycles, or oscillations, but rhythms will do for our purposes. These biorhythms are part of what Minkowski (1970) intended when he referred to as *lived time*. It is not merely that these rhythms mark life's passage, but that chemical, electrical, and physical oscillations comprise life itself (Fraser, 1996, p. 6). From cortical neurons to thermal regulation or cognitive reckoning each process has a certain cadence. Whether we are sensitive to rhythms on a routine basis, we may be jolted into awareness when they become desynchronized. The much-storied jet lag or the malaise sometimes associated with shift work are cases in point, but only two of the more obvious examples. It is not too much of an overstatement to say maintaining the cadences is essential to maintaining life—as the beat declines, so, too, does life's vitality—until it is sapped.

Circadian Rhythms

The category of rhythms occurring in 24-hour cycles are called circadian. There are also longer and shorter endogenous cycles. Many plants and animals have circadian rhythms, and most of us are at least vaguely aware of the diurnal opening and closing of flowers, leaf movement, photosynthesis, or nocturnal animals reflecting oscillating photo or thermal cycles. In humans, circadian rhythms have to do with sleep-wake cycles, thermal regulation, and so on that begin as early as the prenatal phase. A slightly less obvious cycle has to do with optimal cognitive processing normally thought of as attentiveness. In everyday parlance, we speak of "morning people" or "night owls" to characterize people who operate better on one end or the other of the day. Though wakefulness and attentiveness are highly sensitive to external stimuli, they are ready examples of the regularities of our being: there is a time for being attentive and a time for rest.

Many of these rhythms are mediated by environmental conditions and can be reset by light cues, for example, gradually shifting to an alternative cycle if there is reason to do so. To illustrate: scientists know that brain waves can be affected by an array of external stimuli, such as photic activity that can disrupt normal patterns. There may be other environmental factors as well that also affect our internal rhythms. Scientists have barely begun to attend to the possible influences from the earth's magnetism, gravity, barometric pressure, or atmospheric radiation (Orme, 1969).

TIME IN MIND

Regardless of constitutive elements, awareness of time is above all else a social construction. Perhaps more than any other definition, our interpretation of time is what gives it reality. Apart from our experience all else is abstraction. Having said that does not mean those personal concepts of time, what we generally refer to as one's temporal sense, are so ephemeral as to be unrecognizable. In many respects, time is visceral before it is cognitive. That is not to say time is a priori to experience but simply to say some feeling of time exists before we begin to think about it. Yet our concepts of time become both predictive and prescriptive. In everyday use, the way we think about time delimits present and any possible future cognition (Hendricks & Hendricks, 1976).

Sequential thoughts and sequential actions are central to our sense of time though likely as not, time sense cannot be disaggregated to discernable constituents. Friedman (1990) noted we have no sense organs to sense time, the way we sense other stimuli. At the beginning of the twentieth century, William James (1890/1950) provided an American twist to how we think about time. He was particularly insightful in trying to capture cognitive awareness' involvement with time with what he referred to as the *specious present*. It is the interval we call *Now*, created and sensed in terms of intentional focus. James pointed out that *Now* slopes off both fore and aft and is undeniably an abstraction—what might be termed the duration of a sensible present. As a concept, *Now* is more than a mere instant, but it cannot be discerned on any chronometer—it is a state of mind reflecting the "object focus" of consciousness.

The fact that we even think about time is one thing that is uniquely human. Whether we all possess a recognizable, or highly developed sense of futurity is debatable, but likely everyone has a basic notion of now versus then (Bandura, 1986). The same is true of time as is true of most human experience; we attend to those things deemed germane and ignore others. The way people think of time is linked to what they regard as important, individually and collectively, and how motivated they are in terms of their goals. That is not to say there are not breeches, startling intrusions demanding of attention. Generally, however, people organize their expectations according to anticipated futures. They do this in light of a self-referential agenda and the timelines implicit to it. Of course it is a mutually reinforcing process. Consciousness and intentionality are defining human characteristics and concurrently synchronize the various levels of temporality in our lives. In other words, the expectations people have influence how they perceive time. In turn, expectations are facets of one's self-concept, one's sense of well-being, and one's membership in social categories.

From the themes of our life scripts, we construct mental models of "recurrent temporal patterns in our environment" (Friedman, 1990, p. 2). It is important to stress that these mental models mirror personality, age, and experiential factors, and that the mental model itself may shift dramatically without any particular disjuncture being perceived. The time we create is *our* time, but it is not entirely of our own design.

Subjective Experience of Time

The mysteries of time have occupied scholars for centuries. Aristotle's assertion that a perceiving mind must be present to keep track of before and after—otherwise there could be no time—is portentous. Does it allude to the possibility that time started when human minds appeared on the scene or that once upon a time there was no time?

Perplexing questions, to be sure, but the import of Aristotle's claim is that moments in time in and of themselves cannot flow—they can only mark the moment. In short, instances in and of themselves do not lead to continuity; the latter is apperceived via the amalgam provided by the perceiver.

Raynor (1982) was of the opinion that subjective sense of time, especially projected futurity, is linked to the number of steps foreseen for reaching a desired goal. His particular contribution was in differentiating determinate tasks, where all steps are discernible in advance, from contingent tasks wherein each step reveals previously unseen sequela without necessarily providing a sense of gratification or reinforcement. Of course there are steps and there is the time required to take steps—Raynor recognized the two operate autonomously—so the focal length of one's personal future is contingent on specification or anticipation of tasks and extent of the effort required. If Raynor's hypothesis is correct, both dimensions are part of the way we conceive of time's movement.

Duration and Time's Passing

Sense of duration is another aspect of time more complex than first meets the eye. Sometimes tasks define the measure of time, rather than clocks. Sometimes people are absorbed in what may be described as an "object focus" and lose track of time, as it were, working through breaks and mealtimes, past bedtimes or appointments to complete a task. In so doing the same chronological measure of time is experienced very differently. It may be the perception that an event or action is enduring simultaneously provides awareness of time passing. In contrast, losing track of time is analogous to losing track of duration wherein absorption, focus, and experience bridle awareness of the clock's turn. To make the point, we might say that the depth of "focal duration" alters how time seems to pass. Implicit in that assertion is acknowledgment that content and concentration are significant in the perception of time for it is through them that intervals disappear and successive intervals of chronological time are perceived as compressed or as one (Bergson, 1965; Hendricks & Peters, 1986). When this occurs, a person is said to be concentrating very hard. The converse may also be apt. When we are not concentrating at all, or when the content of our attention is monotonous—in other words, when we are bored—each interval is keenly felt and the passing of time seems slower as though each tick of a clock rings loudly. In this instance, people may be said to be lacking an "object focus," and the protraction of time might be thought of as similar to the "watched pot" phenomena (Flaherty, 1999). Incidentally, the same may be true during times of perceived threat; the intervals may seem to expand.

The ebb and flow of episodic temporal awareness has a common-sensical familiarity. Participating in one or another activity we sometimes become aware of time inching or sailing along, out of synch with the uniformity of temporal markings at the moment of engagement. Our temporal awareness, the subjective impression of time, can thus be said to be grounded by content and by focus. Intervals of time seem shorter than intervals where less occurs to occupy attention (Orme, 1969). Many commentators have wondered if the sense of time's passage is a function of the "density of experience," or what we might think of as refracted as a consequence of mental activity levels. In a sense, time is an event system, the ecology of which contributes to temporal perception. In thinking about the shifts in sense of time with age, could it that the perception of time speeding up may not be hinged to age per se but to the fullness of the content or experience of activities, whether that is in terms of mental content or actual encounters?

Figure 2.1 provides a heuristic visual representation of the refractive relationship. The middle horizontal axis is intended to depict the interval nature of Newtonian time as kept by clocks and as most of us have been socialized to think of as absolute and real. The darker hash marks show the "set time" of the momentary present, the lighter hash marks have to do with the ambiguity of time intervals depending on intentionality, object focus, or what is sometimes called one's purpose-at-hand. The convex horizontal axis is meant to suggest that when we lack an abiding object focus, temporal intervals seemingly stretch out, and time feels as though it passes slowly. The concave horizontal axis is the converse: depth of focus refracts perception of temporal intervals so they seem shorter and time seemingly flies by. Of course time is experiential and also a human creation, so the figure is heuristic and not a representation of something that is actual or concrete.

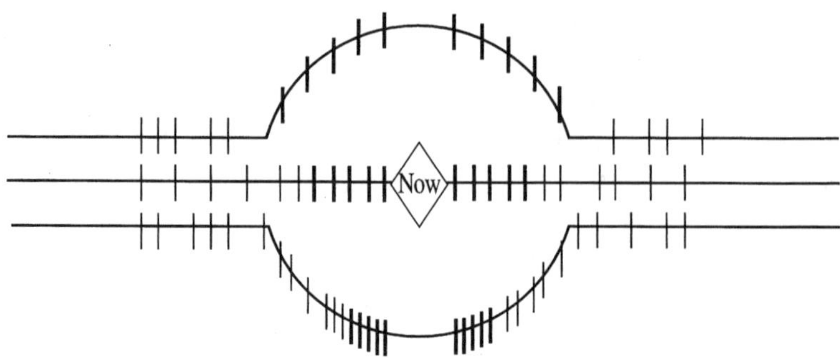

FIGURE 2.1　Chronological and perceptual flow of time.

THE SOCIAL CONSTRUCTION OF TIMELINES

Our personal sense of time also casts back to a consensual process. To paraphrase Humpty Dumpty, in *Alice Through the Looking Glass*, temporality means what people say it means—neither more nor less. Substantially, time and temporality are social constructions agreed to by those involved in similar situations; that is all they can be. Time is embedded in culture, it is part and parcel of social life, and is a principle component of how we think about the life course, not to mention the flow of history. A belief in progress has long been closely coupled with Judeo-Christian teleological traditions and to the Enlightenment's belief that life was getting better and better, day by day. In ancient China, however, history was seen very differently since time was believed to run in approximately 60-year cycles without linearity, essentially beginning anew with the passing of each generation. Everybody saw it that way. There was no such thing as linear progress, merely a turning of a wheel. Social conventions represented that model, and all kinds of ideological beliefs were formulated to accompany them.

The many ceremonial occasions embedded in a culture serve as deft chronological symbols, creating epochal intervals and synchronizing various social and individual times either by design or circumstance. The millennial year provided an excellent case in point. It stands as a marker for the end of an era, the beginning of an era, and will stand as a momentous occasion for anyone who retains memory of participating in its occurrence. The advent of clock time did not do away with social protocols; they still provide utile understandings about the proper use of and tracking of time. Today we have many conventions to help ground time. We celebrate Ramadan, Passover, Lent, the ambiguous "holiday season," or national holidays and use them as hallmarks to track other events. These and other examples are not real times either, but time proclaimed by concurrence and extensively used as lodestars to negotiate all manner of things and events.

How are the many layers of time kept in harmony, or at least how is our thinking about them kept in tune? Society, like nature, provides countless cues to coordinate and integrate people's sense of time. Examples are almost too plentiful, but one underlying theme all have in common is that they structure the pace of life, are symbolized in culture, and are surrounded with moral imperatives. The pace they provide becomes a back beat, as it were; it keeps people oriented to communal time as they go about their individual routines. Think for the moment about the pulse of time derived from memberships— family life, work life, religious observations, national holidays. To illustrate: family life cycles are an indelible part of every individual's frame of reference and they can be the nexus around which other forms of timing evolve. There are gender differences, no doubt, but there are generalizable principles that help in understanding how family life structures time sense and life course reckoning. But then, so too do such prosaic occurrences as meal functions, bell towers, or traffic congestion—each signaling socially significant times of day. How often are temporal notations part of the description of any event? All cultures seemingly do the same thing—relying on locally salient turning points to demarcate both occasion and time boundaries. In nearly all instances the effect is the same: it helps people come together for meaningful interaction, coordinate their schedules, or chronicle the beginnings and endings of various activities. Whether it is a seasonal benchmark or an ordinary daily occurrence, temporal milestones surround us and function as sweeping synchronizers. While cultures vary on issues of punctuality, temporal sequencing, and duration, all have ways of creating temporal regularity and all convey them to members via socialization (Moore, 1963; Zerubavel, 1981).

If sociologists have a contribution to make to the study of human affairs, one that is vital is that individual consciousness is not just personal. Rather it reflects membership in various social categories. The latter provide not only orientation and socialization but resources individuals rely on to make their way. It is because of this that distinctive subcultures can be found among groups that diverge on any of a number of key characteristics. So, for example, many cultural groups differ in terms of how they view time; age-groups are no different. It is the commonalties that create the essential groupness, reflecting both what people regard as important as well as cues in the milieu. This is not to say individuals are passive recipients of cultural messages. Rather, they actively select among potential messages based on relevance to their own purpose-at-hand. People attend to some, ignoring others as less germane. This personal agency is unique to humans and is one fly in the ointment when psychologists talk about stimulus and response—the same event may not be equally apropos to all actors.

ESTABLISHING THE TIMES OUR LIVES

Age-Grading and Social Transitions

Having asserted that time is a social construction defined by agreement, part of the warp and weave of social life, the next question is how? What is the loom that weaves the fabric? Several components have already been broached, but one that still requires attention is one that keeps individual timetables synchronized with those of larger membership groups and simultaneously creates "fellow travelers"—known to all of us as cohorts. I am talking about the concept known as age-grading, practiced by all societies and a mechanism by which shared temporal perspectives are inculcated. Like other social groups, cohorts have distinctive temporal orientations based on the historical period in which members came of age and on other unifying currents of social life (Gurvitch, 1964; Hendricks & Hendricks, 1976). One of the principal mechanisms for synchronizing the time of members of a cohort is through the process of age-grading. People undergo many *rites of passage* to signify transition across age boundaries and by way of the experience, certain communal worldviews are established. In fact, the life course is punctuated by many timelines that create the familiar trajectories we call social maturation and aging.

Birthdays are one surefire form of age-grading. In effect they say, okay, let everyone born in a certain year now enter school, graduate, obtain the right to drive, vote, drink, and so on until we get to the point where retirement is judged befitting and the events that follow are explained by their being age-appropriate. In other words, people pass from one to another status on the basis of recognized points of origination—their birthdates. There are other types of age-grading as well, some fairly ordinary, as in grade in school, age of entry into the labor force, parenthood, exit from the labor force, and so on. Whatever the event, provided it is socially acclaimed, it will stand as an important life episode defining phase, transitions, and trajectories. As Elder and O'Rand (1995, p. 457) put it, the process ensures some degree of *loose coupling* between life course trajectories and recognized societal transitions even if a panoply of intervening factors can potentially alter how the process plays out. In certain respects each phase or status is prologue to what follows. Once set in motion, a disruption is necessary if patterns are not to be played out in later stages of life. It is not deterministic—far from it. After all, personal agency is a defining human characteristic, but age-grading does establish overarching patterns within particular subcultures (Hendricks, 1999; Hogan & Astone, 1986). Age-grading and temporality are inexorably linked in manifold and subtle ways, and they remain influential throughout life.

MARKING TIME

Age-grading or other socially recognized age statuses provide the rhythmic structuring of cultural life by which time and aging are both marked (Hendricks & Hendricks, 1976, p. 27). As has been said, all manner of events are useful time markers for tracking life's transitions. Besides birthdays, other, less formal age-norms and temporal guideposts are integral to our daily lives and are sometimes endowed with ceremonial trappings. Retirement is such a transition; it casts a long shadow, it is an event cloaked in a great deal of lore. Retirement also illustrates those types of transitions creating temporal contexts and imbuing people with recognized status characteristics. These latter are seldom entirely of an individual's own volition, even when transitions may not be so clear-cut. In terms of temporal benchmarks, such as getting a driver's license, certain bodily changes, graduating, becoming a parent, and so on, retirement is a discernible watershed—it marks a before and after that is an indelible component of interpretation for the individual and for how they are seen by others.

Whether temporal structuring is equivalent for women and men is an important question since so many of our *rites of passage* are gender-linked, and some transitions, such as retirement, may be markedly different for various people (Moen, 1996, p. 132). Settersten and Hagestad (1996) discovered that men are more closely bound to a kind of linear clock time than are women, who experience what may be characterized as cyclical or at least not as rigidly linear time and thereby age-grading. If that is indeed the case, it allows for more than a bit of ambiguity in terms of personal definitions of age. Settersten and Hagestad (1996) are of the opinion that the age-graded timelines of a man's life are more patent than they are for women, at least up to the point of retirement. But even then, and throughout, they also found that people with less education, non-Whites, and nonprofessionals referred to an awareness of deadlines and earlier deadlines with greater frequency and more explicitly than their more advantaged counterparts. It would be a miscue to attribute difference to personal characteristics when they may also be traced to social resources contouring a person's ability to negotiate concessions or activate autonomous schedules.

Seemingly, there is an array of socioeconomic linkages incorporated into a person's sense of time. For example, diverse work experiences influence how boldly life's transitions are drawn and temporal trajectories constructed. With a career track laid out ahead that incorporates sequential rungs on a mobility ladder, a person likely develops a more lineal sense of futurity than do people who are engaged in contingent employment opportunities lacking internal mobility ladders. Each helps to denote time's passage but may likely yield different temporal horizons.

SOCIAL DURATION AND THE STRUCTURE OF TIME

All actors are "suspended in webs of significance that they themselves have spun" (Geertz, 1973, p. 5) and part of the consequence of those webs is that they provide the skein for an extensive temporal milieu. As has been noted, every individual's sense of time is rooted in tempos derived from membership in various subcultural categories. Societal time is invariably present: 7-day weeks are endemic, with a broad range of activities specified for each day; we have workdays and weekends, we have vacations and holidays, religious and secular days. We have the aforementioned family groups, work groups, and many other kinds of affinity groups. Think only of the academic year, whether your own or that of children or grandchildren. How vividly does the cadence of the school year structure perception of time. An even better example can be seen in the experiential dimensions of medical school training and how medical students' conception of the phases of their education are only tangentially related to the divisions of the academic calendar. Instead of 4 years or eight semesters, students see five general stages, each characterized by a dominant agenda (Light, 1975). Each illustration points to a cadence, and each permeates life with discernable rhythms. Each of us is conditioned by life events, relationships, socializing experiences, social resources and constraints, not to mention trajectories that emerge from ancillary involvements. In every instance, time consciousness reflects priorities of the moment. So, for example, if an actor is engaged in certain types of activity, that person's temporality will reflect the primacy and pacing bound-up with that activity. Changing to another type of activity will bring a shift in temporal orientation—successive shifts bringing about further reconfigurations of time and temporality even as some residual is carried forward from what has gone before, with its relevance only slowly fading from consciousness.

THE PROMISED LAND: REMINISCENCE AND FUTURITY

Temporal Projections: Thinking To and Fro

Few adults think only of the present; we frequently think back or ahead. Hopping from one dimension to another is seemingly effortless for most people. In ways that are not entirely clear, temporal orientation can shift and shift again, in less than the blink of an eye. It is hard to imagine daydreaming without incorporating future, present, or past. It probably happens, but it is hard to imagine. Part of the reason it seems so normal is that situating oneself in time and context is indivisible from how one thinks about one's self. As people think about their experience or their intentions, timelines are implicit (Wessman & Gorman, 1977). Whether it is because anticipated goals and aspirations are so consequential or because most of our chronological life lies in the past or ahead (assuming normal life expectancies) is difficult to say, but the plain fact is that time is pivotal to how we think of ourselves. Some researchers contend that older people are less prone to think ahead, but that assertion is fraught with complexity, and it is not yet time to draw definitive conclusions. Part of the difficulty is that as people think about their futures they are generally thinking about personal goals, tasks, projects, or concerns. We anchor attention through our personal well-being and future selves. It is important to bear in mind, however, that older people may also think about abstract futures not necessarily revolving around themselves, personally—a more oblique future perhaps, but a future nonetheless. Researchers themselves need to be mindful of how they ask questions about projected futures to make sure "generative futures" encompassing loved ones and others are not overlooked.

REMEMBRANCE OF THINGS PAST

In a very real sense, our personal past exists most vividly in our memory. I am not talking about what is written in history books or geological deposits but about the remembrance of personal experience, those things that have shaped how people think of themselves. It is not an overstatement to say a person's past is a mental construct, subject to the same ambient conditions that affect all other constructs. Because of the purpose they serve, it is not surprising that memory and recollections are seldom "exact" or indelibly "photographic" reproductions. Instead, they are reconstructions. As we summon our past, current needs and our self-referential agenda of the moment mold remembrance. It is not that memories are fantasias but they are not rigorously reportage either. There is nothing wrong about that; the probity of memory may not depend on its fidelity but in its application.

Memories are not unswerving and they do strange things to time. One cannot carbon-date memories to fix their chronology. Part of the muddle is that memories are what keep the past alive and through them continuities with current issues are created. There are distinctive psychological processes involving encoding, retention, and retrieval of either short- or long-term recall. In fact, experimental and cognitive psychologists spend careers in laboratories studying the ways in which information is stored and called forth again. They have written at length about the strength of memory, recency or primacy as factors in how things are remembered. These are important points, but not the aspects of memory that concern me here. Rather, I am interested in the emotional or intentional aspect of personal remembrance—how our pasts are catalogued and how they relate to temporality.

The reason memories refract is that personalities, psychological needs, and one's current focus each shape the remembrance of things past. The psychological emphasis on storage and retrieval processing interweaves with a more dynamic conception of personal past. Retrieval should not be thought of as a random sorting through pigeonholes looking for the right one to bring forth its contents. Instead, retrieval occurs through perceptual lenses configured in terms of self-referential and on-going concerns. When storage is occurring, if a category does not exist, experience is easily forgotten or redefined to resemble something else in memory. But that is not the end of it. Once something is archived, the meaning and outline are not then invariant. Memories are recalled differentially, contoured or redefined as current priorities grow and change so that a sense of congruence is maintained between past and what is happening at present. Personal memories are recoded in light of current focus, and the temporality implied in them is grounded in important aspects of self-concept. Memories of proximate as well as distal experiences have implicit timelines in which the self-relevant significance is the logic by which they are nested. But it is a kind of "fuzzy" or contingent union of past and present, not to mention the way they fit together shifts according to emergent aspects of one's sense of self that are currently of concern.

ECHOES OF TOMORROW

A great many people ask: Where am I headed? What will become of me? On the one hand those questions may be construed as anxiety speaking. On the other hand, they are exactly the questions all of us quietly ask ourselves and probably should be asking ourselves. In attempting to answer our own queries we begin to sketch-out some of the broad parameters of what may happen to us, before it does. How can that be?

In conceiving of life's script, people affect the way it is written. Even when we dream, in the sense of a daydream, we often dream of things that are yet to be as though they already were. Then when we get focused again we proceed toward the goals we envisioned in our reverie. One might say we "recollect the future" much as we reconstruct the past. It is not that expectations are tantamount to destiny, but they do exert a prophetic magnetism—or gravitational pull—over current behavior and thinking. To put it another way, the future is like an Elysian field drawing us forward. Thinking ahead, having a vision of the future, anticipating necessary next steps in the passage is somewhat like using a bright light to pierce the darkness. What falls within the beam of light is known, what does not, remains a mystery. Then the issue becomes where to shine the light and whether to go in the direction of what is illuminated or to set off in another direction toward the unknown.

What lies behind the enigma has to do with conceiving a prospective course and how that then becomes a motivational impetus occurring in the present (Zaleski, 1994, p. 15). Having a sense of futurity enables people not only to extend themselves in time, but to act in accord with a future foreseen. Elsewhere I have described it as a proleptic process in which we imagine a future already accomplished (we think in a future perfect tense), then resolve how to get there (Hendricks, 1982). Over a hundred years ago Guyau averred:

> Time is a strategy of coping with the world; our consciousness of time is a side effect of goal-oriented behavior; time is a product of consciousness. Whereas the present is perceived, the past and the future are represented. (Guyau, 1890, quoted in Zaleski, 1994, p. 13)

A key component of what Guyau termed "represented" has to do with intentionality. Representations are purposely filtered perceptions of the point at issue. Representations mean that events or activities are captured via synoptic-like imaginings, not as a series of discrete data points. As representations, images of the future are not value-neutral conceptions; rather they are prescient delineations replete with personal affect (Lewin, 1939; Nuttin, 1984). Accordingly, personal futures, the summary precis of things to come, stand as desired goals perceived proleptically—as though already accomplished—providing beacons for navigating one's way through what comes next toward a future foreseen. Behavior and experience is then evaluated in terms of whether it is leading toward that desired goal or is tangential. The proleptic future, with its prophetic motivational ramifications in the present provides mechanisms for individuals and groups to plan and implement actions that reach beyond the moment (Hendricks & Hendricks, 1976; Lens & Moreas, 1994).

In large measure people tend to think of the ability to imagine a future already achieved as a personal attribute, somehow unique unto themselves. To a certain extent that is true. Yet, neither our focal length nor its details are entirely of our own volition. No one else shares a duplicate biography to be sure, and therefore it is unlikely anyone anticipates an identical future. But there may be parallels. Whether it is as part of a marital unit, or other close relationship, or as part of a palpable subcultural or socioeconomic category, the way individuals imagine the future is linked to comparable imaginings of others who share a similar social niche. In projecting themselves in time, individuals rely on the same array of personal and social resources they utilize to negotiate other aspects of life. As a consequence, the broad parameters of those resources set forth the extensive and inclusive image of the future and what it will take to get there.

TELLING TIME: PERSONAL NARRATIVES AND TIME TALK

Talking creates explanatory scenarios and talking about time creates time frames that provide important referential cues. Creating narratives about our experiences is a meaning-making endeavor. In a way, these stories, using common language and syntax, provide interpersonal certitude to social meaning since most interaction partners would be hard-pressed to relate 900 billion ticks of a cesium clock ago or from now to anything recognizable. Being told an event was just before the birth of the baby, or about New Year's 2 years from now establishes a referential context that creates a temporal connection for our interaction partners. It converts the reference to something recognizable and is part of others' experience (Hendricks & Hendricks, 1976). The temporal horizons thus created are integral to life, interaction, self-concept and, for that matter, to the structure of knowledge, for they are what provide the synthesizing principles by which connections are drawn.

The narratives created in life-stories bind our life-span into coherent leitmotifs, linking present with past and projected futures (McAdams, 1990). What is interesting is that there are certain parallels among shared status groupings of men, women, members of minority groups, persons of a given socioeconomic status, age groups, and so on. Each has referential group experiences complete with interlocking timelines that are instrumental in shaping the stories woven by individuals. And like a good cover, the point is to provide warmth and comfort (via explanation and coherence)—exactitude being coincidental at best. The stories are self-representations, abstractions, incentives, or deterrents utilized for making sense of what has gone before, what is anticipated, and for establishing interrelationships (Markus & Herzog, 1991).

When you think about it, speaking takes time, writing takes time, and recollecting either seems to imply a spatial dimension. Looking at a sentence on a page is a linear process; so, too, is talking about time. Merely talking about time helps imbue time with structure, almost implicitly, akin to a "train of ideas" that occupies attention in its passing (Sherover, 1989). Whether we perceive words then sentences or sentences that are later broken into constitutive elements is not the issue. The point is that verbalization stretches across time, giving a sense of linearity and succession. Weaving stories is akin to crafting time; doing so provides continuity.

Development and Time's Horizons

Being able to talk about time does not spring full blown from the head of Zeus. Like many other functions, situating ourselves in time is a developmental process. In the early years of life, infants and young children are centered in the moment, with limited, albeit developing, memories but a more equivocal sense of futurity. As children approach their second birthdays, some anticipatory mindset enters into their thinking, even though they cannot yet manipulate temporal concepts other than basic sequencing information. By age two and a half, remembrance and recall become apparent with accompanying vocabulary shifts. By the next birthday, a greater sophistication is evident and it becomes possible to ask a child to delay until an event in the near future has taken place, a partial sense of deferred gratification having emerged (Mischel, 1981). During the same period children employ the past as a concept, even though differences between "yesterday" and "last week" may be idiomatic and intermittent. With each incremental period thereafter, conceptualization of things temporal shows evolutionary change so that by age six or seven, clocks, the seasons, and a developed sense of duration are integrated into children's temporal frontiers, can be readily referenced and are part of their self-awareness, and are manipulated by means of appropriate language structure.

On the other end of the lifecourse it has been widely presumed that older people live extensively in the past since most of their life is behind them. Anecdotal evidence of past-oriented story telling has been taken as evidence of preoccupation with what has already occurred to the exclusion of what may happen next. As implausible as such a view now seems, even on its face, such was the general conception for many years (Kastenbaum, 1982). It is, however, misleading to think older persons have a constrained sense of futurity; mostly it is different rather than circumscribed or shorter. The differences should not be construed to mean older people do not think ahead, only that how they think of the future might be different than the patterns manifested by younger people.

As alluded to above, what may actually be the case is that older persons have a highly developed sense of futurity but not one grounded in narrowly circumscribed personal concerns. As most assessments of psychological processing see higher order thinking, characterized by abstraction and existential transcendence as positive attributes, it would be a mistake to infer negativity to the way older people approach the future. In keeping with maturational processing, an older person's futurity may be more abstracted and thereby a more sophisticated sense of futurity requiring a greater sensitivity in ascertaining its focus. Old people are not fools. They know their life expectancy is limited, but they recognize there is more to the future than their personal presence; therefore time itself is not thereby limited even if their own time is. Via their children or grandchildren, all younger generations actually, older people can anticipate a future unfolding in a more abstract sense than personal futurity implies—it might be called generative futurity—a future conceived through people and issues older persons care about but not necessarily through themselves. Such a perspective may actually be a robust indicator of mental health insofar as they think abstractly, are able to take the role of others in approaching that future, and are not egocentric in that the only future they can foresee is their own.

TEMPORALITY, SELF AND SENSE OF WELL-BEING

There can be little doubt that temporal perspective is a touchstone of well-being. In fact, being oriented to time and place is a widely used diagnostic protocol in assessing mental status since time disorders are closely linked with delusional thinking associated with various forms of distress. Such conditions stand only as extreme cases of more prosaic fluctuations (Aaronson, 1966).

Temporal Balance and Personal Integration

Almost by definition, being reflexive implies a continual temporal reorganization built on environmental screening and evaluation of possible options (Giddens, 1991, p. 32). Refurbishing one's sense of self over adult life is predicated on a rolling reflexivity. It means keeping a particular narrative going through a personal biography that presumes knowing who we are, how we got here, where we are going (Taylor, 1989).

At the risk of overgeneralizing, it is possible to say that the more optimistic a person is, the more expansive the temporal horizon. It is likely that being optimistic or having a positive self-concept is partially attributable to believing there are "mountains left to climb" (Nuttin, 1984). Those "mountains" are emblematic of course, standing for personal projects, aspirations, or goals. Throughout much of life they may be largely personalized, but during the later years they may evolve into abstractions, cast in terms of aspirations for grandchildren, one's reference groups, causes, and so on. Having a purpose in life is tantamount to a mission. It means not living life one day at a time but maintaining an expectant attitude and an openness or receptivity about what the future can become (Rappaport, Foster, Bross, & Gilden, 1993, p. 337). It may be that such everyday processes as activity levels depend on possessing a sense of optimism or anticipation. Raynor (1982) referred to a person's psychological career wherein activities and self-concept are both related to expectations about future prospects and pathways still to come. To a certain extent, people may conceive of themselves as a project, with a "contextual lifespan" (Orme, 1969, p. 9). In many respects, sense of self is analogous to having sense of purpose (Royce, 1903). I would extend that further and assert that being aware of a sense of becoming is to be aware of time.

HEALTH AND SENSE OF TIME

Those individuals dealing with stressors, such as ill health, functional impairment, depression, financial adversity, or difficult relationships have circumscribed temporal extensions constricted by the nature of those conditions and circumstances. As one might imagine, the absence of options and resolution will not only result in some impairment as far as well-being, purpose, and meaning are concerned, but will affect temporal horizons as well. It is hard to escape the moment when adversity looms large.

In discussing health as a possible influence on temporal reckoning, two dimensions come together. To begin with, sense of futurity is related to positive mental outlook, but so, too, is a sense of control. Not having a feeling of autonomy or control circumscribes future thinking (Fingerman & Perlmutter, 1995; Trommsdorff, 1994). Having a sense of autonomy or control is also closely linked to health status. Ill health and impairments that encroach on sense of identity affect one's perception of being able to exercise initiative to affect events and, consequently, one's sense of time. Temporary bouts of ill health are not at issue, but chronic and persistent conditions altering self-image, interaction patterns, or ability to manage our environment are crucial. There is nothing like pain or impairment to focus one's mind on the present or for creating a perception that a person is not on a path leading to anything particularly desirable. As Eisenhandler (1989, p. 163) noted, the reason health matters is that it is a means of access for maintaining customary routines. A disruption of those routines brings about reorganization in one's outlook on life, one's sense of time, one's self-concept, and interaction patterns. Rakowski (1986) and others (e.g., Kenyon, 1996) have repeatedly found that such troublesome displacing factors as ill-health have a profound negative impact on older people's senses of futurity.

In an effort to disentangle the effects of age, per se, from health, Bouffard, Bastin, and LaPierre (1994) reported that age did not affect temporal orientation anywhere near as much as health status. They found that among individuals experiencing the most restrictive health conditions, future time perspective was significantly briefer than among age peers who reported satisfactory health statuses. On top of that, subjective appraisals of quality of life make a difference even in the face of a given degree of functional impairment. Those who judged their lives more positively despite their impairment manifested a correspondingly more positive temporal outlook. In contrast, those who appraised their lives most negatively also expressed the most constricted future time orientation.

SOCIOECONOMIC CONSIDERATIONS AND TEMPORAL HORIZONS

There is one important factor left to consider in terms of its impact on temporal horizons and because it is closely linked with feelings of autonomy, control, and work experience. Socioeconomic background is relevant, as it is a form of social capital integral to an actor's interpretative template. Socioeconomic status is wrapped up in the "natural attitude" actors bring to their affairs and is also a component of institutionally formulated scripts coloring life course development (Bourdieu, 1989; Hendricks, 1999; Kohli & Meyer, 1986). Without putting too fine an edge on it, socioeconomic status undergirds the sociocentric world-views that actors take as their own, including sense of futurity and patterns of the life course. In commenting on the importance of socioeconomic background, Brandt-stadter (1990) is apt, "As these contextualized conditions undergo change, so do the modal patterns and constraints for individual development" (p. 84). The evidence suggests that people's socioeconomic positions are the proximate circumstances that affect psychological functioning if only through ability to establish ideational flexibility, self-direction, and choice (Kohn & Slomczynski, 1990).

Why might the differences matter? For one thing, socioeconomic background is a resource called into play in the face of undesirable life events (McLeod & Kessler, 1990). For another, with little prospect of improving life chances or little opportunity to exercise initiative, being oriented to the present makes all the sense in the world. On the other hand, if education, income, and other personal or social resources are such that there are realistic possibilities of imposing one's will on the environment, a sense of futurity is a likely result. If every day is pretty much like the one that went before and there are few prospects of change, it should not be too surprising that sense of optimism and futurity is restricted. Anything else could well be dysfunctional. Indeed, in their analysis of future time perspective among older persons in Quebec, Bouffard, Bastin, and LaPierre (1994, p. 85) reported a connection between socioeconomic status and futurity—a link that was strongest among males, in younger age cohorts, and for those with the highest levels of functional autonomy. Settersten and Hagestad (1996) found similar results, awareness of life course transitions being most evident for comparable categories.

CONCLUSION

Time comes in many guises and has many faces. Although it is entirely possible that Hawking (1988) is correct, that the directionality of time is inexorably part of the expanding of the universe, the way we think of time has to do with how we keep track of it and the cultural implications of dominant modalities. The synthesis provided by human consciousness is indivisible from time's role in our lives and our conceptualization of it.

We live our lives ensconced in many varieties of social circumstances. Each has an effect on the way we conceive of time and its passage. We have many cultural traditions that are inexorably part of our mindset, regardless of whether they represent current circumstances. Then, too, beginning at birth, various groups and organizations impose varying degrees of precision and temporal suzanantry over our lives. Some reckonings are fairly flexible and permit individual or comparative temporal frameworks; in others there is "a one-sided emphasis on chronological time" such that our thinking and our clocks are closely aligned (Baars, 1997, p. 285).

We begin life grounded in families, then move to the educational system, the world of work, and other organizations and social engagements. Each has a rhythm inherent in its functioning. We adapt to and utilize the cadence of these involvements to structure our own lives and how we distinguish time. As participants in one after another, our time reflects their time and timing and the interface between the time of diverse categories to which we belong. Occasionally there are preemptory clashes or conflicts prompted by one getting out of phase with another. These clashes serve to remind us of the importance of coordination. In every instance, however, a sense of becoming, of forward movement, or potentiality bolster a sense of futurity.

All the ways we calculate time will influence what we think about aging and the human life course. It is not an overstatement to say that as a culture and as a scholarly endeavor many of us have equated aging with its measure. In conceiving of a lifetime, we have spoken nearly exclusively in terms of measurable time (Baars, 1997; Hendricks & Hendricks, 1976). But of course people with the same number of ticks of the clock under their belt can vary greatly in terms of their worldview and how much time might be left to them. This is not to say that having knowledge of the number of ticks a person has experienced will tell researchers nothing, but what it tells is probabilistic knowledge—sometimes "true," sometimes not, depending. In some respects it is fair to say that aging well may relate to a sense of timelessness in terms of not reining in one's expectations (Strumpf, 1987, p. 201). Of course it is mutually reinforcing. Older people who manifest a positive future orientation express great life satisfaction, less boredom, and seemingly experience less stress or anxiety (Neuringer, Levinson, & Kaplan, 1971; Rakowski & Clark, 1985). But the converse may also be true; those who anticipate negativity, personally defined, may incur corresponding consequences.

REFERENCES

Aaronson, B. S. (1966). Personality stereotypes of aging. *Journal of Gerontology, 21*, 458–462.

Bandura, A. (1986). *Social foundations of thought and action.* Englewood Cliffs, NJ: Prentice-Hall.

Baars, J. (1997). Concepts of time and narrative temporality in the study of aging. *Journal of Aging Studies, 11*, 283–295.

Bergson, H. (1965). *Duration and simultaneity,* (L. Jacobsen, Trans.). Indianapolis: Bobbs–Merrill.

Bouffard, L., Bastin, E., & LaPierre, S. (1994). The personal future in old age. In Z. Zaleski (Ed.), *Psychology of future time orientation* (pp. 75–94). Lubin, Poland: Towarzystwo Naukowe KUL.

Bourdieu, P. (1989). Social space and symbolic power. *Sociological Theory, 7,* 14–25.

Brandtstadter, J. (1990). Development as a personal and cultural construction. In G. Semin & K. Gergin (Eds.), *Everyday understanding: Social and scientific implications* (pp. 83–107). Newbury Park, CA: Sage.

Eisenhandler, S. (1989). More than counting years: Social aspects of time and the identity of elders. In L. E. Thomas (Ed.), *Research on adulthood and aging: The human science approach* (pp. 163–181). Albany, NY: SUNY Press.

Elder, G., & O'Rand, A. (1995). Adult lives in a changing society. In K. Cook, G. Fine, & J. House (Eds.), *Sociological perspectives on social psychology* (pp. 452–475). Needham Heights, MA: Allyn and Bacon.

Fingerman, K., & Permutter, M. (1995). Future time perspective and life events across adulthood. *The Journal of General Psychology, 122,* 95–111.

Flaherty, M. G. (1999). *A watched pot: How we experience time.* New York: New York University Press.

Fraser, J. T. (1996). Time and the origin of life. In J. T. Fraser & M. P. Soulsby (Eds.), *Dimensions of time and life: The study of time VIII* (pp. 3–17). Madison, CT: International Universities Press.

Friedman, W. (1990). *About time: Inventing the fourth dimension.* Cambridge, MA: MIT Press.

Geetz, C. (1973). *The interpretation of cultures.* New York: Basic Books

Giddens, A. (1991). *Modernity and self-identity: Self and society in the late modern age.* Stanford, CA: Stanford University Press.

Gurvitch, G. (1964). *The spectrum of social time.* Dordrecht, Holland: D. Reidel.

Hawking, S. (1988). *A brief history of time.* London: Routledge.

Hendricks, C. D., & Hendricks, J. (1976). Concepts of time and temporal construction among the aged, with implications for research. In J. F. Gubrium (Ed.), *Time, roles, and self in old age* (pp. 13–49). New York: Human Sciences Press.

Hendricks, J. (1982). Time and social science: History and potential. In E. H. Mizruchi, B. Glassner, & T. Pastorello (Eds.), *Time and aging* (pp. 12–40). Bayside, NY: General Hall.

Hendricks, J. (1999). Practical consciousness, social class, and self-concept: A view from sociology. In C. Ryff & V. Marshall (Eds.), *The self and society in aging processes* (pp. 187–222). New York: Springer.

Hendricks, J., & Peters, C. B. (1986). The times of our lives: An integrative framework. *American Behavioral Scientist, 29,* 662–676.

Hogan, D., & Astone, N. (1986). The transition to adulthood. In R. Turner (Ed.), *Annual Review of Sociology:* Vol. 12 (pp. 109–130). Palo Alto: Annual Reviews.

James, W. (1950). *The principles of psychology.* New York: Dover. (Original work published 1890)

Kastenbaum R. (1982). Time course and time perspective in later life. *Annual Review of Gerontology and Geriatrics, 3,* 80–101.

Kenyon, G. (1996). The meaning/value of personal storytelling. In J. Birren, G. Kenyon, J. E. Ruth, H. Schroots, & T. Svensson (Eds.), *Aging and biography: Explorations in adult development* (pp. 21–38). New York: Springer.

Kohli, M., & Meyer, J. (1986). Social structure and the social construction of life stages. *Human Development, 29,* 145–156.

Kohn, M. L., & Slomczynski, K. M. (1990). *Social structure and self-direction: A comparative analysis of the United States and Poland.* Oxford: Basil Blackwell.

Lens, W., & Moreas, M-A (1994). Future time perspective: Individual and societal approach. In Z. Zaleski (Ed.), *Psychology of future orientation* (pp. 23–38). Lubin, Poland: Towarzystwo Naukowe KUL.

Lewin, K. (1939). Field theory and experiment in social psychology concepts and methods. *American Journal of Sociology, 44,* 868–897.

Light, D. (1975). The sociological calendar: An analytic tool for fieldwork applied to medical and psychiatric training. *American Journal of Sociology, 80,* 1145–1164.

Lundmark, L. (1996). The separation of time and nature. In J. T. Fraser & M. P. Soulsby (Eds.), *Dimensions of time and life: The study of time VIII* (pp. 97–104). Madison, CT: International Universities Press.

Markus, H., & Herzog, A. (1991). The role of the self-concept in aging. In K. W. Schaie & M. P. Lawton (Eds.), *Annual Review of Gerontology and Geriatrics, Volume 11* (pp. 110–143). New York: Springer.

McAdams, D. (1990). Unity and purpose in human lives; The emergence of identity as a life story. In A. Rabin, R. Zucker, R. Emmons, & S. Frank (Eds.), *Studying persons and lives* (pp. 148–200). New York: Springer.

McLeod, J., & Kessler, R. (1990). Socioeconomic status differences in vulnerability to undesirable life events. *Journal of Health and Social Behavior, 31,* 162–172.

Minkowski, E. (1970). *Lived time.* Evanston: Northwestern University Press.

Mischel, W. (1981). *Introduction to personality* (3rd ed.). New York: Holt, Reinhart & Winston.

Moen, P. (1996). A life course perspective on retirement, gender, and well-being. *Journal of Occupational Health Psychology, 1,* 131–144.

Moore, W. (1963). *Man, time, and society.* New York: Wiley.

Neuringer, C., Levinson, M., & Kaplan, J. (1971). Phenomenological time flow in suicidal, geriatric and normal individuals. *Omega, 2,* 247–251.

Nuttin, J. (1984). *Motivation, planning and action: A relational theory of behavior.* Hillsdale, NJ: Lawrence Erlbaum.

Orme, J. E. (1969). *Time, experience and behaviour.* London: ILIFFE Books, Ltd.

Pixten, R. (1995). Comparing time and temporality in cultures. *Cultural Dynamics, 7,* 233–252.

Rakowski, W. (1986). Future time perspective: Applications to the health context of later adulthood. *American Behavioral Scientist, 29,* 6, 730–745.

Rakowski, W., & Clark, N. (1985). Future outlook, caregiving, and care-receiving in the family context. *The Gerontologist, 25,* 618–623.

Rappaport, H., Fossler, R., Bross, L., & Gilden, D. (1993). Future time, death anxiety, and life purpose among older adults. *Death Studies, 17,* 369–379.

Raynor, J. (1982). A theory of personality functioning and change. In J. Raynor & E. Entin (Eds.), *Motivation, career striving, and aging* (pp. 249–302). Washington, DC: Hemisphere.

Royce, J. (1903). *Outlines of psychology.* New York: Macmillian.

Settersten, Jr., R., & Hagestad, G. (1996). What's the latest? II. Cultural age deadlines for educational and work transitions. *The Gerontologist, 36,* 602–613.

Sherover, C. (1989). *Res cogitans:* The time of mind. In J. T. Fraser (Ed.), *Time and mind: Interdisciplinary issues, the study of time VI* (pp. 279–294). Madison, CT: International Universities Press.

Strumpf, N. (1987). Probing the temporal world of the elderly. *International Journal of Nursing Studies, 24,* 201–214.

Taylor, C. (1989). *Source of the self.* Cambridge: Cambridge University Press.

Trommsdorff, G. (1994). Future time perspective and control orientation: Social conditions and consequences. In Z. Zaleski (Ed.), *Psychology of future orientation* (pp. 39–62). Lubin, Poland: Towarzystwo Naukowe KUL.

Wessman, A., & Gorman, B. (1977). The emergence of human awareness and concepts of time. In B. Gorman & A. Wessman (Eds.), *The personal experience of time* (pp. 3–55). New York: Plenum.

Zaleski, Z. (1994). Towards a psychology of the personal future. In Z. Zaleski (Ed.), *Psychology of future orientation* (pp. 10–20). Lubin, Poland: Towarzystwo Naukowe KUL.

Zerubavel, E. (1981). *Hidden rhythms: Schedules and calendars in social life.* Berkeley, CA: University of California Press.

CHAPTER 3

Aging, Time Estimation, and Emotion

Quinn Kennedy, Helene H. Fung, and Laura L. Carstensen

The ability to monitor time and to anticipate the future is a uniquely human characteristic. Throughout life, especially in adulthood, an increasing number of life events, such as graduations, births of children and grandchildren, and deaths of same-aged peers, serve as reminders that time is passing by. Social endings, such as impending geographic moves or emigrations, also heighten a sense of endings. In addition, unlike any other animals, humans anticipate their own deaths. How does the approach of ending influence emotional experience? The answer to this question remains largely unknown. Endings not only provoke dread and sadness, they also increase the appreciation for what is precious in life. Viktor Frankl wrote (1986, p. 33):

> Passing time is therefore not only a thief, but a trustee . . . the person who takes life [optimistically] is like a man who removes each successive leaf from his calendar and files it neatly and carefully away with its predecessors—after first having jotted down a few diary notes on

the back. He can reflect with pride and joy on the richness set down in these notes, on all the life he has already lived in full. . . . What reasons has he to envy a young person? [This man says to himself] "Instead of possibilities, I have realities in my past—not only the reality of work done and of love loved, but of suffering suffered. These are the things of which I am most proud—though these are things which cannot inspire envy."

Frankl suggests that an anticipation of endings—in this case, the end of life—affects emotional experience in two ways. First, it motivates people to focus on the "pride," "joy" and "richness" of life, not on expanding horizons or seeking new frontiers. Second, it leads to experience characterized by emotional poignancy—the simultaneous experience of positive and negative feeling states. People remember not only "work done and love loved" but also "suffering suffered." They treasure the things of which they are "most proud," but at the same time realize that those things "cannot inspire envy."

In this chapter, we propose that as people age and sense that remaining time is limited, their goal hierarchies change. Long-term goals that are directed at improving the quality of life in a distant future decrease in importance. In contrast, because they are realized in the moment, emotionally meaningful goals become centrally salient. Emotionally meaningful goals motivate people to regulate their emotions and are associated with relatively positive emotional experience. When emotional meaning is sought, even mundane activities of daily life can become tinged with complex, and often poignant, emotions. Having dinner with a spouse, receiving a phone call from an old friend, and sharing holidays with loved ones take on increased importance, in part because they could be among the last. Unlike 20-year-olds who may perceive "reaching 43 as a trillion years away" (Azenberg, 1997, p. 14), older people who perceive restrictions on time may react even to everyday events not just with positive emotions like joy and happiness, but also with negative emotions such as sadness and fear. We begin the chapter by discussing how the theoretical works of Viktor Frankl and Erik Erikson draw connections among aging, emotional experience, and emotional poignancy. We then outline a theory—socioemotional selectivity theory—that argues that changes in perception of time, rather than age, influence emotional experience and poignancy. We then speculate about how these time-related changes can take on different forms among different cultures and religions.

EARLY WORK ON AGING, EMOTIONAL EXPERIENCE AND EMOTIONAL POIGNANCY

Frankl's Theory of Logotherapy

The intertwining of the end of life and emotional experience is implicit in the works of Viktor Frankl and Erik Erikson. Frankl's theory of logotherapy emphasizes recognition of the spiritual dimension of life or the meaning of being human. One principle of logotherapy claims that humans possess a "will-to-meaning" in which there is an innate desire to give as much meaning as possible to one's life and to actualize as many values as possible. Emotional satisfaction is garnered from striving to satisfy and, possibly, satisfying this innate desire. The will-to-meaning is what most distinguishes humans from other animals. It is with the principle of will-to-meaning that aging, and the time perspective associated with it, is most relevant in Frankl's work. Precisely because people recognize their mortality, they are driven to attain maximal meaning from life. As Frankl (1986) states, "Finality, temporality, is therefore not only an essential characteristic of human life, but also a real factor in its meaningfulness. The meaning of human existence is based upon its irreversible quality" (p. 64). The finiteness of human life drives people to create a personally acceptable ending to their lives. Frankl proposes that those near the end of life will conduct a life review to derive as much meaning as possible from their lives. Conducting a life review is an emotional task that can lead to meaningful emotional experience. It can also be an emotionally poignant task, as people review past mistakes as well as achievements.

Erikson's Developmental Theory of Psychosocial Values

Erikson's work (1980) on the development stages of psychosocial values, particularly integrity, also emphasizes emotional goals and emotional poignancy. Erikson's developmental theory of psychosocial values describes the processes by which people mature. According to his theory, people must resolve a particular psychosocial crisis during each of eight life stages. As each psychosocial crisis is resolved, people become more socially mature. For example, during the fifth stage, adolescents strive to achieve self identity. Self identity is achieved by integrating past and future goals, seeking out information from others, and "trying on" different personalities. During Erikson's final stage, older adults strive for integrity. A review of one's life and an attempt to integrate the generational cycle are some of the psychosocial challenges facing older adults during this stage. It appears that older persons attempt to achieve emotional satisfaction with their life histories, particularly in their relationships with others. According to Erikson, in describing their lives older adults mention satisfaction with their relationships, for example, in marriage and as parents. In addition, Erikson argues that older adults have "grand-generativity" in that they see their own parenting as partly responsible for their children's parenting styles and grandchildren's achievements. Grandparenting allows older adults to have a second chance at generativity—to contribute to their grandchildren's development without the responsibility. Also, many older adults attend religious services to maintain an enduring thread in their lives, their family's lives, and the community. Attending religious services in old age is one way to connect childhood—when people first learn the meaning of the services—with the present. It is also an activity that can be shared by all generations on a regular basis. Finally, regular attendance at religious services is a way to maintain social and emotional connections with other members of the community.

Theoretically, according to Erikson, older adults strive to add coherence to their lives and their place in the world by maintaining familial social ties through their roles as parents and grandparents. Erikson's theory of integrating the generational cycle is consistent with the idea that older adults place increasingly greater emphasis on emotional goals, particularly on maintaining and deepening emotional ties with loved ones. In contrast to the fifth psychosocial stage, in which adolescents endeavor to achieve long-term goals, older adults attempt to achieve emotional satisfaction and meaning in the here-and-now.

Erikson's final stage, in which older adults strive for acceptance of their lives, has gained empirical support. In research by Cross and Markus (1991), people of various ages were asked to list images of self that they hoped to achieve ("hoped-for" selves) and images of self that they were afraid they would end up being ("feared" selves). Older adults showed greater self-acceptance by reporting fewer "hoped-for" and "feared" selves than younger adults. In addition, young adults reported a wide range of "hoped-for" and "feared" selves, many of which were unrealistic, whereas older adults seemed to accept the imperfection of life in describing their "hoped-for" and "feared" selves. For example, in describing their "hoped-for" possible selves, young adults made statements such as "being perfectly happy," and "famous." In contrast, older adults made statements that focused on the development of current roles or conception of self.

Further evidence is found in lay formulations of psychological well-being. Ryff (1989a) interviewed middle-aged and older adults about their conceptions of psychological well-being. She found that while middle-aged adults stressed being confident and assertive, older adults emphasized self-acceptance. In responding to an open-ended question about what they would like to change in their life "given the chance," the most frequent response for older adults was "nothing," while that for middle-aged adults was "active self-improvement." Indeed, older adults rated themselves lower than middle-aged and young adults on personal growth—"see[ing] one-self as growing and expanding" (Ryff, 1989b), and goal-seeking—the desire to achieve new goals, to search for new and different experiences, and to be on the move. These findings suggest that older adults place less emphasis on goals related to changing themselves and they are emotionally satisfied with the way things are. Rather than chastising themselves for past errors and lost opportunities, they show greater acceptance of themselves.

Moreover, in old age, most people recognize that they no longer have the time to strive for unfulfilled dreams. According to Erikson, Erikson, and Kivnik (1986), this realization inspires a life review in which older adults come to terms with perceived mistakes and failures and missed opportunities. They state that older adults

> endeavor to integrate, rather than resolutely deny, the mixed feelings
> that inevitably result from comparing the life actually lived with the

life anticipated in youthful fantasy and imagined, over decades, as waiting to be claimed at the next opportunity. (p. 141)

As the end of life nears, older adults not only try to come to terms with their lives, but also with humankind's place on earth. Similar to Frankl's notion of the will-to-meaning, Erikson's life review process is likely to entail experiences of emotional poignancy. One could even argue that it would be impossible to not experience both positive and negative emotions when coming to acceptance of one's life.

SOCIOEMOTIONAL SELECTIVITY THEORY

Consistent with the work of Frankl and Erikson, socioemotional selectivity theory (Carstensen, 1992, 1995; Carstensen, Isaacowitz, & Charles, 1999) postulates that aging is positively associated with a heightened salience of emotionally meaningful goals. However, the theory argues that age per se is not the causal factor. The realization that time left in the future is limited, not some inherent and unidirectional properties about aging, motivates older people to focus on goals that maximize emotional satisfaction from social interactions. In addition, the perception of an anticipated ending tinges everyday emotional experiences with both positive and negative emotions.

Influence of Time on Emotional Goals

People set goals throughout their lives. In general, young people view the future as a large expanse of time and set goals that maximize future payoffs. They are willing to pursue global goals that may take years to accomplish and pursue subgoals on a daily basis that facilitate the attainment of this distant dream. In contrast, with age the number of goals that extend far into the future decreases (Bouffard, Bastin, & LaPierre, 1996). Older adults estimate time to be shorter, view time as nearing an end, and are more likely to set short-term goals that can be achieved in the remaining time (Carstensen, 1995).

Socioemotional selectivity theory postulates that the same essential set of goals operates throughout life, such as establishing and maintaining intimacy and learning about the world and oneself, but the relative importance of specific goals changes depending on whether time is perceived as expansive or constrained (Carstensen, 1992, 1995). The theory focuses on two main classes of social goals: knowledge-related goals and emotion-related goals. Knowledge-related goals consist of acquiring information about one's self and others and about the world. Emotion-related goals include establishing intimacy, feeling good, deriving emotional meaning from life, and verifying the self. Knowledge-related goals help people to reach long-term goals, whereas emotion-related goals are often achieved in the moment of contact.

Throughout life, the relative importance of these two classes of social goals fluctuates. Developmentally, knowledge-related goals are very important during the early years of life and gradually lessen in importance over the course of the life span as knowledge accrues and the future becomes less expansive. Emotion-related goals show a more curvilinear path. Like knowledge-related goals, they are also highly salient during infancy and early childhood. Between middle childhood and young adulthood, however, they are relegated lesser importance than knowledge-related goals. In later adulthood, emotion-related goals increase in importance, becoming increasingly salient throughout old age (see Figure 3.1).

Theoretically, changes in goal salience are adaptive. In early adulthood, emotion-related goals, like feeling good in the moment, can impede achievement of long-term goals, such as developing a career. For example, young adults who value emotional goals over knowledge goals would be less likely to behave to achieve a future goal, nor would they think about the consequences of their current actions. Because emotion-related goals could impede reaching long-term goals, younger adults place less importance on emotion-related goals and greater importance on knowledge-related goals as they strive to achieve long-term goals. However, as people age and the end of life nears, the long-term future is less relevant. The emphasis shifts from long-term to short-term goals, such as feeling good or establishing intimacy. For example, at a party, a young woman may be interested in meeting new people, whereas in her old age, this same woman may be more interested in catching up with old friends.

Socioemotional selectivity theory offers one explanation for what lifespan developmentalists have called the "paradox of aging." Along with decline in physical functioning, the loss of old friends and

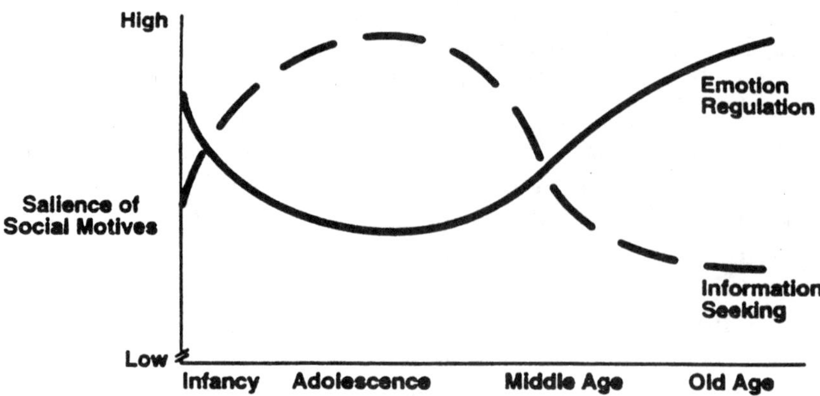

FIGURE 3.1   Idealized model of socioemotional selectivity theory's conception of the salience of two social motives across the life span.

Note: From *Annual Review of Geriatrics and Gerontology* (Vol. 17, p. 331, edited by K. W. Schaie and M. P. Lawton). Copyright 1998 by Springer Publishing Company. Reprinted with permission.

family, and the increased likelihood of illness, old age is commonly believed to be marked by negative emotions and experiences. Surprisingly, it has been found that despite an array of declines and losses, overall emotional well-being seems to be well-maintained in the second half of life.

Socioemotional selectivity theory explains this paradox in motivational terms. It argues that in a relative sense, younger and older people strive to attain different goals in life. While younger people, given their open-ended time perspective, are motivated to seek information and expand their horizon, older people, who perceive time as more limited, are motivated to derive emotional meaning from life and deepen intimacy with loved ones. Because of this motivation, older people in general do not have much more difficulty in achieving personally important goals than do younger people, thus enabling them to maintain a high level of emotional well-being. Moreover, since older people place central importance on emotional goals, they may actually work harder to regulate their emotions, leading to a generally more positive emotional experience.

There is much empirical support for the postulate that emotional goals become more important with age. Studies on age differences in social cognition find that older people pay greater attention to the emotional aspects of their social world than do their younger counterparts. Fredrickson and Carstensen (1990) asked people ranging from adolescents to octogenarians to sort a set of cards describing various types of prospective social partners according to their perceived similarity. They then employed multidimensional scaling techniques to explore the cognitive dimensions that people used to make such judgments and the relative weights placed on each dimension by different age groups. They identified three dimensions that accounted for most of the variance in the mathematical solution: (1) the potential for offering emotional rewards, (2) the potential for providing information, and (3) the possibilities for future contact. Fredrickson and Carstensen found that while younger age groups weighted the three dimensions fairly evenly, successively older age groups placed greater emphasis on the affective potential of social partners. In another study, this effect was replicated in both men and women, blue- and white-collar workers, and African Americans and European Americans (Carstensen & Fredrickson, 1998).

The age-related emphasis on emotions also manifests itself in the cognitive processing of socioemotional information. Carstensen and Turk-Charles (1994) asked people aged 20 to 83 years to read a selection drawn from a popular novel. Then they tested participants' memories for the selection using an incidental memory paradigm. They found that older people recollected proportionately more emotional information than did younger cohorts. In another study, Hashtroudi, Johnson, and Chrosniak (1990) exposed young and older adults to a number of everyday situations simulated or imagined in the laboratory. This was followed by a recall test on both types of situations. Hashtroudi and colleagues found that for both types of situations, older adults recollected more associated feelings whereas young adults recollected more nonemotional information such as colors, objects, sensory information, spatial information, and actions. Similar findings were revealed in a series of studies conducted by Labouvie-Vief and her colleagues with diverse age groups ranging from adolescents to very old persons. In these studies, they consistently found that older people process information with a greater focus on subjective states and symbolic themes (Labouvie-Vief, 1997) and are more likely to emphasize psychological themes in recalling and interpreting text than are their younger counterparts (Adams, 1991).

Importantly, socioemotional selectivity theory contends that chronological age per se does not explain changes in social goals. Rather, the theory holds that perceived time left in life is the causal factor. Because of this, the theory predicts that younger people who are placed in situations where perceived time is limited are as likely to favor emotional goals and thus emotionally close social partners as older people. This prediction has been confirmed. In an effort to disentangle chronological age from perceived time, Carstensen and Fredrickson (1998) examined mental representations of social partners in two samples. One sample comprised Caucasian and African-American adults aged 18 to 88 years. The other sample comprised three groups of young gay men who differed in their HIV-status (HIV-negative, HIV-positive/asymptomatic, or HIV-positive/symptomatic) but were comparable in age. Thus, age in the second sample was held constant, but place in the life cycle varied. Both samples completed a card-sort task in which they sorted descriptions of prospective social partners according to their perceived similarity. Multidimensional scaling techniques were again employed to reveal the dimensions along which these categorizations were made and the relative weight subsamples placed on specific dimensions. The same three dimensions as found previously accounted for most of the variance: emotional qualities, informational potential, and future prospects. Importantly, the pattern of dimension weights for young, middle-aged, and older adults closely resembled that for HIV-negative, HIV-positive/asymptomatic, and HIV-positive/symptomatic men, respectively. Both older people and younger people who were HIV-positive and experiencing AIDS symptoms placed greater weight on emotional qualities of social partners than on informational or future possibilities. These findings support the contention that perceived time left in life influences the ways people think about social partners. Moreover, they suggest that perceived constraints on time shift attention from information seeking and future prospects—knowledge-related goals—to emotional goals.

The increased focus on emotional goals with age is also reflected in social relationships. Knowledge-related goals are more likely to motivate contact with peripheral and novel social partners because these social partners are more likely to provide novel information.

In contrast, when emotional goals instigate behavior, emotionally close and familiar social partners are sought. Older people, who prioritize emotional goals, display social patterns that focus more on emotionally close social partners than do younger people. Age-related reductions in social contact have been widely documented in many studies, both longitudinal (Lee & Markides, 1990; Palmore, 1981) and cross-sectional (Gordon & Gaitz, 1976; Harvey & Singleton, 1989; Lang & Carstensen, 1994; Lawton, Moss, & Fulcomer, 1987; Montero, 1980). However, there is no evidence that older people withdraw from close social relationships. Indeed, the decline in social interactions with age is selective. Contact with close social partners remains stable with age, while contact with peripheral social partners is reduced. This targeted reduction of social network partners was examined in three studies. The samples for the first two studies (Lang & Carstensen, 1994; Lang, Staudinger, & Carstensen, 1998) came from the Berlin Aging Study, which included older adults aged 70 to 104. The sample for the third study (Fung, Carstensen, & Lang, in press) included Americans aged 18 to 94 years. Participants in all three studies were asked to nominate social partners who were either "very close," "close," "less close," or "not close." It was found reliably that the decline in social contact with age was due to reductions in the number of "less close" and "not close" social partners. Number of "very close" social partners did not differ across the wide age range. Thus with age, the number of emotionally close social partners remains stable, even after controlling for personality and family status (Lang et al., 1998).

Longitudinal studies reveal a similar pattern. Carstensen (1992) examined emotional closeness, satisfaction, and frequency of interaction in six types of relationships—acquaintances, siblings, parents, close friends, children, and spouses. She found that as people progressed from early to late adulthood, both satisfaction and the frequency of interaction declined for acquaintance-type relationships. In contrast, the frequency of interaction for close social partners, such as spouses and close friends, remained constant with age, and the satisfaction garnered from these relationships increased over time. Likewise, Field and Minkler (1988) also found that both frequency of interaction and satisfaction with adult children increased with age. These findings suggest that as one ages, peripheral relationships are weeded out while those relationships from which one receives the most emotional satisfaction are maintained and fostered. This proactive selection process appears to contribute to the emotional richness found in older adults' everyday lives.

These studies that examined social relationships and social networks consistently show patterns predicted by socioemotional selectivity theory. However, descriptive studies such as these cannot demonstrate the theoretically predicted causal mechanism, namely, time perspective. In a series of experimental studies, time perspective has been manipulated to determine its influence on social partner preference. In each study, similar methods have been used: participants are asked to imagine that they have 30 minutes of free time and then choose one of three social partners with whom they wish to spend that time. Representing the three dimensions found in the Fredrickson and Carstensen (1990) and Carstensen and Fredrickson (1998) studies, subjects choose from (1) a member of your immediate family, (2) the author of a book you've just read, and (3) a recent acquaintance with whom you have much in common. The immediate family member represented the affective dimension and was coded as "familiar social partner." The author represented the information dimension, and the recent acquaintance represented the future potential dimension. The author and recent acquaintance were coded as "novel social partners."

In the first study (Fredrickson & Carstensen, 1990), participants aged 11 to 92 were asked to indicate their preference for one of the three social partners under two experimental conditions. In one condition, they were asked to imagine that they had 30 minutes of free time and to choose a social partner. Given that old age itself imposes constraints on time, it was hypothesized that older adults in this condition would prefer the familiar social partner for the emotional value, whereas younger adults would prefer novel social partners for the potential gain in information. In the other condition, time perception was experimentally limited by asking participants to imagine they were about to move across the country, but they currently had 30 minutes of free time, and to choose a social partner. In this condition, when time was manipulated such that both young and old both perceived a social ending to be near, it was hypothesized that both young and older participants would prefer the familiar social partner. These hypotheses were confirmed. Findings from this American sample were replicated in Hong Kong, Taiwan, and China (Fung et al., 1999). They were also replicated in another American study with a different set of social partner choices: an old friend (familiar social partner), a new roommate/housemate and a famous person you admire (novel social partner) (Fung et al., 1999).

Another study used essentially the same paradigm, but expanded time perspective rather than limiting it (Fung et al., 1999). The control condition was the same as the one described above. In the time-expanded condition, participants were asked to imagine that they had just received a phone call from their physician, who told them a new medical breakthrough would likely add 20 years to their life in relatively good health. Although older adults preferred familiar social partners in the control condition, the bias disappeared in the time expansion condition. In contrast, young adults did not show a bias in either condition. These findings suggest that it is perceived time, not age per se, that causes the observed age differences in social goals.

Apart from micro-level time manipulations, real-life society-wide changes in temporal contexts also shift social goals. This hypothesis was tested in Hong Kong 1 year before, 2 months before and 1 year after its return to the People's Republic of China in 1997 (Fung et al., 1999). A year before the handover, only older Hong Kong people preferred familiar social partners to novel ones. Younger Hong Kong people did not. Two months before the handover, when the ending was more salient, both age groups preferred familiar social partners. A year after the handover, when the time constraint no longer existed, once again only older Hong Kong citizens preferred familiar social partners. Younger Hong Kong citizens no longer showed such a preference.

Together, this series of time manipulation studies shows that it is perception of time left before an ending (death, geographic move, political endings) rather than age that influences social preferences. When people, old or young, perceive that an ending is near, they prioritize emotional goals and prefer to interact with familiar social partners. Interactions with familiar social partners can be more emotionally rewarding than interactions with novel social partners, and thus, enhance emotional experiences.

Influence of Time on Emotional Experience

One aspect of emotional experience is the regulation of emotion. If older people pay increased attention to and place greater value on emotional aspects of life, this should logically lead to better regulation of emotion. Those who place value on emotional goals are likely to monitor the emotional quality of their social interactions and use strategies that will optimize the emotional aspects of important social relationships. In addition, those who show preferences for familiar social partners, as a result of a heightened sense that time in the future is limited, are more likely to enjoy social interactions that are more emotionally meaningful and often more pleasant. If this is the case, according to socioemotional selectivity theory, those who perceive time as more limited, such as older people, should show better emotion regulation and consequently more positive emotional experience. Further, the perception of limited time contributes to the sense that each experience may be the last one of its kind, enabling people to gain a perspective that heightens appreciation for positive experiences and mitigates the overall negativity of negative experiences. Better emotion regulation would be reflected in how positive or negative one perceives emotional experiences to be. This hypothesis was tested in a study by Gross and colleagues (1997) that examined emotional experience and regulation across diverse ethnic, religious, and regional groups, ranging from Catholic nuns, African, European, and Chinese Americans, to Norwegians. Across these diverse samples, older adults reported better control of their emotions and experienced fewer negative emotions than younger adults. The use of diverse samples in this study reduces concern that the observed age differences reflect stable differences among age groups (viz., cohort effects) rather than age changes.

Further evidence for better emotional regulation with age comes from research on emotional expression and regulation in interactions between middle-aged and older happily and unhappily married couples as they discuss emotionally charged topics (Carstensen, Gottman, & Levenson, 1995; Levenson, Carstensen, & Gottman, 1994). Spouses identified a mutually agreed upon conflict and discussed the conflict for 15 minutes. The discussion was videotaped and coded for discussion content and emotional expression. Both subjective reports and direct observations of the discussions showed better emotion regulation in the older couples. Even after controlling for global marital satisfaction and severity of the conflict, older couples expressed lower levels of anger, disgust, belligerence, and whining in the discussions and were more likely to express affection to each other than middle-aged couples. Since both age groups showed similar levels of involvement, the findings cannot be explained by older couples' disengagement from the task.

These studies used either self-report measures or examined a specific emotional experience—marital conflict. The question still remains as to whether older adults experience better emotion regulation in everyday life, outside of the laboratory. This question was recently addressed in a study based on experience sampling method (Carstensen, Pasupathi, Mayr, & Nesselroade, in press). Participants, aged 18 to 95, carried electronic pagers and were paged randomly five times a day over the course of a week. Each time they were paged, they completed questionnaires about the feelings they had just before they were paged. To examine the duration of people's emotions, conditional probabilities that an emotion would occur given that it occurred on a previous page were computed. Analyses of the conditional probabilities showed that while the duration of positive emotions was similar across the age range, older adults experienced a shorter duration of negative emotions than younger adults.

Better emotion regulation is associated with less frequent negative emotional experiences. The study described above (Carstensen et al., in press) found that while the frequency and intensity of positive emotion remained stable across age groups, the frequency of negative emotion declined with age. The age trend continued well into old age, at which point there was an increase in the frequency of negative emotion. However, at no point in old age were negative emotions experienced more frequently than in young adulthood.

The overall emotional profile in old age appears to be quite positive. There is little or no change in the experience of positive emotions among younger and older adults. In addition, except for the very old, older adults experience negative emotions less frequently and for shorter durations than younger adults. While there may be a few reasons for these findings (for example, that older adults perceive themselves to be in better health than is generally expected at that age), we argue that this positive emotional profile in old age is partly due to the fact that older people perceive time as limited and thus place greater importance on emotional goals and emotional regulation.

Influence of Time on Emotional Poignancy

Despite enjoying better emotional regulation, older people are not simply hedonists who seek uniformly positive emotional experience. Rather, socioemotional selectivity theory suggests that awareness of constraints on time leads older adults to experience emotions that are richer, more complex and poignant, and perhaps more meaningful.

Although the frequency of negative emotional experience declines with age, older adults experience emotional poignancy in their daily lives. In the experience sampling study in which participants carried electronic pagers, Carstensen et al. (in press) examined age differences in emotional poignancy by computing a simple correlation between positive and negative emotional experience. Thus, emotional poignancy was defined as the simultaneous co-occurrence of positive and negative emotions. They found that the correlation was higher among older adults than among younger adults, suggesting that the elderly are more likely to experience mixed positive and negative emotions than are their younger counterparts. Furthermore, with the use of factor analysis, Carstensen and colleagues measured emotional complexity by computing the number of factors that best characterized the emotional responses of each research participant over the course of the study. They found that more factors were required to account for older adults' emotional responses, suggesting that their emotional experiences are more complex than are those of younger adults.

In another study, participants aged 19 to 94 read several positive and negative scenarios (Kennedy, Carstensen, & Pasupathi, 1999). They were asked to imagine that each scenario was actually happening to them, and to indicate the extent to which they felt eight positive and eleven negative emotions in response to each scenario. No age differences were found in the frequency and intensity of positive and negative emotions in the response to the positive scenarios. However, older adults endorsed a higher frequency and intensity of negative and positive emotions than younger adults in response to the negative scenarios. Further analyses indicated that older adults endorsed higher intensities for the emotions of accomplishment, boredom, happiness, and pride than younger adults in response to the negative scenarios. While these findings are based on hypothetical situations, they suggest that when faced with a negative event, older adults simultaneously experience both negative and positive emotions. Younger adults, on the other hand, are more likely to experience negative events as purely negative emotions.

Similar evidence is found in studies from other laboratories. For example, Gatz, Kasl-Goodley, and Karel (1996) found that while the frequency of clinical depression declines in old age, the number of subclinical depressive symptoms increases with age. We speculate that the increase in subclinical depressive symptoms is actually a sign of the emotional poignancy experienced in late life. As time becomes more limited, everyday events may be tinged with sadness. Yet most older adults maintain positive emotional well-being: they do not succumb to clinical depression.

To the best of our knowledge, there has so far been no experimental study examining how time perspective contributes to emotional poignancy in old age. Socioemotional selectivity theory postulates that it is the realization that every moment and event may be the last that leads older people to react to everyday activities with more complex and poignant emotions. Further studies are needed to test whether manipulating time perspective can shift the observed age differences in emotional complexity and poignancy.

Taken together, empirical evidence supports socioemotional selectivity theory's contentions that, as compared to younger adults, older adults place greater importance on emotional goals and thus regulate their emotions better and have more positive, richer, and more poignant emotional experience. We argue that the causal factor is perception of time left in life, not age per se. Those who perceive the end of life as near are more motivated to invest in the emotional aspects of social interactions, leading to better emotion regulation and a more positive emotion profile. Moreover, perceived limitations on time also lead to an awareness that every moment and every interaction may be among the last, contributing to emotional poignancy in everyday experiences. In the following section, we discuss how these processes may affect religious practice and spirituality.

Time Perspective and Religion

The two main components of socioemotional selectivity theory are perspective of time left in life and the relative importance of knowledge-related and emotion-related goals. These two components are reflected in the spiritual and religious practices of older adults. There are many reasons why people maintain spiritual and religious practices. However, due to the purpose of this chapter, we focus specifically on the relationship between time perspective, emotion-related goals, and spirituality and religiosity.

As noted by Viktor Frankl (1986), the realization of our own mortality is what distinguishes humans from other animals. For many people, the aging process elicits existential questions regarding the meaning of life and death. Religion is one source of answers to these questions (McFadden, 1996). People often look toward religion to explain the meaning of the existence of humankind and help them accept their own mortality (Idler & George, 1998; Sinnott, 1998). As people near the end of life and perceive time as limited, religious beliefs and practices offer people resources for coping with illness and death (Koenig, George, & Siegler, 1988). This idea is consistent with the suggestion by some researchers that older adults maintain spiritual and religious beliefs and practices due to a perception of limited time and the increased salience of emotion goals (McFadden, 1996).

The second component of socioemotional selectivity theory focuses on the relative importance of knowledge and emotion-related goals as time perspective changes from expansive to limited. As people age and view time as increasingly more limited, the relative importance of emotion-related goals becomes greater. Religiosity has been linked with emotional well-being for people of all ages. It is positively correlated with life satisfaction, happiness, and emotional adjustment and negatively correlated with depressive symptoms, chronic anxiety, and loneliness (Levin & Chatters, 1998). However, religiosity may be even more beneficial for those nearing the end of life. Research indicates that maintaining religious practices has a stronger effect on the emotional well-being of older adults than of younger adults. For example, happiness is more strongly correlated with religious attendance in elderly persons than in young adulthood (Veenhoven, 1994). Given that religious attendance and prayer is more frequent with age (Levin, Taylor, & Chatters, 1995) and older adults place greater importance on emotion-related goals, older adults may view religious attendance and spiritual practices as ways to achieve emotion-related goals. These practices can help older adults retain or enhance their emotional connections with others and experience positive emotions, such as hope and love (McFadden, 1996). Thus, there is some empirical evidence to suggest that the relationship between time perspective and importance of emotion-related goals may be reflected in spiritual and religious practices.

The empirical work mentioned in this section has focused primarily on Christians and Jews living in the United States. The relationship between time perspective and the relative importance of emotion-related goals may vary across a broader range of religions. One may wonder if different religious beliefs about an afterlife affect people's estimation of time left in life, and consequently, the relative emphasis placed on emotion-related and knowledge-related goals. For example, one could imagine that because Buddhists believe in reincarnation, they may value knowledge-related goals over emotion-related goals throughout their lives. To our knowledge, no studies have examined time perspective and different religious beliefs, leaving the question open for future research. However, socioemotional selectivity theory argues that given the perceived approaches of endings—ranging from graduations to the end of political eras to the ultimate ending, death—emotion-related goals will become relatively more important than knowledge-related goals. For Buddhists, then, death would mark an ending—an ending of the present life before starting the next. We would expect that, like the Hong Kong citizens before the British handover of Hong Kong to mainland China, Buddhists approaching the end of life may place relatively greater importance on emotion-related goals than knowledge-related goals.

CONCLUSION

In several domains, such as everyday life, existential thought, and empirical research, the importance of time perspective on emotional experience is clearly evidenced. In this chapter, we have attempted to explain this relationship and describe its implications. A focal point of both Viktor Frankl and Erik Erikson's theories is that as older adults approach mortality, they strive to accept and maximize the emotional meaning of their lives. In this way, socioemotional selectivity theory is consistent with Frankl's and Erikson's theories. However, socioemotional selectivity theory disassociates age from time. Empirically, the relationship between time perspective and emotional experience is depicted in the paradox of aging—while old age is a time of loss and decline, such as the decline in social contact, older adults report high levels of emotional well-being. Rather than age per se, it is perception of time left in life that influences the importance of social goals. Indeed, the tenets of socioemotional selectivity are compatible with certain cultural beliefs and customs, self-identity, religious practice, and existential thought. As we perceive time to be limited, daily occurrences and life events become increasingly meaningful, and, we expect, poignant.

REFERENCES

Adams, C. (1991). Qualitative age differences in memory for text: A life-span developmental perspective. *Psychology and Aging, 6*(3), 323–336.

Azenberg, E. (1997, November 2). Back at that infuriating but irresistible Broadway. *New York Times*, p. 14.

Bouffard, L., Bastin, E., & LaPierre, S. (1996). Future time perspective according to women's age and social role during adulthood. *Sex Roles, 34*, 253–285.

Carstensen, L. L. (1992). Social and emotional patterns in adulthood: Support for socioemotional selectivity theory. *Psychology and Aging, 7*, 331–338.

Carstensen, L. L. (1995). Evidence for a life-span theory of socioemotional selectivity. *Current Directions in Psychological Science, 4*, 151–156.

Carstensen, L. L., & Fredrickson, B. (1998). Influence of HIV status and age on cognitive representations of others. *Health Psychology, 6*, 494–503.

Carstensen, L. L., Gottman, J. M., & Levenson, R. W. (1995). Emotional behavior in long-term marriage. *Psychology and Aging, 10*, 140–149.

Carstensen, L. L., Isaacowitz, D. M., & Charles, S. T. (1999). Taking time seriously: A theory of socioemotional selectivity. *American Psychologist, 54*, 165–181.

Carstensen, L. L., Pasupathi, M., Mayr, U., & Nesselroade, J. (in press). Emotion experience in the daily lives of older and younger adults. *Journal of Personality and Social Psychology.*

Carstensen, L. L., & Turk-Charles, S. (1994). The salience of emotion across the adult life span. *Psychology and Aging, 9,* 259–264.

Cross, S., & Markus, H. (1991). Possible selves across the life span. *Human Development, 34,* 230–255.

Erikson, E. H. (1980). *Identity and the life cycle.* New York: Norton.

Erikson, E. H., Erikson, J. M., & Kivnick, H. Q. (1986). *Vital involvement in old age.* New York: Norton.

Field, D., & Minkler, M. (1988). Continuity and change in social support between young-old and old-old or very-old age. *Journal of Gerontology: Psychological Sciences, 43,* P100–P106.

Frankl, V. E. (1986). *The doctor and the soul* (Winston, R. & Winston, C., Trans.). New York: Vintage.

Fredrickson, B. L., & Carstensen, L. L. (1990). Choosing social partners: How old age and anticipated endings make people more selective. *Psychology and Aging, 5,* 335–347.

Fung, H. H., Carstensen, L. L., & Lutz, M. A. (1999). The influence of time on social preferences: Implications for life-span development. *Psychology and Aging, 14,* 595–604.

Gatz, M., Kasl-Godley, J. E., & Karel, M. J. (1996). Aging and mental disorders. In J. E. Birren & K. W. Schaie (Eds.), *Handbook of the psychology of aging* (4th ed., pp. 365–382). San Diego: Academic Press.

Gordon, C., & Gaitz, C. (1976). Leisure and lives. In R. H. Binstock & E. Shanas (Eds.), *Handbook of aging and the social sciences* (pp. 310–341). New York: Van Nostrand Reinhold.

Gross, J. J., Carstensen, L. L., Pasupathi, M., Tsai, J., Skorpen, C. G., & Hsu, A. Y. (1997). Emotion and aging: Experience, expression, and control. *Psychology and Aging, 12,* 590–598.

Harvey, A. S., & Singleton, J. F. (1989). Canadian activity patterns across the lifespan: A time budget perspective. *Canadian Journal of Aging, 8,* 268–285.

Hashtroudi, S., Johnson, M. K., & Chrosniak, L. D. (1990). Aging and qualitative characteristics of memories for perceived and imagined complex events. *Psychology and Aging, 5,* 119–126.

Idler, E. L., & George, L. K. (1998). What sociology can help us understand about religion and mental health. In H. G. Koenig (Ed.), *Handbook of religion and mental health* (pp. 51–62). San Diego: Academic Press.

Kennedy, Q., Carstensen, L. L., & Pasupathi, M. (November, 1999). *Aging and emotional response to negative situations.* Paper presented at the Annual Meeting of the Gerontological Society of America, San Francisco.

Koenig, H. G., George, L. K., & Siegler, I. C. (1988). The use of religion and other emotion-regulating coping strategies among older adults. *The Gerontologist, 28,* 303–310.

Labouvie-Vief, G. (1997). Cognitive-emotional integration in adulthood. In K. W. Schaie & M. P. Lawton (Eds.), *Annual review of gerontology and geriatrics* (Vol. 17, pp. 206–237). New York: Springer.

Lang, F. R., & Carstensen, L. L. (1994). Close emotional relationships in late life: Further support for proactive aging in the social domain. *Psychology and Aging, 9,* 315–324.

Lang, F. R., Staudinger, U. M., & Carstensen, L. L. (1998). Perspectives on socioemotional selectivity in late life: How personality and social context do (and do not) make a difference. *Journal of Gerontology: Psychological Sciences, 53B,* P21–P30.

Lawton, M. P., Moss, M., & Fulcomer, M. (1987). Objective and subjective uses of time by older people. *International Journal of Aging and Human Development, 24,* 171–188.

Lee, D. J., & Markides, K. S. (1990). Activity and mortality among aged persons over an eight year period. *Journal of Gerontology: Social Sciences, 45B,* S39–S42.

Levenson, R. W., Carstensen, L. L., & Gottman, J. M. (1994). Influence of age and gender on affect, physiology, and their interrelations: A study of long-term marriages. *Journal of Personality and Social Psychology, 67,* 56–68.

Levin, J. S., & Chatters, L. M. (1998). Religion, health, and psychological well-being in older adults: Findings from three national surveys. *Journal of Aging and Health, 10.*

Levin, J. S., Taylor, R. J., & Chatters, L. M. (1995). Religious effects on health status and life satisfaction among Black Americans. *Journal of Gerontology: Social Sciences, 50B,* S154–S163.

McFadden, S. H. (1996). Religion, spirituality, and aging. In J. E. Birren & K. W. Schaie (Eds.), *Handbook of the psychology of aging* (4th ed., pp. 162–177). San Diego: Academic Press.

Montero, D. The elderly Japanese American: Aging among the first generation immigrants. *Genetic Psychology Monographs, 101*(1), 99–118.

Palmore, E. (1981). *Social patterns in normal aging: Findings from the Duke Longitudinal Study.* Durham: Duke University Press.

Ryff, C. D. (1989a). In the eye of the beholder: Views of psychological well-being among middle-aged and older adults. *Psychology and Aging, 4*(2), 195–210.

Ryff, C. D. (1989b). Happiness is everything, or is it? Explorations on the meaning of psychological well-being. *Journal of Personality and Social Psychology, 57*(6), 1069–1081.

Sinnott, J. D. (1998). Development and yearning: Postformal thought and spirituality. In J. D. Sinnott (Ed.), *The development of logic in adulthood: Postformal thought and its applications* (pp. 255–266). New York: Plenum Press.

Veenhoven, R., and coworkers. (1994). *World database of happiness: Correlates of happiness.* Rotterdam: Erasmus University.

CHAPTER 4

Meaning and the Tenses of Time: A Whiteheadian Perspective

Paul R. Sponheim

To probe the "meaning of time" it is important to ponder the distinctions and connections of past, present and future. Attention to the fundamental significance of time built in the twentieth century, as suggested at the two-thirds mark by Stephen Toulmin and June Goodfield in their book *The Discovery of Time* (1966). Moreover, increasingly authors have come to recognize that to fathom the significance of time one must focus on the tenses in their several relationships. Thus in writing of "The Rediscovery of Time" Nobel prize winner scientist Ilya Prigogine (Prigogine & Stengers, 1984) did not settle for a merely formal assertion:

> Today we are becoming more and more conscious of the fact that on all levels, from elementary particles to cosmology, randomness and irreversibility play an ever-increasing role: science is rediscovering time. (p. 434)

There are authors who would not draw from their study of science either the formal recognition of the "ultimate significance of time" or the material emphasis on irreversibility (Griffin, 1986; Polkinghorne, 1988). Bertrand Russell and Albert Einstein can be cited as not inconsiderable dissenters. Douglas K. Wood (1982) has noted that in the early twentieth century influential voices (T. S. Eliot, Nicolas Berdyaev, Aldous Huxley, and Carl Jung) together spoke as *Men Against Time.* John Polkinghorne (1988) has described the patterns evident in such dissent: time as "a trick of human psychological perspective" or time as a secondary construction "reflecting the emergence of properties in certain physical situations" (pp. 330–337). These objections are not trivial. Nonetheless, increasingly the testimony of the sciences is that our human experience of temporal order (we do not remember the future or anticipate the past) expresses a fundamental fact about the nature of reality. This essay will develop the perspective of someone who shares that testimony, the mathematician and philosopher Alfred North Whitehead (1861–1947). He titled his magnum opus *Process and Reality,* and the multidisciplinary stream of influence that has flowed from his writings for more than a half century is aptly known in popular terms as "process thought." In the vast secondary literature there do not seem to be many studies explicitly relating Whitehead's work to gerontological issues, though John B. Cobb, Jr. and Thomas Au have authored a helpful chapter (1995). The potential in process thought for contributing to the understanding of aging seems considerable and warrants further work.

Whitehead was not isolated from influences that could have worked against developing a strong emphasis on the reality of temporality and against the theological elements that came to be contained in that emphasis. His first professional career was in mathematics, and it was with the "great atheist" Bertrand Russell that he wrote *Principia Mathematica.* But he came to recognize that the presumed universality of mathematics rested on abstraction. Thus he stated "there is no such entity as a mere static number. There are only numbers playing their parts in various processes conceived in abstraction from the world process" (Whitehead, 1938/1966, p. 93). Accordingly, he turned in midlife to the development of a descriptive metaphysics that would be more responsive to the dictates of actual human experience. He argued against defining that experience in reductive terms, critiquing views such as David Hume's exclusive valuing of sense perception. Rather, "experience drunk and experience sober, . . . experience normal and experience abnormal" must be consulted (Whitehead, 1967, p. 226). In between these pairs he lists ten others, including "experience religious and experience skeptical" and "experience in the light and experience in the dark." In this range and elsewhere we hear an echo of Whitehead's acknowledged influence by William James' probing of the wilder and often repressed elements of human experience. In *Process and Reality*, while he develops both "rational" and "empirical" criteria, he insists "the ultimate test is always widespread, recurrent experience" (1978, p. 17).

Metaphysical description is not easily managed however, for it seeks the universal. Are we not stuck fast in the particular? Perhaps this is one reason metaphysics has fallen into disuse and disrepute in philosophical circles. Whitehead acknowledges the problem:

> We habitually observe by the method of difference. Sometimes we see an elephant, and sometimes we do not. The result is that an elephant, when present is noticed. . . . [But] metaphysical first principles can never fail of exemplification. We can never catch the actual world taking a holiday from their sway. (1978, p. 4)

Accordingly, Whitehead proposes an alternative method:

> When the method of difference fails, factors which are constantly present may yet be observed under the influence of imaginative thought. Such thought supplies the differences which the direct observation lacks. It can even play with inconsistency; and can thus throw light on the consistent, and persistent elements in experience by comparison with what in imagination is inconsistent with them. (1978, p. 5)

His image for the metaphysical venture is that of the airplane flight with a method that

> starts from the ground of particular observation; it makes a flight in the thin air of imaginative generalization; and it again lands for renewed observation rendered acute by rational observation. (1978, p. 5)

What Whitehead saw from the air and found on the ground does not leave him in doubt about the fundamental character of the experience of temporality. He makes this point vividly in a passage deep in the dense pages of *Process and Reality:*

> That "all things flow" is the first vague generalization which the unsystematized, barely analyzed, intuition of men has produced. It is the theme of some of the best Hebrew poetry in the Psalms; it appears as one of the first generalizations of Greek philosophy in the form of the saying of Heraclitus; amid the later barbarism of Anglo-Saxon thought it reappears in the story of the sparrow flitting through the banqueting hall of the Northumbrian king; and in all stages of civilization its recollection lends its pathos to poetry. Without doubt, if we are to go back to that ultimate, integral experience, unwarped by the sophistications of theory, that experience, whose elucidation is the final aim of philosophy, the flux of things is one ultimate generalization around which we must weave our philosophical system. (1978, p. 208)

In this task of metaphysical description he found the making of God claims to be essential. Perhaps this justifies Allan B. Chinen (1994) taking Whitehead as "perhaps the most dramatic example of the process" of returning "to spiritual concerns despite social pressures against such a development" (p. 206). In any case, he offers us detailed reflection on the meaning of time, reflection informed by work in the natural sciences, but also by wide humanistic reading. His work may well represent a major contribution of the twentieth century to this new century's pondering of the meaning of time. It is a contribution that connects with many of the elements of Western modernity, while also resonating to Eastern, particularly Buddhist, impulses. Regarding that resonance, John B. Cobb, Jr. and Masao Abe (1995) have been leaders in developing a series of Buddhist-Christian conversations from a Whiteheadian perspective. Whitehead's seminal thought does not remain stuck in the modern world and in a series of postmodern volumes David Griffin (1989a) has taken up the constructive task he anticipated. In both of these developments the fundamental significance of time's tenses is decisively recognized.

THE MEANING OF TIME: A METAPHYSICAL SKETCH OF THE POWER OF THE PAST

The power of the past is secured by the irreversibility of time's arrow. In this understanding, we are two moves beyond Newton's world view with its changeless substances and states of motion. In that view, time and space appear as passive containers of matter. Ilya Prigogine (1984) notes that the first move beyond Newton was made by Einstein, whose general theory of relativity holds that "space-time is no more independent of matter but is itself generated from matter" (p. 444). Prigogine can well speak of this rejection of a container view as Einstein's greatest achievement. But Einstein's understanding of the four-dimensional continuum (the three dimensions of ordinary space and a fourth corresponding to time) may be portrayed as a spatialization of time. At times Einstein himself seems to have seen it so. He could comment "it is a characteristic of thought in physics . . . that it endeavours in principle to make do with 'space-like' concepts alone" (Einstein, 1954, p. 141). And yet he can be quoted as saying "that the time-coordinate is defined physically wholly differently from the space co-ordinates" (Einstein, 1950, p. 31). Clearly, the idea of localization in space-time was important to Einstein, as was the concept of a God "who does not play at dice." Robert John Russell (1989) formulates succinctly the question emerging from Einstein's work: "From the standpoint of physics, are irreversible processes at the macrolevel reducible to reversible microprocesses, or is there an irreducible physical basis for time's arrow?" (p. 211).

Can one have it both ways? Nobel laureate Prigogine's response seems right: "Irreversibility is either true on all levels or on none; it cannot emerge as if out of nothing, on going from one level to another" (Prigogine & Stengers, 1984, p. 285). Whiteheadians are not indecisive in opting for "all levels." Thus process philosopher of science Ian Barbour (1986) argues that for any specific observer the concrete occurrences that constitute time are connected irreversibly:

> In relativity theory there are some events that are past for one observer and future for another observer, but for any two events that could be causally related there is an absolute distinction of past and future for all possible observers. There is no way in which a future event could influence the past or present, according to relativity theory. (p. 168)

This conviction of temporal irreversibility does not arrive as special revelation from the *cognoscenti* of relativity theory. At the basis of the

Whiteheadian emphasis is the ordinary human experience that we derive our present from the past, not from the future. Whitehead (1959) wrote:

> Time in the concrete is the conformation of state to state, the later to the earlier; . . . pure succession is an abstraction of the second order, a generic abstraction omitting the temporal character of time . . . the immediate present has to conform to what the past is for it, and the mere lapse of time is an abstraction from the more concrete relatedness of "conformation." (p. 36)

We do take up our lives in the present from the past. While I will indicate in the next section of this essay that Whitehead does not see this transition in deterministic terms, the past does have objective power—it bears in on us.

Whitehead makes two further points about this temporal process. First, there is nothing about us as human beings that is somehow exempted from this process. He spoke of the "principle of process": "that how an actual entity *becomes* constitutes *what* that actual entity *is*; so that the two descriptions of an actual entity are not independent. Its 'being' is constituted by its 'becoming' " (1978, p. 23; emphasis his). We can, of course, commit "the fallacy of misplaced concreteness," supposing there is some mental or spiritual part of us that transcends becoming. We may forgetfully misplace our concreteness, but the body tends to remember. Rita Nakashima Brock and Susan Brooks Thistlethwaite (1996) have made this point well in an insightful study of prostitution. They write of how "the body stores our spiritual and material legacy. And the longer our life expectancy, the more the accumulation of such legacies becomes evident" (p. 277). The truly fundamental status of the self's embodiment is gaining greater recognition, as represented by the interdisciplinary team Warren S. Brown, Nancey Murphy, and H. Newton Malony (1998) have put together at Fuller Theological Seminary to articulate a "non-reductive physicalist" position. Whiteheadians would hope that this emerging emphasis would gain widespread recognition as well for the essentially temporal character of the self.

Secondly, Whitehead understands that concreteness in a very atomic manner. Reality is the process of myriad pulses of becoming. The solid familiar (misleadingly so, I will argue in the next section of this essay) world dissolves into pulses of energy. As Whiteheadians like to say, the rock of Gibralter exists, happens, from moment to moment. We human beings are complex "societies" of occasions, but the fundamental creative energy is in the process not the product. "Thus the ultimate metaphysical truth is atomism," so that "actual entities are the only reasons" (1978, pp. 35, 24). Whitehead gathers these two points in a single sentence, saying flatly "there is a becoming of continuity, but no continuity of becoming" (1978, p. 35).

Is that too flat? This severely atomic emphasis has alienated some authors who otherwise join Whitehead in the recognition of the ultimate significance of time. Thus John Polkinghorne (1988), while recognizing such specific discontinuous moments as "the collapse of the wave packet," writes:

> The punctuated, discrete event ("actual occasion") picture of physical process presented in the thought of A.N. Whitehead and his followers, is very difficult to reconcile with scientific knowledge. (p. 342)

Indeed many who otherwise think very well of Whitehead's work do question the adequacy of his understanding of the continuity of the human individual. Robert Neville (1974) has attempted to develop the notion of a "discursive individual," "an irreducibly basic concrete entity on a cosmological par with actual entities or actual occasions" (p. 47). Others (for example Janusz and Webster, 1991) appeal to Whitehead's own reflections in *Science and the Modern World* regarding "organic unities." Some kind of "top-down" causality seems evident in such a passage as this:

> The concrete enduring entities are organisms, so that the plan of the *whole* influences the very characters of the various subordinate organisms which enter into it. (Whitehead, 1967, p. 79; emphasis his)

Proposals are also made about nested occasions' collective field (Bracken, 1989) and about "inclusive occasions" (Ford, 1988).

These proposals for adaptation or correction represent a significant conversation within process thought, but they do not constitute a fundamental challenge to Whitehead's understanding of the nature of time. We can confidently proceed to consider the bearing of temporal irreversibility on the understanding of human agency.

Whitehead himself did not fail to address questions of broad social relevance for human beings, and persons working in his tradition have combined in their careers close analysis of microscopic matters with issues concerning economics and ecology. A stunningly clear example is John B. Cobb, Jr., who having written early in his career an intricate Whiteheadian study of *Christian Natural Theology* (1965) turned decades later to work with Hermann Daly in an economic proposal *For the Common Good* (1989). It may be that work on actual human matters, including the reality of aging, will gather sufficient empirical force to double back to modify the metaphysical description of time. In any case we proceed, recognizing the stubborn empirical testimony that somehow a person is one over the seasons of her life.

So what does follow for the understanding of aging? First, with this perspective, we will recognize aging as an expression of the fundamental reality of change. It is not as if human beings were essentially unchanging substances who somehow suddenly begin to age. To speak of our aging is to speak of temporal process, and we are thoroughly temporal beings. Indeed, process thought does not speak of occasions *in* time, as if some qualitative distinction could be made such that the door is opened for us to regard human beings as less than thoroughly temporal. John B. Cobb, Jr. (1965) warns against such an understanding that would seem once again to move back toward a container view of time. He writes:

> . . . we are not to think of four-dimensional space-time as a fixed reality into which all entities are placed. Space-time is a structure abstracted from the extensive relationships of actual entities. (p. 69)

Further, within this perspective the fact that we change, including that we change in aging, is to be seen as just that, a metaphysical fact. It is given with the nature of reality; process and reality do belong together. Obviously, this bears on the evaluation of the fact of change. Theologically, it would be well nigh preposterous and surely arrogant for a believer claiming a creator God to bracket all of this pulsing reality of change—people and plants and the universe as process—under something said to be unnatural, namely "sin." Yet the power of a Platonic privileging of the unchanging in classical theism does seem to be reflected in practical terms in a piety for which change is at least suspect. A Whiteheadian perspective will warn against such tendencies. Distinctions within change, and within the change that is aging, will need to be made, of course. But *that* we age calls for acceptance as a sheer metaphysical given.

Two other things follow from the givenness of the discontinuous in the atomic character of becoming. There is a kind of aloneness in the moment, which can be recognized as fully natural. I am reminded of the distinction between being alone and being lonely, as discussed by Barbara Payne and Susan McFadden (1994). Moreover, the several moments that together make up a human life span stand somewhat apart in subjective immediacy, so that one could speak of a "daily dying," what Whitehead termed "perpetual perishing" (1978; pp. 29, 340).

Such affirmations and appropriations of the discontinuous do help us to recognize the naturalness of aging. But the point can be overplayed. Indeed, there are impulses in the deconstructive form of postmodernism that threaten to flatten out necessary distinctions about human identity and how well or how badly we age. Those currents have led Edith Wyschogrod (1990) to plead for the category of "saint," for the compassion that can be present only when "there are more than disseminated drops of desire" (p. 234). And the same cause has been addressed by process theologian Catherine Keller (1990) in asserting the need to "stand one's ground":

> Some of us will go on working and playing at an alternative sense of self, one quicksilvery enough to elude the fixed centers of essence, one firm enough to stand its ground. Standing one's ground: this allows the persistence needed not to remain self-identical, which only blocks the flow of relation and energy, but to face difference, conflict, loss, reality, future. (p. 221)

Aging people do not delude themselves about remaining self-identical; they know more than a little about difference and loss. They could well recite the question of Shakespeare's sixty-fifth sonnet:

> . . . O, how shall summer's honey breath hold out
> Against the wreckful siege of battering days,
> When rocks impregnable are not so stout,
> Nor gates of steel so strong, but Time decays?

The question is not at all an idle one. Caught so in time's grip, what can one do? What might a Whiteheadian perspective commend for a self so radically located temporally?

MEANING IN AGING: AN ETHICAL PROPOSAL FOR PRESENT FREEDOM

I have stressed the power of the past bearing down on, or—better—flowing into the present moment. This could be understood in deterministic terms, and as we age we may begin to sense more fully the reality of consequence. Decisions made decades ago continue to work their powerful effects in our lives. We may seem simply the deposit of the past, bereft of any fresh initiative. Moreover, the sense of the past as determining power may combine with a present context that encourages a sense of dependency in the aging person. The deterministic and characteristically pessimistic reading of this causal efficacy of the past is readily available, for example, in many nursing homes. Rabbi Dayle Friedman (1995) has written insightfully of the "tyranny of routinized time" in which days are structured by tasks "that must be done 'to' the residents." She continues:

> . . . paradoxically, despite the degree to which time is structured, to the resident, time seems empty and burdensome. . . . Much of the institutionalized older person time is spent *waiting*. . . . Time seems limitless when one is waiting. . . . Time clearly weighs heavily without meaningful markers and momentum toward them. (pp. 362–363)

Friedman's summary characterization is that of "learned helplessness," and that phrase captures well a broader cultural construct of aging.

Into this framework a Whiteheadian perspective introduces a radically different understanding. The causal efficacy of the past is empower*ing*. The past becomes resource for present decision and action. Of course there are patterns of habituation that work their ways in the older (as, in principle, in any) person. But fundamentally the present moment has an openness about it, an openness toward the future. Here the troublesome sentence "there is no continuity of becoming, but a becoming of continuity" carries the promise of genuine freedom. It will make a difference as well that Whiteheadian thought resists elevating time into a metaphysical machine abstracted from actual events, thought able to rule inexorably over those events. To the contrary, this metaphysical description does make way for an ethical proposal, for present responsibility is affirmed. One could put the point thusly: against strong tendencies in the modern world a fact/value split is not to be accepted. It matters what the recipient of the efficacy of the past "does" with it. Whiteheadians stress the fundamental character of time, but they do not level out all differences in this. Change is constant, but not to be evaluated in a singular way. As Whitehead (1938/1966) wrote: "When fundamental change arrives, sometimes heaven dawns, sometimes hell yawns open" (p. 95).

How do we effectively lay claim to the empowering presence of the past? A candidate might be memory, for in memory we repossess certain experiences "from the inside," as it were. John Cobb, Jr. (1965) has written of how we identify ourselves with our memories (p. 77). It is not only process theorists who make this point. James Ashbrook, senior scholar in Religion and Personality at Garrett Theological Seminary, has written a book entitled *Minding the Soul* (1996). It carries the intriguing subtitle "Pastoral Counseling as Remembering." Ashbrook writes: "Soul expresses 'meaning,' and the making of meaning depends on memory" (p. 169). Obviously this discussion seems to run aground on the stark reality of memory loss. But a Whiteheadian understanding does *not* require that memory be understood in the terms of conscious mentality. Ashbrook, while not appealing explicitly to Whiteheadian epistemology, well expresses this deeper and broader view of memory. He (1966) writes:

Is soul the repository of memory? Memory can extend to all systems of the body [to every cell of the body]; can be the nerve endings that pain in the stump of the arm that has been amputated; can be ancestral memory such as the fear of falling; can be the dread of darkness.

Is it just my stomach that remembers the fullness of fasting; just my taste buds that carry the succulence of watermelon in the heat of summer? As I understand it, it is the mind and senses together that ritually make the first bite into the first apple of the season real and ritual to me, so that the season, the taste, the recognition of change all celebrate the occasion as ritual event calling on memory as it reaffirms me living in this event of the apple season from the past, and moves me along in the reality of life in this new apple season.

Memory draws from my gut, from my physical senses, from my brain, from my knowledge of time's passage in the instance of the apple season, forming an experience of life that is my life, that bears my history. (I draw on memories of apples stored for winter in the straw above the horses' barn; the wind-fallen apples in the orchard; the memory of baking apples for supper the night I received news of my sister's death, so I don't bake apples any more because of this memory. I remember going with my father with a wagon load of apples to the cider mill, sensing his excitement of this event, which now I call his richness in the world.)

All of these are part of apple memory. But it's brain, senses, gut—all the systems [and cells] of my body together—that form an image of the person I know in the name I bear. Thus might soul be summed up as all the parts of the body creating in unison a particular view of the reality of being with memory as the linchpin that holds all in place. (p. 170)

Ashbrook's eloquent statement does help us to recognize how a person suffering from what we call "memory loss" nonetheless can efficaciously claim the empowering presence of the past in the present moment. However, this is not to deny the value of using the conscious memory to whatever degree is possible. Mel Kimble (1995) has written of the task of "life-review" in these terms:

One of the developmental tasks of aging is to maintain a past scanning function that reclaims the past. Personal experiences are always located in time. Memory implies time elapsed. The fear of forgetting and the need to remember both mark the last stage of life. Memory enables persons to hold fast to their identity and to shape and interpret it in new ways. People do not merely have these memories; they are these memories. By remembering, connections can be made and the patterns and designs of our lives can be discovered. (p. 139)

Again a Whiteheadian perspective uncovers an additional resource for memory's work. Whitehead emphasizes that sense perception is a secondary mode of perception, offering typically rather insignificant information about the reality surrounding the deciding self. But sense perception—what he terms "presentational immediacy"—is secondary in that it is derivative from the far more primary mode of causal efficacy—the empowering presence of the past. The resource to be claimed in this case is termed "symbolic reference," a knowing that connects with the link between the two modes of perception (1978, Part II, chapter 8). In *Adventures of Ideas* Whitehead (1933/1961) applies what may seem like a rather dense set of distinctions and connections in a set of sentences invoking concrete aesthetic substance:

> Music, ceremonial clothing, ceremonial smells, and ceremonial rhythmic visual appearances, also have symbolic truth, or symbolic falsehood. ... Music elicits some confused feeling into distinct apprehension ... by introducing an emotional clothing which changes the dim objective reality into a clear Appearance ... (p. 249)

To summarize the argument of this section: the older person does not need to learn to be helpless, for a richly empowering past is present even if consciousness does not function fully with regard to it. Moreover, there is a symbolizing capacity in human beings such that sense perception can be employed to bring the resources of the past into a position where the person can employ them more effectively. Indeed one might well say that the older person has more than a resource available; there is here a present ethical responsibility in relationship to the past metaphysically given. There is excitement in this mix. No wonder Whitehead (1933/1961) calls us to turn away from "the tedium of indefinite repetition" and toward "adventure," "the search for new perfections" (p. 258).

And what is to guide the older person in the adventure of decision? Again, we can use religious language to express what is metaphysically revealed: "the primordial appetitions which jointly constitute God's purpose are seeking intensity, and not preservation" (1978, p. 105). To that end of intensification an ordering of experience is needed, such that one "has simplified the welter of occasions, individually insignificant, into a few significant individual things" (1933/1961, p. 263). Whiteheadians emphasize pattern as essential to human identity at any age. Robert C. Atchley (1995) has summarized the connection between pattern and a sense of personal continuity in the aging:

> The central thesis of continuity theory is that in adapting to aging, people attempt to preserve and maintain the long-standing patterns

of living and coping that they identify as being uniquely them. They tend to use familiar ideas and coping strategies in familiar environments, activities and social relationships. Thus adaptation takes place in ways that preserve the continuity of character, setting and plot. Change is designed and redefined to be integrated with one's prior history and anticipated future. (p. 69)

Whitehead places significant ethical value in a particular pattern. This is the experience of "harmony," deriving "strength from the concurrence of significant individual objects" (p. 263). This strikes me as a microscopic description able to serve what Eugene Bianchi, citing Teilhard de Chardin, has called a kind of "growth through diminishment" (1991, p. 61). Similarly, Payne and McFadden (1994) speak of "the opportunity for growth through the kind of emptying practiced by mystics across the centuries" (p. 25). But such growth does require an integrating process, as in the constructing of a life journey that has "pulled together the themes of life and climactic events into a coherent whole" (Quinnan, 1994, p. 174). The older person needs this kind of ordering, given the wealth of the past available. And perhaps the circumstances of aging, the confrontation with real and potential losses, provide an occasioning setting for this process.

We began this section with the question provoked by the metaphysical analysis: "What is possible for a self located so radically temporally?" The answer would seem to be, "Quite a lot, really." The older person will not be at a loss for "things to do" in the present. Nonetheless, even as we busy ourselves from moment to moment, we do look ahead toward the future. We lean into that future. Indeed, Whitehead recognizes that it is the prospect of the future that endows the present decision of the individual with significance. He put it pointedly in an infamous quotation: "in the real world it is more important that a proposition be interesting than that it be true" (1978, p. 259). In the very next sentence he quickly adds, of course, "the importance of truth is that it adds to interest." But the point is not lost. Time is real and matters. What is important is not some recital of the timeless, but the proposition that is a proposal into the future. Such a proposal interests us; it draws us toward that future. Thus Whitehead writes (1933/1961) that a factor in the enjoyment of harmony "is the intuition that the future, where its objective immortality lies, is increasing the grounds for harmony" (p. 263).

But what kind of prospects exist for an individual self if reality is as thoroughly temporal as Whitehead suggests? He does have a response to that question, and it brings us to the ground of religion.

TIME AND AGING: A RELIGIOUS PERSPECTIVE OFFERING FAITH FOR THE FUTURE

It is worth underlining the point made in this section's title because it opposes strong tendencies in thinking about religion. Outside circles of faith, and even within, it is sometimes thought that religion turns us back to some real or imagined distant past, some Golden Age. Even if God is not defined in essentially nontemporal terms, the religious appeal still is seen to call us "back to Eden." Theistic Whiteheadians will not relinquish talk of God the creator. There is, to be sure, a debate as to whether God's originating creation should be understood as creation out of nothing or out of chaos. Whitehead himself did not speak of creation out of nothing, though he could speak of how God "at once exemplifies and establishes the categoreal conditions" (1978, p. 344). Many process theologians have turned away from *ex nihilo* talk, as does Tyron Inbody (1997) in worrying that this notion weakens the connection between God and the world (pp. 173–174, 184). Yet if one recognizes that in divine self-limitation a free act of creation does constitute genuine limitation, one may well speak of the strength of the Creator/creature relationship. In any case, theistic Whiteheadians do lay claim to the doctrine of creation. Accordingly, there will be some basis for "re" language: redemption, restoration, and the like. But such Whiteheadians will soon move to speak very strongly of the future when they speak of the way God talk functions for faith. The conviction of temporal irreversibility, the point made so prominently in the first section of this essay, pushes the Whiteheadian person of faith to look ahead. How, then, would the Whiteheadian have the person of faith look to the future?

The most readily available way is what process people call "objective immortality," connected with what was said in the first section regarding the power of the past. While there is in this perspective a recognition of the perishing of subjective immediacy every moment (noted in section one as "perpetual perishing," in Whitehead's language), the flow of time carries the content of our lives into the future objectively. In a lecture on immortality at Harvard Divinity School near the end of his life, Whitehead put the matter so: "What does haunt our imagination is that the immediate facts of present action pass into permanent significance for the Universe" (1941, p. 698).

Two aspects of this passage must be made clear. First, our lives pass into the future in that they pass into God. In this there is some kind of transformation involved such that Whitehead can speak of it as a "perfecting." The perishing actuality is received—"its sufferings, its sorrows, its failure, its triumphs, its immediacies of joy—woven by rightness of [God's] feeling into the harmony of the universal feeling" (1978, p. 346). The image Whitehead offers at this point (noting "it is but an image") "is that of a tender care that nothing be lost" (1978, p. 346). This is what Whitehead spoke of as the judgment of God, and many a believer will find a gospel in it in that the judgment is not merely the summation of cold consequence that our deeds live after us.

The second point that must be made about this objective immortality is that our lives, thus received and judged by God, do pass back into the world. On the last page of *Process and Reality* Whitehead phrases it thusly: "For the perfected actuality passes back into the temporal world, and qualifies this world so that each temporal actuality includes it as an immediate fact of relevant experience. For the kingdom of heaven is with us today" (1978, p. 351). Here is a metaphysical and religious formulation that connects with Robert L. Rubinstein (1994) in his effort to avoid juxtaposing "generativity" and "narcissism" (171–173). Rubenstein notes that the Eriksonian call to generativity seems to run counter to the American ideal of selfhood, which emphasizes such themes as "autonomous, commercial, goal-oriented, independent, proactive, self-reliant" (1994, p. 170). His recognition of an "ambiguous" relationship between generativity and narcissism is accepted and deepened in a Whiteheadian understanding of objective immortality. In such a way feminist theologian Sallie McFague (1987) has written of the importance of "universal parenthood, for "whether or not one is a biological or adoptive parent, . . . we all want to be life-givers, to pass life on, and when we do we can face our own deaths more easily" (p. 120). This "objective" theme is strongly present in the Hebrew scriptures, and a Whiteheadian perspective provides a strong metaphysical basis for this emphasis in looking to the future.

Is there anything more? Does religious faith in turning to the future manage somehow to speak of *subjective* immortality? It is clear that many believers cling to such a hope, not the least as later years come. And it is clear that Whitehead himself struggled to find a formulation of that hope that would fit his framework. In 1926, in *Religion in the Making,* he could say that his philosophy was "entirely neutral on the question of immortality" (107). But by 1929 he was at work in the last part of *Process and Reality* to show that "there is no reason of any ultimate metaphysical generality" why process must entail loss (1978, p. 340). As we have noted, for process thinkers the reality of an enduring personality is already remarkable for what Whitehead calls "some peculiar completeness" (1978, p. 350). But Whitehead offers a visionary sketch of "an even more complete unity of life in a chain of elements for which succession does not mean loss of immediate unison" (1978, p. 350).

There is much debate in the process community as to whether this sketch is convincing. The most extensive effort to develop the sketch is that of Marjorie Suchocki (1988). Working deeply in Whiteheadian formulations, she interposes a stage of "enjoyment" between subjective immediacy and objectification and reaches for transcendence in three ways:

> First a transcendence of seriality into the fullness of the self; second, a transcendence of selfhood through the mutuality of feeling with all other selves and occasions, and third and most deeply, a transcendence of selves into the Selfhood of God. (p. 108)

Suchocki's Claremont colleague, David Ray Griffin, has raised a number of troubling questions about the fit of this proposal with Whitehead's basic metaphysical principles (1989b). In any case, this formulation offers a *telos* that would well serve many believers, even if it is not to be reached by the metaphysical route Suchocki has sketched. Regarding subjective immortality, Whitehead himself (1926) stated "there is no reason why such a question should not be decided on more special evidence" (p. 111).

This second move toward the future is clearly not one without difficulties. There are not only the difficulties having to do with whether the move "works" metaphysically within Whitehead's description of reality. There are also the very considerable difficulties involved in the way some people of faith have formulated the hope and in the way they have focused on that hope. As to formulations, Whitehead did not overstate the matter in his Immortality lecture in saying that "the various attempts at description are often shocking and profane" (1941, p. 698). As to the focusing, process theologian Catherine Keller has warned against the dangers implicit in the notion of apocalypse (1996). Surely Whitehead would not accept a view of the final future that either trivialized the present or justified violent behavior in that present. In the very section in *Process and Reality* in which he is discussing "God and the World," he contrasts the God concept deriving from "the Galilean origin of Christianity" to the image of "the ruling Caesar, or the ruthless moralist, or the unmoved mover." He indicates that he is speaking of love and adds "it does not look to the future; for it finds its own reward in the immediate present" (1978, p. 343).

So, how could an older person live fully and productively in the present—whether or not clinging to a hope for subjective immortality. I believe such a life is available, and religion can well serve it. Whitehead uses his last chapter in *Adventures of Ideas* for "peace," "that Harmony of Harmonies which calms destructive turbulence and completes civilization" (p. 1933/1961, p. 285). This is not a state of anesthesia, for "it is a positive feeling which crowns the 'life and motion' of the soul" (p. 285). Here one is beyond "the stress of acquisitive feeling arising from the soul's preoccupation with itself" (p. 285). There is, instead, "a grasp of infinitude, an appeal beyond boundaries" (p. 285). And in this there is "the intuition of permanence" (p. 286). I have indicated that Whitehead sought to distinguish this peace from "its bastard substitute," anesthesia. That distinction still needs to be made, as does the distinction of this peace from the familiar religious frenzy of self-sacrifice. Rather "peace is self-control at its widest—at the width where the 'self' has been lost and interest has been transferred to coordinates wider than personality" (p. 285). His final paragraph spoke of how "at the heart of the nature of things, there are always the dream of youth and the harvest of tragedy" (p. 296). And so it is that "the immediate experience of this Final Fact, with its union of Youth and Tragedy, is the sense of Peace" (p. 296).

That we are on religious ground may be suggested by the scope of the claims made for this peace. But Whitehead speaks directly of "an Adventure in the universe as One" (p. 295). But this everywhere present One is not a cold metaphysical fact. Whitehead's famous definition of religion has to do with what one does with his or her "solitariness" (1926, p. 16). And he came to speak of God as "the fellow sufferer who understands" (1978, p. 351). So it would be that the older person can sing with Whitehead the hymn he cites in the midst of the dense thickets of *Process and Reality* "Abide with me; fast falls the eventide" (1978, p. 209). Believing persons trust that God will go forward into whatever future there may be, just as—in some sense—they will also. For faith that is enough.

Thus one may find in Whiteheadian thought metaphysical wisdom concerning the power of the past, ethical wisdom for life in the present, and religious wisdom as one anticipates the future. To do so will be to contribute to our understanding of the meaning of time in relation to the reality of aging.

REFERENCES

Ashbrook, J. B. (1996). *Minding the soul: Pastoral counseling as remembering.* Minneapolis, MN: Fortress.

Atchley, R. C. (1995). The continuity of the spiritual self. In M. A. Kimble, S. H. McFadden, J. W. Ellor, & J. J. Seeber (Eds.), *Aging, spirituality and religion: A handbook* (pp. 68–73). Minneapolis, MN: Fortress.

Au, T., & Cobb, J. B. (1995). A process theology perspective. In M. A. Kimble, S. H. McFadden, J. W. Ellor, & J. J. Seeber (Eds.), *Aging, spirituality, and religion: A handbook* (pp. 444–459). Minneapolis, MN: Fortress.

Barbour, I. (1986). Bohm and process philosophy: A response to Griffin and Cobb. In D. R. Griffin (Ed.), *Physics and the ultimate significance of time* (pp. 167–171) Albany, NY: SUNY.

Bianchi, E. C. (1991). A spirituality of aging. In L. S. Cahill & D. Mieth (Eds.), *Aging* (pp. 58–64). London: SCM.

Bracken, J. (1989). Energy events and fields. *Process Studies, 18,* 153–165.

Brock, R. N., & Thistlethwaite, S. B. (1996). *Casting stones: Prostitution and liberation in Asia and the United States.* Minneapolis, MN: Augsburg Fortress.

Brown, W. S., Murphy, N., & Malony, H. N. (1998). *Whatever happened to the soul? Scientific and theological portraits of human nature.* Minneapolis, MN: Fortress.

Chinen, A. B. (1994). Fairy tales and the spiritual dimensions of aging. In L. E. Thomas & S. A. Eisenhandler (Eds.), *Aging and the religious dimension* (pp. 85–103). Westport, CT: Auburn House.

Cobb, J. B. (1965). *A Christian natural theology.* Philadelphia: Westminster.

Cobb, J. B., & Abe, M. (1995). *Buddhism and interfaith dialogue.* London: Macmillan.

Cobb, J. B., & Daly, H. (1989). *For the common good.* Boston: Beacon.

Einstein, A. (1950). *The meaning of relativity.* Princeton: Princeton University.

Einstein, A. (1954). *Relativity: The special and the general theory.* London: Methuen.

Ford, L. (1988). Inclusive occasions. In E. Wolf-Gazo (Ed.), *Process in context: Essays in post-Whiteheadian perspectives* (pp. 107–136). New York: Peter Lang.

Friedman, D. A. (1995). Spiritual challenges of nursing home life. In M. A. Kimble, S. H. McFadden, J. W. Ellor, & J. J. Seeber (Eds.), *Aging, spirituality and religion: A handbook* (pp. 362–373). Minneapolis, MN: Fortress.

Griffin, D. R. (1989a). *God and religion in postmodern theology.* New York: SUNY.

Griffin, D. R. (1989b). Marjorie Hewitt Suchocki, The end of evil. *Process Studies, 18,* 57–62.

Griffin, D. R. (Ed.). (1986). *Physics and the ultimate significance of time.* New York: SUNY.

Inbody, T. L. (1997). *The transforming God: An interpretation of suffering and evil.* Louisville, KY: Westminster John Knox.

Janusz, S., & Webster, G. (1991). The problem of persons. *Process Studies, 20,* 151–161.

Keller, C. (1990). "To illuminate your trace": Self in late modern feminist theology. *Listening, 5,* 211–223.

Keller, C. (1996). *Apocalypse now and then.* Boston: Beacon.

Kimble, M. (1995). Pastoral care. In M. A. Kimble, S. H. McFadden, J. W. Ellor, & J. J. Seeber (Eds.), *Aging, spirituality and religion: A handbook* (pp. 131–147). Minneapolis, MN: Fortress.

McFague, S. (1987). *Models of God: Theology for an ecological, nuclear age.* Minneapolis, MN: Fortress.

Neville, R. (1974). *The cosmology of freedom.* New Haven, CT: Yale.

Payne, B. P., & McFadden, S. H. (1994). From loneliness to solitude: Religious and spiritual journeys in late life. In L. E. Thomas & S. A. Eisenhandler (Eds.), *Aging and the religious dimension* (pp. 13–28). Westport, CT: Auburn House.

Polkinghorne, J. (1988). Natural science, temporality and divine action. *Theology Today, 55,* 329–343.

Prigogine, I., & Stengers, I. (1984). *Order out of chaos.* London: William Heinemann.

Quinnan, E. J. (1994). Life narrative and spiritual journey of elderly male religious. In L. E. Thomas & S. A. Eisenhandler, *Aging and the religious dimension* (pp. 85–104). Westport, CT: Auburn House.

Rubenstein, R. R. (1994). Generativity as pragmatic spirituality. In L. E. Thomas & S. A. Eisenhandler, *Aging and the religious dimension* (pp. 169–182). Westport, CT: Auburn House.

Russell, R. J. (1989). A response to David Bohm's "Time, the implicate order and pre-space." In D. R. Griffin (Ed.), *Physics and the ultimate significance of time* (pp. 209–218). Albany, NY: SUNY.

Shakespeare, W. (1925). *Shakespeare's sonnets.* New Haven, CT: Yale.

Suchocki, M. H. (1988). *The end of evil.* Albany, NY: SUNY.

Toulmin, S., & Goodfield, J. (1965). *The discovery of time.* New York: Harper.

Whitehead, A. N. (1961). *Adventures of ideas.* New York: Free Press. (Original work published 1933)

Whitehead, A. N. (1941). Immortality. In P. A. Schilpp (Ed.), *The philosophy of Alfred North Whitehead* (pp. 682–744). New York: Tudor.

Whitehead, A. N. (1926). *Religion in the making.* New York: Macmillan.

Whitehead, A. N. (1959). *Symbolism: Its meaning and effect.* New York: Macmillan.

Whitehead, A. N. (1966). *Modes of thought.* New York: Free Press. (Original work published 1938)

Whitehead, A. N. (1967). *Science and the modern world.* New York: Free Press.

Whitehead, A. N. (1978). *Process and reality: An essay in cosmology.* New York: Free Press.

Wood, D. K. (1982). *Men against time.* Lawrence, KS: University Press of Kansas.

Wyschogrod, E. (1990). *Saints and postmodernism: Revisioning moral philosophy.* Chicago: University of Chicago Press.

PART II

Experiencing Time and Aging

CHAPTER 5

Learning, Aging, and Other Predicaments

Armin Grams

When I shared the title of this chapter with a colleague, she promptly dubbed it "provocative." Little did she know how much discussion that title had already provoked at home between my wife Sophie and me. I got the idea from a statement by George Santayana that I liked so much, I attached it to our refrigerator door. It read "Life is not a spectacle, it is not a feast, it is a predicament." When Sophie first saw it she protested vigorously and promptly crossed out both "nots" and inserted an "and" between the second and third phrase, thus rendering it "Life is a spectacle, it is a feast, and it is a predicament."

I share these domestic details because they illustrate a central theme in this chapter, namely, that as the years pass it becomes increasingly clear that life is much more a matter of "both/and" than of "either/or." Though Santayana pronounced life a predicament, his definitive conclusion, gloomy though it was, in a sense settled it for him. But Sophie's observation unsettles things by suggesting that it can be many things besides a predicament to one who remains open to life's experiences.

The following old story about a rabbi is instructive here. Two men asked his help in settling a dispute. The first man stated his case, after which the rabbi said to him, "You are right." After the second man made his case, the rabbi said, "You are right." Now the rabbi's wife, who had heard these exchanges, confronted him. "How can they both be right?" Following a thoughtful pause, the rabbi replied, "My dear you are right."

My dictionary defines predicament as a problematic situation about which one does not know what to do. Applying that to life confirms the observation that life is not easy, and yet we all know that it can have its splendid moments. How then to harmonize and integrate these quite discrepant perceptions is the principal predicament that I hope to explore here by reflecting on what I think I have discovered and am still discovering about learning and aging, particularly in the last dozen or so years. In a sense it can be summarized in the words of a well-known Pennsylvania Dutch adage: "Ve get so soon oldt, und so late schmart." We do find ourselves old before we know it, and, probably not as wise as we once thought we were. In 8 A.D. the poet Ovid observed:

> Time in its stealthy gliding, cheats us all without our notice;
> Nothing goes more swiftly than do the years.

Or, as I heard someone quoted recently, "You don't grow old gradually, or on purpose, the way you go downtown on a subway. It's more like finding yourself standing in the last station and wondering how you got there." For me, like for the subway rider, time has flown. Life was a busy business, marked by an almost frenetic involvement with many things. I often felt, in the midst of doing something, that I should be doing something else.

So much for the "soon oldt" part. What about "getting so late schmart?"

In younger years I thought learning was getting to know as much as possible, at least more than my students, so that I could merit the title "teacher" and be looked up to as an authority. Only much later did I come to see the truth in Cicero's words, "The authority of those who teach, stands for the most part in the way of those who would learn." It was a long time before I learned that great teachers do not claim to be experts, and that the best of them are "learners among learners." The predicament here, of course, is that it is not easy to say, "I don't know" when one believes that as a teacher, one should. Or to say "I need to learn more about that."

Although pioneer developmental psychologist, G. Stanley Hall, at the turn of the last century, authored a volume entitled *Adolescence* and another entitled *Senescence,* early in my career, my field was known as child development. Gradually, however, Hall's prescience was recognized, and we came to accept that development is a lifelong process. In my youth I longed to be "grown up," and later thought I was. Most young people today still do. How often have my students reacted with both disbelief and deflation when I suggested that there was no such thing as a "grown-up;" "almost," perhaps; "completely grown-up," no. Again, early in my career I would not have understood the statement on the cover of the Fall 1981 journal *Aging,* "An elder is a person who is still developing, still growing, still a learner, still with potential, whose life continues to have within it promise for and connections to the future." Yet in the last 15 years I have referred to that statement in almost every class or lecture I have given. My neat compartmentalized conception of life, which seemed so simple and reasonable, one that Matilda White Riley entitles "age differentiated," where first comes education, next work, and finally leisure, had to be abandoned and replaced by one that saw each of life's successive stages as being, to use Riley's terms, "age integrated," that is, consisting of elements of each of the three components, education, work, and leisure (Riley, Kahn, & Foner, 1994). But, again, that kind of thinking insists that life is "both/and" rather than "either/or."

What was left then, but to look into the possibility that our intellectual endowment can be stretched to meet the challenges of a "both/and" view of the world. In later years, increasingly confronted with the wrenching realities of life, the importance of postformal thought to an understanding of what living involves has proved simultaneously stimulating and depressing. Postformal thought, beyond what Piaget (1967) described as formal operations (hypothetical deductive reasoning), requires accommodating ambiguity and uncertainty, irony and contradiction, with the integrative process of finding meaning in life. Gradually, I am coming to understand that adult learning and aging today need to be informed by certain characteristics of postformal thought as well as by some of the principles that can be derived from our continuing study of life-span development.

BEYOND FORMAL OPERATIONS

Going beyond Piaget's adult stage of cognitive development makes heavy demands on those who would do so. And certainly not all adults do. Many are content to leave unexamined their moral convictions and beliefs and to reason at the earlier level of concrete operational thought. My favorite illustration of this kind of thinking was the sign I once read that a shop keeper, in a community known for its conservatism, had printed on the back of the shade of his show window. When he closed his shop, pulled down the shade, and left for home, he left a message to all who passed his establishment. It read "Some open minds should be closed for repairs."

UNCERTAINTY AND AMBIGUITY

To go beyond formal operations requires that we give up the sureness, the certainties that I, for many years, believed would form the basis of a stable, predictable, adult life. I acquired this way of thinking as a result of being brought up in a fairly traditional home by parents who wanted me to be a teacher; worked hard to support me through normal school at $200 per year for room, board, and tuition; helped me get my first job; and then prayed that I would "settle down" with wife and children; and live out my life in a way that would bring no dishonor on the family in much the same way as they had done.

But, for some reason or other, I did not settle down. I was discontented and edgy. As a result, in Robert Frost's words, I chose "the path less taken." But oh, what a predicament that resulted in. My basic equipment—a belief in an orderly, predictable world, a conviction that people were basically good and that honest effort would be rewarded—was a serious mismatch for the world I was encountering. While I managed to keep my head above water, a lot of crazy stuff happened to me on the way to learning to think at the level of postformal operations, the defining elements of which are illustrated in the process that stretches across the years—of coming to accept uncertainty, to tolerate ambiguity, to wonder at the spectacle that life can be, to enjoy the feast it offers, and to make peace with its being a predicament.

What I for many years thought would be a settled and systematic journey to a clearly defined goal in life instead became a pilgrimage on which I still find myself today. The pilgrimage metaphor conveys life's open-endedness, incorporating both certainty and uncertainty. As Kurtz and Ketcham (1992) have it, "a pilgrimage is in essence a winding, turning, looping, crisscrossing, occasionally backtracking *peregrination*." The contemporary American artist Kitaj, who lived most of his life in England, writes that at age 54 he withdrew for 3 years into his family life and "grew more and more unsure of what I could do in painting. I felt I had no method and I was driven nearly mad, experimenting with more painterly painting and feeling I was going nowhere" (Kitaj, 1994).

A pilgrimage is a journey that involves uncertainty and ambiguity, often taking us places we never expected to go. Life is certainly a predicament if it means being open to uncertainty, taking ambiguity in stride because, as we will consider later, there is within us such a strong drive to attain closure. A recent essay about Lionel Trilling describes the open-ended life this way, "Thinking against himself, endlessly reweaving and unweaving his own point of view, keeping the world at arm's length, he resisted closure as a matter of principle" (Dickstein, 1998). But learning to think that way is not easy, especially for folks, reared as I was, to think in quite a more concrete and absolutist manner.

Toward the close of World War II the German theologian Dietrich Bonhöffer (1967) in one of his letters from prison wrote that in his view the world had come of age. I believe what he meant was that perceptive adults would never again enjoy the luxury of simplistic thinking about right and wrong, but would have to deal increasingly with ambiguities, the relativistic, nonabsolute nature of reality and knowledge.

One of the meanings to be derived from what has just been said is that the process of enjoying the spectacle, of savoring the feast, and of attempting to deal with the predicament is the important thing. I know it, and have taught it, but I still have difficulty living the idea that life's fulfillments are found in the process rather than in the achievement of the perfect product. It helps when I remind myself what the 90-year-old Pablo Casals said when asked why at his age he continued to practice. "Because I am making progress," he said. But the predicament for many of us is that we want to believe that he could be at peace with his competence. We want to believe that he was perfection. But the predicament is clear in the lives of other artists as well. It is reported that Cezanne's widow told Matisse that Cezanne often had no idea how to finish a painting.

CONTRADICTION AND IRONY

Another facet of postformal thought requires the thinking adult to accept contradiction. For a person who was reared believing that God was in His heavens and all was right with the world, and who as a parent and a parent educator wanted children to learn to believe that the world was good and that they could count on it, it was hard to learn that life is not fair. I remember how remorseful, confused, and angry I felt the first time I said to our already grown daughter that life was a "crock." And yet adult cognition requires the recognition of contradiction as a part of reality. A well-developed sense of irony, the ability to accept the fact that circumstances are frequently quite the opposite of what one would expect, is a valuable quality for committed thinkers of any age in today's world.

When I was a boy it was not infrequently observed by elders that "the good die young." The irony of that was lost on me for many years. Only later was I to begin to learn that life is not fair; that to be human is to err; that we are both saint and sinner, strong and weak, competent and incompetent; and that it is not our assignment in life to become perfect, for to do so is to rob ourselves of our humanness.

Recently a friend suggested that I read a book entitled *Spirituality of Imperfection*. I recommend it to those, who like me, have serious problems accepting our own and, of course, others' imperfections. I would like to believe that I used to be a perfectionist, but that I gave it up because I was not good enough at it. An eye-opener for me at the outset of this book is a statement by former commissioner of baseball, Francis T. Vincent, Jr. "Baseball teaches us, or has taught most of us, how to deal with failure. We learn at a very young age that failure is the norm in baseball, and, precisely because we have failed, we hold in high regard those who fail less often—those who hit safely in one out of three chances and become star players. I find it fascinating," he goes on, "that baseball, alone in sport, considers errors to be part of the game, part of its rigorous truth" (Kurtz & Ketcham, 1992).

Early in my career I dabbled in counseling (I also gave that up because I felt I wasn't good enough at it) and I read, and suggested that others read, a book with the catchy title *I'm OK, You're OK.* In later years I am beginning to understand how simplistic this is and am coming to accept the contradiction "I'm not all right, and you're not all right, but that's OK, that's all right." Sound familiar? Remember my wife's objection to the Santayana quote? Remember the story about the rabbi? Learning and aging are predicaments because they both confront us with the fact that things are not "either/or," but rather "both/and."

To be a serious user of postformal cognitive processes challenges the best of us to apply levels of intellectual energy that, while on the one hand are stimulating, even exhilarating, are on the other time consuming and fatiguing. Small wonder, then, that many embrace the simpler solutions that fundamentalist thinking offers. But our contemporary world seems steadily to be embracing complexity. Elders today are being given options in realms that were formerly structured and straightforward. The Social Security Administration has often been cited as a model of efficiency. Considering its size, its operation has been incredibly error free and user friendly. For most of us, here was something we could count on precisely because we understood how it worked and what to expect. Unfortunately, despite the best efforts of elder advocates, the lure of profits to be made by partially privatizing the system will now introduce choices about which many elders will be troubled, if not seriously confused. How disillusioned already are many Medicare recipients, who, at the prospect of coverage for prescription drugs, chose to affiliate with HMOs, but are now being refused further coverage as a cost cutting measure. And, while favored by most of us in the aging business, the elimination of mandatory retirement has, however, confronted many individuals with yet another predicament. Our challenge is how to deal with these and other predicaments encountered with increasing frequency as the years fly by. Can what we think we know about postformal thought help us find our way, or does its emphasis on openness, uncertainty, and contradiction condemn us to going around in circles? Are there fundamental principles about our nature and development that adult thinkers can embrace as they seek to deal effectively with the challenges of our contemporary society? I believe that there are, and I want to devote the closing portions of this paper to them.

INTEGRATION

Paradoxically, while the first two components of postformal thought relate to our individuality, our strengths and weaknesses, and our need to see life as open ended, the third aspect of this kind of thought is that it seeks to be integrative. It seeks to help us harmonize the risks of uncertainty with our need for seeing relatedness and meaning. Again here, however, we confront a "both/and" situation. As maturing adults we must learn to be comfortable with seeking certainty while continuing to experience uncertainty, to seek completion while recognizing that to be human is to be incomplete, to seek wholeness, while recognizing that we are broken. I am reminded by this of Emerson's remark that there is a crack in everything God has made.

The search for relatedness is aided by the kind of thinking involved in integration. Many older individuals tend to combine categories and eliminate detail in organizing information. They concern themselves more with wholes, with synthesis. It has been demonstrated that, when confronting problems, in contrast to younger ones, older executives came to fewer solutions, but those they came to were more often successful because they eliminated those that experience showed did not work. This boiling down of life experience is integral to the quest for relatedness, to our seeking wholeness, to our making sense out of life, especially as we see it inevitably drawing to its close. It is the process by which extraneous details, which often consume so much of our time and energy, are eliminated, permitting us to reflect on the basic principles that undergird our development as human beings. Let me quickly mention a few that have special relevance for learning and aging.

The principle of priority is clear from the outset. The direction of development is from the top down and the inside out. First things first, those systems most vital to our successful survival, notably the autonomic and cerebro-spinal nervous systems, are the best developed at birth and prove to be the most resilient across time. We ignore at our psychological and social peril the lesson of priority in life's affairs. Earlier I mentioned often feeling in the midst of doing something that I should be doing something else. How often in the process of preparing this material did I have to struggle with my priorities. My predicament was that it was not always my highest priority. Especially in a world as complex as ours, sound personal priorities are crucial if a frenetic and exhausting existence is to be avoided.

A second principle that some of us learn to respect only too late in life is that of the importance of a rhythmic pattern of work and rest. As I described earlier, during much of my early career I rather resembled a grasshopper leaping about from notion to notion, and to some extent, from place to place with little, if any, time spent sitting still and thinking in a connected way about family, community, and the meaning of life. I shall long remember my father's consistent comment when I would get involved in something new: "Armin, when are you going to settle down?" Though he died soon after I began my career in Vermont, I am sure he would have been pleased that I am still there after almost 30 years. And yet, settling down, in the sense of staying put, is not what this principle is all about. What it does embody is finding the proper balance between activity and contemplation. To find that balance requires taking the time to understand what we have been, who we are, where we are headed, and how what we are doing is or is not in harmony with that understanding. I am sure I am not the only person who finds this a major predicament in life.

The pilgrimage metaphor I referred to earlier illuminates a third principle of human development, namely, that every gain we make is at a price. The child who ultimately succeeds in walking, relinquishes the comfort and security of being carried. Arriving at "independent" adulthood carries with it the cost of personal responsibility for one's behavior. In my case the price exacted was a protracted loss of contact with the tradition in which I was reared. It meant disavowing beliefs I once accepted, but that gradually failed to speak to what I was experiencing. On numerous occasions I was torn by doubts and fears, but continued on the way less taken, in spite of the fact that another important principle in development is that of respect for tradition. The cry of the fiddler on the roof haunted my attempts to deal with the predicament I found myself in.

It is the principle of continuity that demands respect for tradition, for refusing to learn from the experience of those who have gone this way before is a costly and time consuming error, to say the least. It is this principle that points up the importance of listening as elders tell their story. Indigenous people in many parts of the world share a saying that when an elder dies a library goes up in flames. We can ill afford to ignore the heritage of our humanity. But it was critical for me to learn that there is a world of difference between the unthinking acceptance of a corpus of beliefs and the challenging process of distilling from that extensive corpus, the fundamental ideas contained, avowing them, and attempting to make them operative in my life.

This making sense of life, so inexorably bound up with what has been termed reintegration, can result, when it is successful, in wisdom. I think Samuel Johnson put this so well when he wrote: "Deign on the passing world to turn thine eyes, and pause a while from learning, to be wise."

It has been said that wisdom embodies cognition and affect, and it has been suggested that this integration is what adult cognitive development is all about. For this reason most observers agree that the experience that comes with age is a prerequisite to but not a guarantee of wisdom. Foolishness is not the exclusive domain of children and youth. But what wisdom we can muster is sorely needed if we are some day soon to be faced with the decision of whether to extend the life-span. Returning momentarily to the principle of continuity, we are reminded here that adult cognitive capacity is both informed by what we have learned from past experience and the determinant of further learning endeavors. Perhaps, at the risk of oversimplifying, one might venture that the old both colors, and is colored by, the new. Do I hear "both/and" again?

With age comes a strong urge to find meaning, to somehow put it all together, to achieve at least some degree of wholeness. This, it seems to me, is the other side of the integration coin. It is here that adult intellectual prowess is explicitly challenged, and it is here that another principle of human development, namely indigenous motivation, plays a significant role. This principle simply refers to the fact that our abilities, of whatever kind, are dynamic in nature. That is, they carry with them a drive to be utilized; the greater the ability, the stronger the drive. Discovering meaning and purpose is a challenge that our cognitive capacities cannot ignore. The need to harmonize our urge to explore unknowns, to risk continuing openness to experience and the learnings to be found in it, with those stable and fundamental elements of our being that provide meaning and continuity, that need for wholeness will not be ignored.

But the quest for wholeness pushes us beyond ourselves into community—beyond dependency and independence toward interdependence. It is in community that our individuality, our uniqueness, finds its *raison d'être*. And we are unique because no one else has our exact pattern of weaknesses nor our selfsame profile of strengths. But without others there would be no succor for our weakness, nor needs in others for our strengths to serve. As maturing adults we are simultaneously both dependent and independent—the "both/and" business again—and achieving a proper balance between these is the predicament that interdependence incorporates. But while we are pushed toward community, we hesitate to reveal both our weaknesses for fear of exploitation and our strengths for how they might be perceived. The temptation is to try to hide our uniqueness by adopting a role, a mask, even at the risk of cutting ourselves off from the fellowship we are designed to enjoy and through which we can find fulfillment and meaning in life. In a review of Newton Arvin's critical biography of Nathaniel Hawthorn, we find the following: "The essential sin (Hawthorne would seem to say) lies in whatever shuts up the spirit in a dungeon where it is alone, beyond the reach of common sympathies and the general sunlight. All that isolates, damns; all that associates, saves" (Worth, 1998).

But a prerequisite to association, to full participation with others, is addressed in the final developmental principle that I wish to articulate. Essentially it speaks to the importance of commitment as opposed to lip service; faithfulness and accountability rather than duplicity and expediency. Without the assurance of the faithfulness of others we hesitate to reveal our weaknesses, and thus are deprived of the gift their strengths can bring us. The converse, of course, is equally true. We cannot use our strengths in the service of others if they fear that disclosing their needs will lead to their being exploited.

Our need for community is clear. But what community, and what kind of relationship, remain perplexing issues. The community that my father knew as a child in feudal Europe was limited to perhaps a few hundred people inhabiting a few thousand acres. No telephones, newspapers, or radio linked his world promptly and easily to that of others. But the meaning of community today confronts me in my old age with a predicament my father in his youth never faced; namely the fabled "world community." In the December 1998 *American Psychologist,* Anthony Marsella reviews our irreversible ties to a world community whose complex problems challenge our sense of identity, control, and well-being. He asserts that to help cope with these problems will require that "psychology reconsider some of its fundamental premises, methods, and practices that are rooted within Western cultural traditions, and expand its appreciation and use of other psychologies" (Marsella, 1998). The same challenge probably confronts most other disciplines as well. Surely the burden of open-endedness continues to challenge our capacity for integration.

So where does this leave us? For me this means that the older I get the more I must accept that I am very much in the dark, and must continue to do my best to seek what light I can discern. Ironically, the more we know, the more we know we do not know. The challenge for me now is to say "That's all right," that is what it means to be an imperfect human, or put in another way, perfectly human. So I continue my quest, my pilgrimage is not over. I will continue to cultivate more fully my sense of humor, to value the community I am privileged to have, and to be myself, a learner among learners. I invite any or all who read this to join me.

NOTE

This material was first presented as the Clark Tibbitts Award Lecture at the meeting of the Association for Gerontology in Higher Education, St. Louis, Missouri, 26 February 1999.

REFERENCES

Bonhöffer, D. (1967). *Letters and papers from prison* (Rev. ed.). London: SCM.

Dickstein, M. (1998, September 20). Bookend: A man nobody knew. *The New York Times Book Review, 148,* 43.

Kitaj, R. B. (1994). *R. B. Kitaj: A retrospective* (R. Morphet, Ed.). New York: Rizzoli.

Kurtz, E., & Ketcham, K. (1992). *The spirituality of imperfection: Storytelling and the journey to wholeness.* New York: Bantam Books.

Marsella, A. (1998). Toward a "Global-community psychology": Meeting the needs of a changing world. *American Psychologist, 53,* 1282–1291.

Piaget, J. (1967). *Six psychological studies.* New York: Vintage.

Riley, M. W., Kahn, R. L., & Foner, A. (1994). *Age and structural lag: Society's failure to provide meaningful opportunities in work, family, and leisure.* New York: Wiley.

Worth, B. (1998, October 5). The scarlet professor. *New Yorker, 74,* 56–67.

CHAPTER 6

Voyage in Time

Carter Catlett Williams

The world of space surrounds our existence.
It is but a part of living, the rest is time.
Things are the shore, the voyage is in time.
—Rabbi Abraham Joshua Heschel (p. 96)

My father, Landon Carter Catlett, Jr., died July 17, 1925 in an airplane crash when he was 27 years old. At the time my mother was 25 years old, and I was 22 months old. I have no memory of him whatsoever. He was a legend to me—the brilliant young man of sterling character, a West Point graduate and aviator in the U.S. Army Air Service, whose promising life was snuffed out when he crashed in what he had described in a July 6 letter to his parents, as a "tiny, fast, single-seater" pursuit plane that he was beginning to master (Figure 6.1).

I remember my sense of self-importance as a small child when occasionally my grandfather told the tragic tale to a visitor. For me, this story belonged to my grandfather and others. I had no sense of relationship with my father. He and I were merely characters in the story, but that was enough to give me a feeling of importance.

FIGURE 6.1   Landon Carter Catlett, Jr.

After my father's death, my mother, Catharine Mott Catlett, returned to the only sources of help she had—to his family for a year, and then to hers, settling down with me in the old house and farm called Toddsbury, situated on an inlet of the southern Chesapeake Bay. My family household, beginning just before I turned 3, was that of mother, aunt, grandfather, invalid grandmother, and great aunt, and the latter's companion. My mother and aunt shared the housekeeping and parent-care duties. By the time I was 22, with college behind me and making preparations for a job away from home, deaths had reduced the household to three. Only my mother, aunt, and I remained.

My mother died at age 86, never having remarried. At her funeral service 13 years ago, I experienced a moment of consciousness new to me. Toward the close of the service, the minister offered a prayer for my father and mother together. Here in this very church where they had married 64 years earlier and where my father's funeral took place less than 3 years afterwards, a prayer was offered for them in their reuniting. The prayer was a complete surprise to me and was accompanied with a solacing, and literally first time thought, hard as that is for others to believe, that once I had had two parents together at the beginning of my life, just like everybody else. This was an entirely new feeling, a new way of viewing them and me, and still brings tears to my eyes at the wonder and comfort of it.

Always on my mother's bureau, next to two small pictures of my father in airplanes, was a framed poem that began, "I cannot say, I will not say that he is dead—he is just away." One very special portrait of the three of us together hung beside her bureau, but there were no family stories or anecdotes from my mother or others telling me about us as a family, my father's ways with me, or his love (Figure 6.2). Except for that one portrait, there were virtually no mementos of our life as a family, only indirect allusions by means of two other objects in the bedroom we shared—a little paperweight showing a field of bluebonnets and a picture of moon-lit palms. These indicated the locations of the two airfields at which they had been stationed, the first in Texas and the other in Hawaii. What little else there was of her married life—some china and silver, melting waxed parasols from Hawaii and a pair of Japanese sandals for a small child—were locked away in a steamer trunk in the back hall. There was nothing to recall or remind us of our life as a young family.

FIGURE 6.2   Catharine Mott Catlett, Landon Carter Catlett, Jr., and baby Catherine Carter Catlett.

The uses of memory are many. Beyond its practical functions, memory makes a special offering to the elder: the means of sorting through experience, to trace the paths taken and not taken, to emerge with fresh and deeper understanding of one's life. Some have called it reconstructing a life and see it as a necessary task in old age.

But what if there is a void in early life where there is no memory? How can one set about this review and reconstruction? In time present, how does one cope with the void in time past? I had been left with a sense of emptiness at my core, an emptiness that took me years to recognize for what it was. In retrospect, the unfolding discoveries and my growing consciousness may appear obvious and almost orderly. But this was not the case. What appear now as obvious signals, were, at the time, only sudden, unrelated blips on the screen, certainly not coherent messages.

My first signal came late one night about 7 years ago, after a day of clearing and sorting things in the attic of my mother's house. I was digging through a box of paper—old legal papers from my mother's family—when I noticed a letter in my father's handwriting, totally out of place in this particular box. It was written from Luke Field, Territory of Hawaii, not many weeks before his death, to his mother on Mother's Day, 1925. He wrote about me, his small daughter:

> ... But on the whole she is a very happy, healthy youngster, understands perfectly, obeys intermittently, and tries to talk incessantly. . . . I don't try to sneak away when I leave the house. I kiss my hand to her and say "bye-bye" and she runs to the window and climbs into the rocker to wave and kiss her hand as long as she can see me. Her face is always serious then but she never cries unless she is cut up over something else.

For the first time in my life, I wept for the little girl who blew kisses to her father on July 17, 1925 and never saw him again. Sobs of loss—as well of the joy I discovered in his words—racked me as I lay in bed that night. My father and my 22-month-old self were present to me for the first time (Figure 6.3).

The next morning, however, still focused on my clearing and sorting task, I returned to work in the attic. Midst the old books and

FIGURE 6.3   Catherine Carter Catlett and her father, Landon Carter Catlett, Jr.

piles of household odds and ends, I found a large, sturdy cardboard box, and took it downstairs to examine its contents in daylight. There lay a wool army uniform and, in a yellowing towel, a fine American flag folded in a triangle, military style. The uniform, with the Army Air Service insignia, was of course my father's, and the flag, from its manner of folding, was surely the flag handed my mother at the conclusion of his funeral service.

I spread the uniform out and looked at it with wonder. Then, returning it to the box, I gently ran my hands over the khaki coat to smooth out the wrinkles. Child and elder folded into one. I tenderly stroked my father's broken body, to comfort and console. I wept for him, yet sealed away this moment, keeping it to myself. I did not want to dig deeper into this pain. I closed the box and returned it to the attic.

I did not yet suspect the complexity of what lay behind the tears. Several years passed before another clue came to me, sparked by a certain group of family photographs. I had assembled this collection to accompany my mother to the nursing home. There are pictures of her as a child, her home on the river (actually an inlet of the Chesapeake Bay) and the boat that plied the route between Baltimore and numerous wharves on those bay inlets, as well as her grandmother, parents, sisters and brother, and pictures of her as a bride, young mother, and Army Air Service wife. I grew up poring over these pictures, soaking up the stories that older family members recounted. They were very much a part of me; they helped me know who I was.

But here it was, 10 years after my mother's death, and I felt alone and bleak from just a passing glance at those photographs. No one but me knows the life shown there, I thought. It's over, it's gone, dead and done. A dreary grayness settled on me. I was losing part of myself, and there was no one to take notice. There was only that sad, empty space I felt inside.

Then I realized a curious thing: I had never lived the life depicted in the photographs. The Old Bay Line steamers stopped coming up our river 3 or 4 years before I was born. I don't remember my great grandmother. I certainly don't remember myself, a tiny newborn in my mother's arms. After all, these were the pictures I had collected and framed for my mother to have with her in her room in the nursing home. They were about *her* life, not mine.

I was so puzzled by my reaction that I wrote many pages trying to explain to myself why I felt such loss and emptiness. I centered my thoughts on the heavy inheritance of family story and tradition that had been mine as the only child in a household of six adults. Yet this did little to explain my desolation.

About the same time, I had started on another path that, remarkably, I viewed as unrelated. On January 28, 1995, I began to sort the contents of a poor little beat-up box, that had been lodged in several storage closets and at least three attics over the course of the last 80 years. I represented the third generation to oversee the fate of well over 400 letters. Most were my father's, but with a substantial sprinkling of letters from his parents and sisters, and a few from friends. I had always known the letters were there, and, many years before, had tried a couple of times on our summer vacations at my mother's to look at them. But reading one or two had filled me with so much sadness for my parents and the early end of their marriage, I quickly put them away and made no more attempts. They were nowhere on the radar screen of my busy life.

Now, at the beginning of 1995, I set about work on the letters in earnest. I sorted them all into chronological order, sampling just a few as I sorted, but enough to toss me about from delight to despair, from the moments of high hope to the aching sadness of condolence letters following my father's death. Then, taking them in the order of their writing, I began the serious business of transcribing every one of them, without reading ahead. With the exception of three, the letters begin in September 1914, when, at age 16, my father left home for the first time to attend The Episcopal High School near Alexandria, Virginia. Though less than a 3-hour drive today, it was then usually an overnight trip, involving boat and train travel, from Gloucester County, in the Tidewater region of the state, up to the outskirts of Washington, DC.

At times, reading the letters hurt so much I could hardly bear it. I woke up nights worrying about my father, going over and over his life and hopes, always in the knowledge of his death. I was left tearful and exhausted from reading years of hopeful and vital letters, encouraging, instructing, reporting on big and little daily events, anticipating—so much anticipating—only to have my father go up in a pursuit plane he was just learning to fly and crash into the blue-green waters of Hawaii. I went to see a therapist in the midst of this after many months of low spirits and poor sleep.

After some exploration of my childhood family relationships, the therapist said it seemed I had grown up in a family that was largely undemonstrative, and then he posed this startling question: From whom did you get your warmth? I volunteered that my aunt was expressive, and my father's family was. The therapist said firmly, "I think the source of your warmth was your father." My response was one of disbelief and perhaps a touch of derision. "How could that possibly be? I never knew my father—I have absolutely no memory of him!" The therapist spoke quietly and authoritatively about the significance and importance of relationships in the first years of life, of how a baby absorbs the feelings, attitudes, and ways of relating from those closest to her, that is, her parents.

This was perfectly reasonable, well-established knowledge about infancy but when applied to me personally, was completely astounding. I began to realize that for me having no conscious memory of my father had meant no father. I had equated absence of memory with absence of experience.

The therapist's question sent me skipping over hundreds of unread letters straight to my father's letters of 1923, the year of my birth, through July 1925, willingly breaking my rule of not reading ahead. I set aside an afternoon, turned off the telephone, and closed myself into the bedroom with his last 36 letters.

I read with total absorption and gratitude, the flooding tears obscuring the pages before me. I heard in my father's words—with what approached a flesh-and-blood reality—his complete involvement in my life. Here are some excerpts, beginning 3 weeks after my birth on September 2, 1923; the first three being from Kelly Field, Texas, the balance from Honolulu and Luke Field, Territory of Hawaii:

September 23, 1923

Dear Mother,

All goes well with your eldest grandchild. She is now imbibing nourishment close to my elbow, lying on our porch couch, which is an army cot with a West Point blanket on it. She is 3 weeks old today and weighs 8 lbs. and 5 oz., a gain of nearly a pound since birth. She is getting along finely since we put her on a 3-hour schedule . . .

Her bowels have done their fair share today. When they get a little slow she kicks and smacks boots and blankets all over the place. But she drinks a little warm water and soon follows an explosion, after which come clean clothes and sleep. That was yesterday. Today she has cried only at bathing time, when she almost stands up and jumps out of the tub. She likes it when turned on her stomach and scrubbed on the back however. It makes her purr like a kitten . . .

Little Catharine[1] doesn't often spit up any. She has a few hiccoughs now and then, but she loves warm water in a bottle almost as much

---

[1]Though baptized Catharine Mott Catlett, my mother changed my middle name to Carter after my father's death, and called me "Catharine Carter." When I went away to boarding school, where there were several Catharines in the class, my double name was shortened to Carter.

as her mother's milk and takes a little nip of it to go to sleep on after nearly every meal. Getting it away from her when she is asleep is a ticklish job. She often knocks it out of her own mouth, which hurts her feelings worse than anything.

October 1, 1923

Dear Mother,

. . . After she finishes drinking [her water bottle], she gets up on her hands and lifts her head several inches, peering around with her eyes bucked and mouth open. She also makes quarrelsome noises like a setting hen when she feels restless. Once she rolled herself over on her back and smack up against the side of the "kiddie koop." Then she squalled. What will she do in a few more months?

. . . My face seems to inspire her with amusement. She is not prone to smile at her mother, who goes to great lengths to induce her to. Such is the perversity of human nature, from the cradle to the grave . . .

March 12, 1924

Dear Mother,

. . . [In earlier arrangements for home leave,] when we planned to stay at your house overnight, we didn't know Mr. Mott would have the truck. I know you will understand that the change is to make the trip as easy as possible on the baby, as all our plans are. She can sleep in a clothesbasket in the back of the truck going to Toddsbury and not awaken till morning . . .

July 25, 1924

Dear Mother,

. . . She does not get fed till 6 in the morning, after her 6 o'clock supper. All during the day she turns the house upside down, exactly like a puppy, but more persistent . . .

August 10, 1924

My darling Mother,

. . . Little Catharine has been fretting to get up, so I have given her some of your letters to play with. She seems interested and rubs her fingers over the marks. She is even now scraping a pencil (unsharpened) over them. . . . Falls are not exactly rare, but are the exception rather than the rule. She will pick up a shoetree, stocking or piece of clothing and carry it around the house for an hour. Consequently when I go to dress, I may find my socks in different rooms . . .

September 2, 1924

Dear Father,

. . . Little Catharine is 1 year old today. She enjoyed the picnic and the other little girl thoroughly. She is not always such a squirmer as of yore. She has pensive moments when she will sit looking off into space and singing to herself and she will neither answer nor pay the slightest attention to words or shaking—decidedly like her grandmother, when her mind is engaged . . .

November 11, 1924

Dear Mother,

. . . Catharine killed our holiday sleep at 5 a.m. by squalling until we gave her a cracker and a doll baby. It gets cool enough in the early morning to need a little cover and she will not stay under any, so she often gets cold and arouses all the neighbors. At 6 p.m. she goes to sleep without a murmur, so we really can't complain. . . . Catharine talks a blue streak now, but never an intelligible word except "Daddy," which she calls out the first thing in the morning and "Mum-mum-mum," which she groans when she is hungry, catching her mother by the skirt and impeding the preparations. She . . . is crawling over me, playing with the stamps and inkbottle . . .

March 15, 1925

My darling Mother,

. . . Peggy Post and Catharine have become very much attached to each other. Peggy often runs away from home and turns up in our back yard where she is greeted with the utmost enthusiasm. . . . Catharine is just as busy as she can be, while Peggy will sit still and chuckle at her activities. Peggy's great stunt is to toddle over and sit in somebody's lap—she sits there too. Catharine sits down for the purpose of squirming and jumping up and down.

April 5, 1925

My dear Father,

. . . Little Catharine climbs everything in sight, walks curb stones like a tight rope performer, writes with a soft rock on the pavement and pencils the white kitchen wall when she gets a chance . . .

June 4, 1925

My dear Father,

... She is still a pest about books and magazines. She doesn't intentionally tear them. She just wears them all out. She loves to write on the margins with a pencil too and will put the pencil in her mouth. Today she poured a glass of water in her mother's handbag.

June 16, 1925

My precious Mother,

A year ago we were making preparations for a long, long journey. How fast the happy days go by for those upon whose youth Dame Fortune smiles. The principal change the year has brought forth is little Catharine. Her teeth, her prattle, her little goodnight kisses, and her eternal vigilance are more and more a delight. . . . I think the older she grows the more attractive she will be. A frank, whole-hearted, energetic child is never gawky or awkward, especially if taught to obey and to regard its parents with affection rather than fear. And Catharine surely holds her parents above everybody.

[Letter fragment, 1925]

... I raised my voice and said "No" this morning. She sat down and burst into tears. I must try never to raise my voice in speaking to her. When we have a visitor with a loud voice, her eyes nearly pop out. Her mother is always quiet with her. . . . Each day finds her more at home in the water. She rides on my back while I swim and she paddles too, but won't kick her feet yet. She complains when we let her head go under, but isn't frightened. . . . She attracts a lot of attention. Yesterday she took one hand off my neck to wave to an old fat gentleman and nearly lost her balance . . .

July 6, 1925

My dear Father,

... Little Catharine . . . runs around singing words she knows over and over like this "Ball—Daddy—Ball—Mudder—Ball—Peggy—night-night—Peggy—"cow-cow" (Japanese for eating food, etc). She constantly tries new combinations. Her best sentence so far is "Mudder, Peggy gone." This upon investigation, proved true. . . . We went for a wonderful picnic on the 4th. . . . A big wave came in and threw sand all over them but little Catharine didn't seem to mind. She did a piece of shivering in the breeze, until we rolled her in a blanket. . . . Our first view of her the following morning was when she was discovered trying to draw on her bathing suit over her clothes! So we took her down to the meager shore here and let her play. She lay on her stomach in the water.

This final entry is from the last of his letters handed on to me. Eleven days later his plane crashed. And my life with my parents crashed, leaving me no recollections of the three of us together or of my father as parent.

Now I devour his words about me. I cannot get enough of them. No detail is too small to give delight. His motivation to keep four grandparents in distant Virginia in touch with their only grandchild is now a gift of life to me. I read, and read again, and again, and not only for his words about me. I soak up every detail his letters tell me about himself and his relationship with me. I fall in love with my frank, caring, responsive, practical father, whose wryness in telling of his daughter's escapades hints at his humor and good humor.

I am entranced with the news that I slept in a clothesbasket in the back of a truck! I wonder if the whole family rode the 14 miles from the boat to Toddsbury in an open truck. And I am proud to have had a father who broke the mold. When making a visit to friends he did not call his wife and say, "The baby needs changing." He quietly did it himself.

I have been transported through many layers of time to my very own family, to the beginning of my life. Indeed, my life extension comes at life's beginning, not the ending.

Memories of my own children are revived as I read his accounts of me. His observations have sharpened mine as I watch our youngest grandchildren, ages 3 and 2. The glimpses of my own first years, the memories of our children's babyhood, and current experiences with our grandchildren meld.

I have become two selves, a 76-year-old woman delighting in her grandchildren, and a 2-year-old child receiving such delight. I see my little grandson anchored to both mother and father, each hand clasped by one of them. I see his satisfaction and fast on that observation is a satisfaction of my own: "My hands were once held like that, and I absorbed that assurance of parent presence and love." In my father's words: "... Catharine surely holds her parents above everybody."

This past summer, the two selves within me watched our youngest granddaughter at 22 months holding up her arms to her father, then request granted, snuggling her head in the curve of his shoulder and neck. My father tells me: "She rides on my back while I swim ... "

The void within begins to fill with my father's words. The once bare and empty spaces of my early childhood are becoming richly furnished.

There is a price for giving up the void. The price is grief, at times deep, exhausting grief. As I hungrily savor my father's words, I long actually to hear his voice, to know his manner of speaking, to recall sitting on his lap and the feel of his wool uniform against my face as he reads to me, to know him through all my senses—to see, touch, taste, smell, and hear him.

I catch at little threads. I remember his parents', sisters', and cousins' speech, as well as that of nine great aunts and uncles—slow and deliberate, in the gentle, now archaic, Tidewater Virginia "Broad A." I know he used it, not only because all the family did, but also because the nickname printed in his West Point yearbook is "Cyahta." In this accent the letter R largely disappeared and a Y sound was injected when A followed a consonant. And A was pronounced with an AH sound, as Britishers do. So in the speech of his family, it would be "Cyahta walked down the gyahden pahth to pick cyahn- ations." How in the world did he handle this way of talking at airfields and West Point?

Another thread I fondly trace is his affectionate ways, consonant with those of his family. His letters open with salutations ranging from "Dear Mother" to "My darling Mother," and sometimes to "Most precious Mother," and similarly affectionate greetings to his sisters. His farewells most commonly are "With a heart full of love to each and everyone," and on one occasion, "Love to all, every chicken thief in Gloucester included."

I glimpse his demonstrative ways when I look closely at the few snapshots I have of him and my mother. His arm is around her or his hand is resting on her shoulder. He writes his family before she sets out with me on her first trip home since their marriage (he is to follow in a month):

We never for a moment considered postponing the trip Home. You "must don't know how bad we're home-struck" . . . anyway Catharine will be with you for supper Saturday night. Kiss her roundly for me. I shall be missing her by then.

I yearn to see him, to know his physical presence. Though in my mind my mythical father was always a giant in all respects, and therefore a tall man, I found that he was 5 feet 8 1/5 inches tall, only 3 inches taller than my mother, and weighed about 160 pounds. His height is now obvious to me when I study his few pictures with my mother, but when one is in the grip of a legend, one doesn't see "obvious" things. He was very erect in posture and took pains with his clothing and appearance. His eyes and hair were dark brown, his nose prominent. He looks at me from his pictures very directly, and sometimes with the hint of a twinkle in his eye.

What had been the familiar taste and scent of him, when I put my head on his shoulder? There would have been no stale smell of tobacco or alcohol because he had no truck with either. Maybe in the mornings there would have been a little scent of talc, because he abhorred anything more than that. And in the evenings, especially at the end of the long, hot Texas days, there might have been a lingering sweatiness, though his pleasure in the refreshment of a shower would have wiped that out.

There are times of unalloyed delight in getting to know my father, but they are few. Always the getting-to-know-him takes place in the knowledge of the loss of him. The more I long to see him, the more acute is his absence. I have come to know my father in the sharpness of his absence. I have absorbed that absence over and over again, cutting into me ever more deeply.

At a time when this pain was almost more than I could handle, I read Rabbi Abraham Joshua Heschel's words in his book, *The Sabbath* (1951).

There is a realm of time where the goal is not to have but to be, not to own but to give, not to control but to share (p. 3). . . . In our daily lives we attend primarily to that which the senses are spelling out for us: to what the eyes perceive, to what the fingers touch. Reality to us is thinghood, consisting of substances that occupy space (p. 5). . . . The result of our thingness is our blindness to all reality that fails to identify itself as a thing, as a matter of fact. This is obvious in our understanding of time, which, being thingless and insubstantial, appears to us as if it had no reality (p. 5). . . . Time, however, is beyond our reach, beyond our power. It is both near and far, intrinsic to all experience and transcending all experience. It belongs exclusively to God (p. 9) . . . . The likeness of God can be found in time, which is eternity in disguise. (p. 16)

There it was before me: I was longing, weeping, yearning, wanting desperately for "what the eyes perceive, to what the fingers touch." I had been wanting to "have" my father through things physical—flesh and blood—not perceiving that his life now is in the dimension of time. I too dwell in time, but my voyage has not yet got free of things that are the shore. I am still anchored there, but my father is purely in time which "belongs exclusively to God, . . . eternity in disguise." Someday, in God's time, free of the fetters of space, I will know my father in a manner beyond present understanding. Sadness abides, but a healing peace begins.

Old age has offered me the chance to be open to discovery and new understanding beyond my brightest expectations. Earlier in life I had not been able to arrange the blocks of uninterrupted time necessary for such exploration, nor was I drawn to it. The child-rearing years and those of increasing commitment to my professional work carried me forward on a current of unceasing activity. Now, though still with effort, to be sure, I am able to pull back and allow experience and the life my father has given me in his written words to mingle. Sometimes moments separated in chronological time collapse one into another, and the grief a little one cannot express, finally finds expression. Grief waits, but will have its day.

Things, in the form of clothing, gave me moments with my father, and things, in the form of letters, were the instruments for making the past resonate in the present. Letters have catapulted me into unexpected growth and discovery. In the reading of them, the chronological bounds of time have been broken. My life's beginning has been extended even as I approach, in the dimension of space, my ending, then to continue the voyage in time.

ACKNOWLEDGMENTS

The author wishes to thank Wendy Lustbader and Thomas Cole for their comments and suggestions in the preparation of this chapter and their companionship on the journey of discovery recounted here.

REFERENCE

Heschel, A. J. (1951). *The Sabbath: Its meaning for modern man.* New York: Farrar, Straus and Giroux.

"It's 1924, and Somewhere in Texas, Two Nuns Are Driving a Backwards Volkswagen": Storytelling With People With Dementia

Anne Davis Basting

Filofaxes, Dayrunners, Palm Pilots—activity bulletin boards, orientation exercises, mini-mental exams. Monitoring and mastering time is how we organize and measure reality. This essay shares the story of a creative storytelling project with young adults and people with Alzheimer's disease in Milwaukee and New York City. Time was suspended in those storytelling sessions. It hovered above us like the ghosts made of torn sheets that the day center staff hung from the ceiling by strings on Halloween. In this essay, I explore how and why the storytelling workshops felt enchanted, and how the suspension of time in the ritual of storytelling enabled participants to breech cognitive and generational gaps.

In 1998 I received a 2-year grant from the Brookdale Foundation to support Time Slips. I broke the project into two parts. In the first year, I trained and coordinated a team of artists and undergraduate volunteers to run creative storytelling workshops for an hour each week for 18 weeks in Milwaukee and 9 weeks in New York. In the second year, we shared what we learned with family and staff caregivers, and with the communities in which the stories emerged. We designed a Web site, made training manuals, created a museum exhibit of photographs and handmade books, and produced a play based on the stories told in both cities.[1]

THE OUTSIDE

Me

Even when I sit still, perfectly still, I feel like I'm moving. Maybe it's caffeine. Maybe it's the fact that I live in Brooklyn and I work in Milwaukee. I know, I know, there are people in sales who live in their cars or corporate types who fly so often they know what's hiding behind all those secret doors in airports. So my story is mild. But it's enough for me. It's enough to make me fantasize about reading Rilke by flashlight as I fall sleep under the stars in a desert without snakes. But I don't do it. Instead I make charts on sketch pads of newsprint with brightly colored markers. September, October, November, December . . . in orange, blue, red, and green, each with a corresponding list of presentations, grant deadlines, writing projects, and a few birthdays.

Students

It's 10:00 a.m. in the circular driveway in front of the student union. After waiting 10 long minutes (my mind flipping back and forth—should I wait? should I go on without them?) Kim calls "Shot gun!" and Elyse folds herself into the back of my rusty Corolla. Kim sighs to release the rush of her morning. She's been in classes for nearly 3 hours already. Elyse's hands clasp a huge cup of something hot.

---

[1]The "Inside/Outside" vignettes are an amalgam of experiences and images at each of the four participating day centers.

She poises her chin on the rim as if using the rising steam to slowly pry open her eyelids. Up until 3. Class at 8. By 10, she is numb with fatigue. Elyse's beeper vibrates on her hip. She gives a little yelp, but doesn't pick up her head which has fallen to rest on the back ledge of the car. The sun glints off her nose-ring. Kim had rehearsals until 11, then homework to do. She's spacey, but awake. "Ok, ok— what are we doing again?" she asks breathlessly. "I need food," mumbles Elyse. I pull into Burger King. We'll be late to the day center for sure now. But after 6 weeks of storytelling sessions, I've learned that it's best to keep the students fully fueled.

INSIDE

Staff

Chancy is calling bingo numbers in the common room. I can't tell if anyone is actually responding. Bonnie is looking for Ed, with a paper cup full of applesauce laced with medication in one hand and a plastic spoon in another. Janie tucks the phone between ear and shoulder and waves from behind the glass wall of her office. I say hello to Mary who flashes a perky smile as she rounds the corner to help someone in the bathroom. "Another busy day!" she warbles. Our photographer and videographer are already set up in the back of the room waiting for us. After turning off the alarm on the front door, the students, my assistant Niki, and I stand in the front hallway for a minute, letting the wheels of the car stop moving inside us, and adjusting to the greased millwork rhythms of the day center. Bingo. Snack. Pills. Exercise. Lunch. These are highly structured places. The structure seems to work like scaffolding for the staff, holding them up when the sorrow of their jobs threatens to sink them.

Residence

The main entrance to the day center opens up into a lobby for staff and visitors. The common rooms are deeper inside the building, buffered from the busy daily routine of comings and goings by a cloakroom. When you pass through the cloakroom the building opens up into a large, bright room filled with residents. Several older men and women sit at long tables and fight with paintbrushes to put color on white paper. Others sit in the back of the room, in a quiet, carpeted area, lifting their legs and swinging their arms to the gentle rhythm of exercise music. It's a separate, incubated world. Of paint, movement, the smell of lunch cooking, and occasionally the sound of someone who has forgotten where they are. A low moan, or a lilting wail. But only occasionally. Otherwise there is a sense that the residents are comfortable in this world apart where time is restructured for them in holiday celebrations and daily routines.

Residents

Ed stares directly at me with no readable expression. Then he gets up, puts on his hat, and walks into an empty office in the back of the center. His movements are decisive. Once in the darkened office, he turns in a slow, continuous circle, his expression empty. Eleanor isn't technically part of our group, but she's almost always sitting nearby. When we enter, she walks up to us immediately as if we bring packages that are long overdue. She has almost no words left, and the ones that remain float out of her mouth in a broken, diaphanous line.

The most eloquent description of the experience of dementia that I've heard is by Cary Henderson (1998) whose journal entries are collected in *Partial View*. He said that when he "wandered," it wasn't just a symptom of the disease. He wasn't aimless. He was looking for something. Anything. Anything to make sense of his disorienting world. The pace of walking calmed him. I imagine it is the same for Ed, for Eleanor, for the woman at the day center who rocks, sometimes violently, in a soft chair designed for just that purpose.

HOW TO BRING THEM TOGETHER

The theory at the root of the storytelling project is that one's personal control of memory is just one of several components of identity.

When older persons develop severe problems with memory, commonly as a result of a stroke or Alzheimer's disease, they are often described as having lost their "self." The very core of who they were seems to have evaporated. But common sense and critical theory demonstrate to us that "the self" is relational. It is created through relationships with people and institutions. When one's personal control of memory falters, one's *social identity* remains and can be strengthened to improve one's quality of life, and to retain, in Tom Kitwood's terms, one's personhood (1997). For Kitwood, personhood is "a standing or status that is bestowed upon one human being by others, in the context of relationship and social being. It implies recognition, respect and trust" (p. 8).

Time Slips' aim was to train staff and undergraduate students to facilitate storytelling workshops that recognize the personhood of people with Alzheimer's and other dementias by creating new social roles of "storytellers." Finding meaning in their words, no matter what those words might be, can help both facilitators and storytellers to trust in the value of those words and of people with dementia. As the storytellers regain trust in their ability to communicate, staff and student facilitators learn that persons are more than their ability to link past, present, and future.

But these were two wildly different worlds. The outside. Where people, styles, objects, and information move at high speeds. Where mistakes in timing can be catastrophic. Where nose rings, platform shoes, and blue lipstick are statements. The inside. Where people and objects move at a snail's pace. Where information travels inefficient paths and often never arrives. Where today's statements are read in yesterday's context—and yesterday might be 70 years ago. The groups of students and storytellers were equally racially diverse. But differences of age and cognitive abilities separated the groups considerably.

TIME, THE GREAT DIVIDER

In Western culture, in spite of Einstein, daily life is lived according to the idea that time is linear and progressive. Our ability to place ourselves in linear time is considered a mark of personhood and distinguishes us from primates who live only in the present. If I am unable to demonstrate my mastery of linear time, I am in jeopardy of losing personhood, particularly in American culture, which over-emphasizes physical and psychological autonomy. Standard mini-mental exams, for example, commonly used to measure one's progress into Alzheimer's disease, ask patients to name the date and the year. Many mini-mental exams ask test takers to draw numbers on the face of an empty clock. And too often a person diagnosed with dementia in Western medicine falls from personhood status to being treated as an object in need of tending.

In the fields of history and anthropology, the concept of linear, progressive time has been used to categorize and separate entire communities, countries, even races. Those groups of people who fall "behind" the expected pace of modernization and progress or who believe time to be circular are seen as stagnant, backward, even as failures of evolution. Anthropologist Johannes Fabian (1983) explores this theme in *Time and the Other*. He suggests that the only way to avoid the bias between notions of "self" (one who masters linear, progressive time) and "other" (one who does not) is to find a way for the two to exist in the same sense of time, a shared present moment.

Over the last several decades, anthropologists and sociologists have found that common, shared present by focusing on the relationship between the interviewer and interviewee in ethnography. Finding common ground in the storytelling sessions presented its own unique challenges. I felt removed from the pace of the students' lives and I'm only 10 years from it. Day center staff not only punch timecards, most were also seriously overworked. And how might it be possible to find common time when people with dementia cannot draw numbers on a clock face?

Rather inadvertently, the creative storytelling workshops found that common time. We began with the aim of drawing people with dementia into creative expression. We quickly realized that to do so, staff and student facilitators would have to suspend their own sense of linear logic. We would have to let go of the idea that a "story" has a beginning, middle, and end, cohesive characters, and logical plot development. In our weekly storytelling circle, a "story" could be anything. All answers would be validated, written down, and repeated back in the retelling of the story, regardless of whether they made sense to the facilitators. We would have to trust in the process and let go of hopes for coherency—hopes tethered to our own desires to make sense of this disease, to shape the stories into answers of some sort that would relieve *us* from the fears and insecurities that dementia stirs up in our own lives.

THE WEEKLY JOURNEY

We held the storytelling sessions for 1 hour, once a week at two adult day centers in Milwaukee and two in New York. Center administrators helped select participants with Alzheimer's and related dementias who were in the middle stages of the disease. The four centers were all quite distinct, and each in turn had a widely diverse group of clients. To unify the storytelling process, we created a ritual that we repeated each week at each center. It consisted of five basic phases: the greeting, the story from last week, this week's story, the final retelling, and the farewell.

We began by inviting participants to sit in a circle of chairs away from other activities that might be happening at the same time. To help give the sessions a "special event" status, we freed ourselves from the long tables around which most activities take place in day centers and long-term care residences. We welcomed the storytellers to the circle and greeted them by name. Students wore name tags and introduced themselves each week. After the greeting phase, one student took out an over-sized sketchpad on which the stories were written, and read back one of the stories from the week before. Other students passed around the image that had prompted that story, being sure that all the storytellers could see it (Figure 7.1). In the retelling, students were careful to acknowledge who had provided which answers. If songs were part of the story, the group sang them once again. The retelling reminded storytellers that the stories were not factual, and that there were no right or wrong answers. This can be a surprising message for those fresh from daily orientation exercises in which they are commonly asked the day, date, season, or the name of the President.

Before telling this week's story, students asked storytellers to help them pick out an image for the week. The images we pulled from greeting cards or magazine ads shared several qualities. They were large enough to see and suggested a fantastical story. If images

FIGURE 7.1 Project Director Anne Basting facilitates a storytelling session.

appeared too realistic, or featured recognizable people, participants assumed there was a "real" story that they had forgotten, or never knew, and were reluctant to make up stories about them. But staged, somewhat surreal images invited creative expression. Our favorite images were taken from greeting cards—three women playing accordions, a woman riding an ostrich, and a man sitting underwater in deep contemplation menaced by fish.

The storytelling began with students distributing the image around the circle. One student served as "the writer," and sat in the center of the circle with the over-sized sketchpad (so participants could see what she was doing) and a box of brightly colored markers. Other students sat around the circle and asked questions of the storytellers such as "What should we call her?" "Where should we say they are?" Questions focused on the sensory ("What does the farm smell like?") and included the world outside the picture as well ("Does the woman riding the ostrich have a family?"). The storytelling became improvisational at this point. Storytellers' answers carried the questions in new directions, and in turn the questions carried the storytellers deeper into the world of the story.

The workshops quickly developed their own momentum. Students were mindful to ask only one question at a time, but even then, several people might answer at once. All answers were folded into the story. If more than one name was provided, the main character would have a hyphenated name. Often the storytellers themselves interpreted each other's answers ("He meant this . . . ") or countered a certain direction of the story they didn't like ("She isn't jumping off the building, she's jumping to the next building to see her friend."). If storytellers got lost in the story, the students would call for a "retell," and the "writer" would read back all that had been answered until that point (Figure 7.2).

Retelling the story, interpreting a sometimes random list of answers into a "story," demanded a certain theatrical flair. It was also a time when students and staff often demonstrated their own reluctance to let go of linear narrative. But as one student said in an interview after the 18 weeks had closed, giving up the desire for linear narrative was what eventually made the sessions successful:

> I think one thing that I learned was that we weren't looking for some type of product to come out of it. I think that at the beginning I was looking for the product. I was looking for the good story to come out at the end. And it was so hard! We just had to pull and push, and it was like nothing was happening. And then it kind of hit me that we were not really there to get this good story. We were there to be with these people and, you know, maybe appreciate them for being individuals. You know it's to *our* advantage that we are there sharing with them their ideas and wisdom and creativity.

One story could go on for nearly an hour. Most commonly, we told two stories each week. At the end of the session, the writer would do one last retelling of the story, reminding storytellers who had supplied which answers, and leading the group in songs if they had added any to the story. Finally, the students said good-bye to each member of the group, individually thanked them for sharing in the storytelling process, and let them know they would return the next week.

FIGURE 7.2   Project Associate Nichole Griffith shows the group an image. Fantastical images spark the best stories.

STORY-TIME

The five-phase ritual felt awkward at times. Students commented on this in their interviews and journals, and I felt it too. Sometimes even the storytellers joked about it ("I *know* you're here for storytelling . . . " said one participant). But joking aside, the ritual process was very effective as a transition for all three groups involved, the storytellers, the staff who were observing, and the student facilitators. For the storytellers, the ritual provided actions that triggered emotional memories. From week to week the storytellers would not remember our names. But the ritual greeting, the circle, and the story images became familiar to them, and with it they quickly associated trust, play, and the freedom to speak. Some even began to associate "performance" with the sessions, as they would clearly play to the entire group as they answered questions. I refer to "performance" here with Richard Schechner's (1995) definition in mind, in which performance is "behavior heightened, if ever so slightly, and publicly displayed; twice behaved behavior" (p. 1). The heightened and publicly displayed behavior was clear in the sessions when storytellers projected their voices or came up with humorous responses to entertain the group. But storytellers also repeated their behavior several times in the sessions, repeating their answers or even singing songs with each of the multiple retellings of the story.

For the staff, the ritual created a separate space in which they could, at least partially, let go of their authoritative roles. In this circle, they did not have to orient or correct the storytellers. They simply asked questions and repeated answers. With no right or wrong answers, staff began to release into the stories, to laugh and sing along with the group. Said one staff person in New York,

> I can't even describe it. By doing the storytelling, it's like they are telling their own life story. They are putting it together and they are loving it. They are living what they are doing. And it makes us feel good! Because I really can get into the storytelling.

For me, the sessions became living, stream-of-consciousness poems. Our questions always began somewhat stiffly, with logical questions about names, weather, and geographic locales. But as the answers accumulated, the storytellers ushered us away from the logic of the outside and into a realm between imagination and memory—ours and theirs. Retelling the story became an incantation that temporarily suspended the usual rules of time and authority that guide the institution and our lives outside. Certainly lines of power and authority still encircled the storytelling. If anyone became aggressive or "inappropriate," they would have been quickly taken out of the group. But the lines were also certainly blurred by no longer looking for symptoms of the disease in the spoken word. Language was free to carry emotional, rather than literal, logical meaning. Staff, volunteers, and storytellers were under the spell of the present moment and our ability to communicate in it, occasionally in complete nonsense. For all of us, story-time was a place where fragments of memory could launch us into new places that we built together rather than lock us into labels of loss or badges of control.

WHAT HAPPENED, REALLY?

Story-time and the stories that emerged from it opened a rare window into the experience of dementia. Many biographies have been published by spouses and children of people living with Alzheimer's and other dementias, but it is rare that we are able to hear the voices of the people directly experiencing the disease. The exceptions are three autobiographies published by people with Alzheimer's disease (Davis, 1989; Henderson, 1998; McGowin, 1993). The stories are unique in that they demand a group effort. They retain the traces of the students' questions, of multiple answers, and even of disagreements between the storytellers. But they also contain projected hopes, fears, dreams, anxieties, regrets, and desires of the storytellers themselves. Here, for example, is a story from a New York group, based on the image of the woman riding an ostrich:

> This is the story of a woman named Holding On (because she's really holding on), who is famous for having no inhibitions.
> She's from England, but makes her living as a can-can dancer in Paris. Her reputation is widely known.
> She dances with her pet ostrich "The Seeable One," but there is a rumor that the ostrich is no pet—and that she is really part animal with lovely legs.

She's a joker, with a good sense of value. She's not ridiculous, and looks quite at home. She is very at ease with herself, and looks happy enough to be all by herself.
Right now, she's on vacation in Africa, relaxing. The weather is very pleasant if a little humid.
She is riding her ostrich and singing to herself "Imagination is funny. It makes a rainy day sunny. It makes a lalalalalalalala."
She is happy to be alone and has a lot of charm.
After vacationing in Africa, she'll go back home to England.
She might perform again—she does whatever comes naturally.
She doesn't have any children, and she thinks she might have missed something.
But she has a very complex sense of happiness.

Gradually, over the course of the 18 weeks, the majority of storytellers expanded their participation. Without expectations of right or wrong answers, storytellers could hone what fragments of speech and gesture they retained. By validating and incorporating all responses into the stories, the workshops created an atmosphere in which storytellers could learn to trust in communication again. The words didn't matter. It was the exchange that was important. In a New York workshop, one woman was unable to do more than share one repeated sound. "Babababababa" she said, the urgency of her sounds and the intensity of her eye contact expressed her strong desire to add something to the story. When we read the story back, saying "Babababababa, said Dorothy," her eyes would light up.

Some storytellers were naturals. They slipped into the role as if they'd always been there. And indeed, some had always been there, but had lost the forum in which to perform their role. One participant came to the group 9 weeks after storytelling began, having heard about the sessions from a local television news program. When he joined the group, his wife explained that he had always been a wonderful storyteller and that she knew he would blossom given the chance to do it again. She was right. He responded to nearly all the questions and cajoled quieter storytellers to respond as well.

In contrast, other storytellers were slow to share responses, unsure whether to trust their imaginations. One, who had been a career military man, sat rigidly in his chair for the first several weeks, giving only an occasional one-word answer. He was part of a group of storytellers who rarely added songs to their stories, in spite of the students' coaxing. In one of the last sessions, students made a last ditch effort and asked if the storytellers heard any music in the background of the story based on an image of a 2-year-old in a tutu. The career military man responded by singing a delicate rendition of "Beautiful Dreamer," which he repeated with each retelling of the story. The director of the day center came out from her office, stood on the edge of our circle and listened, incredulous.

At times, one or two storytellers would opt for silence. In one session, a Milwaukee woman defiantly crossed her arms and flatly refused to participate, leaving students perplexed. Had they done something wrong? Had they insulted her in some way? They never knew. It seemed to depend on the image and the storyteller's frame of mind that day. While some chose silence, others deliberately shared memories rather than creative responses. A few weeks earlier, the same woman who had crossed her arms and chosen silence told me that a picture reminded her of her sisters when they were all little. She and her sisters used to do each other's hair and she had made all their clothes. I asked if it was all right if we included her response in the story and she agreed. The story, based on three women playing the accordion, became:

> Persephone, Mary, and Rosemary are accordion playing sisters in a group called the Three Musketeers. It is also known widely as the Triple Group.
> Their eyes are talking, saying "Listen to Me!"
> Right now they are in a studio playing accordions (partly because they don't know how to play anything else . . .).
> They are loud and happy. You can tell because their mouths are wide open in big smiles.
> They usually play for free, but they are especially happy today because they're about to become rich and famous. Donald Trump has invited them to play for a party for 500 in New York City, a party in celebration of—himself!
> They'll play the Too Fat Polka, and the Beer Barrel Polka, and of course, requests. They'll eat anything that tastes good, but not too much or they won't be able to play.
> There will be cheese, ham, buns, wine, fruit cocktail, chitlins, and of course, beer.
> Mary is the oldest, and Persephone is the youngest.
> Their mother died when they were young. The three sisters grew up fixing each other's hair, teaching themselves the accordion, and Mary made all their fancy clothes.
> They are smiling and happy.

Answers emerged from memory, imagination, and illness (odd or misplaced words). Distinctions between the three became nearly impossible. One woman would give strange names to characters. At first we thought the names were linked to her Alzheimer's. But when we interviewed her about whether she enjoyed the storytelling process, she said, "Oh yes. I like to make up funny names. It stretches my mind."

Almost all the staff we interviewed and several family members commented on the improvements they saw through the storytelling. The most dramatic success story came from the daughter of a woman who had suffered a heart attack and then dementia as a result of lack of oxygen to the brain. The daughter told us about an encounter that surprised her own son:

> Did I tell you about the day my son picked her up out at the day care center? He picked her up and he brought her home here to Illinois. And he just couldn't stop talking about how terrific she was. Apparently when he picked her up, either you were in the middle of or had just finished one of the sessions out there. And she was so excited and so fun and so up. And in the car, rather than have my son initiate all the conversation, which is the usual, she did. And she could remember and talk about the story that was being made up. And he said it was amazing. He had never seen her that good from the 5 years earlier when she initially had the brain damage.

The majority of feedback from staff, however, observed smaller changes. An activities director in Milwaukee said:

> We have a few people who are in the project who are very, very quiet, and I'm very happy to see them coming forward. The first couple sessions that they had they were very quiet, and you really had to pull everything out of them and be very direct. And now I've noticed that as each class has been happening, they are more and more open. And they are so happy when you leave. And honestly, I mean we can really get a lot out of them for the rest of the afternoon.

At two of the day centers, staff were integrally involved in the storytelling from the beginning. At the other two centers, staff used the sessions as a break or to attend to other residents. One was seriously understaffed, and the strain on the workers was clear. They would occasionally stop for a moment to watch the storytelling, but never participated. At the other center, in one of the first sessions, aides took naps in the back of the room while we ran the storytelling. As the weeks progressed, staff from all areas of the center began to stand in the back and watch the sessions. By the end of the 9 weeks, our storytelling circle had grown to include the four or five staff members, from kitchen aides to recreational therapists. They are now continuing the sessions themselves.

GROWTH AND LOSS

The storytelling process is not a success story. The most powerful lesson of the project was that a "success" story for people with Alzheimer's and other dementias is always, simultaneously a story of loss. As facilitators, letting go of desires for coherent narratives also meant shedding expectations of clear endings—that dementia is a living funeral, or that storytelling offered some sort of cure.

Some days were joyful, and some days were hard for *all* the participants. At a Milwaukee care center, one storyteller died during the 18 weeks of storytelling and another went into long-term care. At that same center, a woman who was a very active participant in the early weeks grew increasingly disoriented as the program progressed. In a New York center, one very poetic participant stood up one day and demanded a stop to the storytelling. "Every person has a story," she said emphatically, "There's not a human being that doesn't have a story. But making it mish mosh is bad. It's like a bomb." With a strong increase in her medication, she could no longer tolerate more than one person talking at a time.

Some days I left the day centers dragging the sketchpad behind me, embarrassed of my exaggerated hopes for the benefits the storytelling might have. The next week I'd return to find that the session was an exhilarating, visionary exchange of words and images among caregivers, students, and storytellers.

I do not romanticize dementia. Interviews with family caregivers don't allow it. Dementia can involve dramatic emotional and physical changes and frightening disorientation. But the storytelling sessions suggest that Americans, in the tradition of Western European thought and American rugged individualism, romanticize autonomy. The stories, which emerged from a collaboration between young adults and people with Alzheimer's and other dementias, suggest a more relational model of self. In Arthur Frank's terms (1995), all participants were "communicative bodies," creating meaning together where neither group could do it alone. The story of the storytelling sessions is simultaneously one of dependence *and* independence, of loss *and* growth. They demanded we suspend, as much as possible, our expectations for progressive plots whether they be in the story we were creating together, or in the narrative of the disease. And in the thickness of the present moment, we created a new story together.

Students' journals and interviews reveal that they gained a sense of the fickleness of time, its density, and its true speed. Here I do not mean speed in terms of instant communication on the Web, but speed in terms of how quickly our lives seem to jump from 16 to 86 in a matter of minutes, speed that leads one to a deep appreciation for the present. Staff interviews suggest that they were energized by the sessions, and that seeing *people* where they had seen *patients* gave them hope for their own futures and pride in their work. One staff caregiver in New York said: "It's a really good project, and I commend you. I hope you continue, you know. And what they say, I mean, some of these stories . . . I gave them to the [the director of the day center] and she said, 'Gee, these guys are smart! And funny!' And the family members, Ida's daughter, she read it. And she said 'That story is funny!' She loved it. And I said, 'See? That's what we're doing here on Thursdays!' "

For me, the sessions reawakened a dormant sense of dark-edged whimsy and rekindled my awareness of the tightly turning circle of life and death. They introduced me to living in the moment and made my eyes play games with my mind. I began to see a world unbound by linear time. Volkswagens were driving along the streets of the 1920s. My own 35-year-old hands were a series of steep hills and valleys, cut by blue rivers of veins, punctuated with thickened joints. The young girl on the subway across from me looked 90. The 90-year old at the center looked 14, then 34, then 64. I am left looking at a world in which people, places, and objects are dense knots of time (Figure 7.3).

WHAT ARE THOSE DAMES DOING IN THAT CAR?

Woooooweeee!
It's 1924 and somewhere in Texas, two nuns are driving a backwards Volkswagen. Now you might wonder where two nuns got such a nice car . . .
but it was a gift from Goodwill.
The two Catholic nuns, Sister Maria and Sister Marybeth, are looking for something.
They're in love, but they can't remember with whom.
They're off looking for something—a church.
They're looking for a medium-sized church, because they're in a small car.
They're looking for the church to see what it's like.
When they get to the church, everyone will say "Sit Down and Listen." They'll sing Christian songs, do an entrance prayer, and say "Nice Hair!"
It's late fall, and birds are flying to warmer climates.
Sister Marybeth is a bit of a showoff.
She stands up in the car, clasps her hands in prayer (because that's what nuns do).
When she gets up there, she sees that a car is coming right at them. She prays to have it avoid them.
But Sister Maria is a very very careful driver, and they are going too slow for the other car to hit them.
Sister Maria and Sister Marybeth are strong, funny nuns, if a bit shy. But they are only funny after mass.
When they finally get to the church, they stay for more than an hour. Then they eat and go home to the convent.
You'd be surprised how much fun they have . . .

ACKNOWLEDGMENTS

The storytelling phase of the Time Slips project received the generous support of the Brookdale Foundation, the Helen Bader Foundation, Inc., and was based at the Center for Twentieth Century Studies, the College of Letters and Science, and the Graduate School of the University of Wisconsin-Milwaukee. I thank my collaborative team for creating and sharing this experience with me: the day center staff, the storytellers and their families, the student facilitators, the

FIGURE 7.3   **A storyteller responds to an image. Every response is written down and woven into the story.**

artists, and the advisory board. Kathleen Woodward, Beth Meyer Arnold, Nichole Griffith, Karen Stobbe, and Dick Blau gave more to this project than they know, and they have my warmest thanks.

REFERENCES

Davis, R. (1989). *My journey into Alzheimer's Disease.* Wheaton, IL: Tyndale House Publishers.

Fabian, J. (1983). *Time and the other.* New York: Columbia University Press.

Frank, A. (1995). *The wounded storyteller.* Chicago: University of Chicago Press.

Henderson, C. S. (1998). *Partial view: An Alzheimer's journal.* Dallas, TX: Southern Methodist University Press.

Kitwood, T. (1997). *Dementia reconsidered.* Buckingham, UK: Open University Press.

McGowin, D. F. (1993). *Living in the labyrinth.* New York: Delacorte.

Schechner, R. (1995). *The future of ritual.* New York: Routledge.

CHAPTER 8

A Personal Journey of Aging: The Spiritual Dimension

Melvin A. Kimble

At a certain point, one's perceptions of aging become intertwined with perceptions of oneself. In the experience of aging, my credentials get better every day! As a pastoral theologian, I live in a creative tension between the established dogma and practice of my personal faith on the one hand, and the more generic, encompassing spiritual dimension that is presented here without any primary or specific religious connotation on the other hand. The spiritual dimension is the energy within that strives for meaning and purpose. It is the unifying and integrating dimension of being that includes the experience of transcendence and the *mysterium tremendum fascinans,* the mystery that is at once overwhelming and fascinating, that renders my existence significant and meaningful in the here and now. It is also a mystery in that it is unmeasurable, unprovable, and lacks universal definition.

A review of my personal history reveals a journey of aging punctuated by a number of milestones that I regard as spiritually significant. I am these life experiences old! They made me what I am. They include my faith commitment and choice of vocation and life partner, as well as other experiences and commitments that have shaped and altered my life at all levels.

Samuel Johnson once remarked, "a hanging has a way of focusing the mind." So does a diagnosis of cancer, especially if it is of the more lethal variety like malignant melanoma. Some 10 years ago I had such a diagnosis, followed by major surgery and a grim prognosis. As healing miraculously took place in my body and the cancer went into remission, I felt like Abraham Maslow, who described the time after his first heart attack as his "postmortem life." So with me; every day was now a bonus, and every person in my life more previous and valued. I began to understand what Paul Tillich meant by the phrase, "the eternal now." Life, faith, and grace seemed to break into my life with greater intensity and sharper focus than ever before. With a greater awareness of my finitude and mortality, time and its passing took on deeper meaning. I was learning and experiencing the difference between *chronos,* calendar time, and *kairos,* eschatological time that involves my ultimate destiny. Both have meaning and value and are interwoven into my life in a unifying whole.

During this period, my personal faith orientation and commitments were of particular importance. The salvific symbols and rites of my faith tradition and praxis provided powerful sources of meaning in formulating the existential order of my life at this anxious time. Keeping the door open to the transcendent was crucial for me. This meant putting myself in positions and places where such transcendent experiences could break through. Organ concerts that included music of Bach and Langlais were particularly poignant and soul stirring. Even sunrises and sunsets as well as full moons were events not to be missed, especially sunsets shared with loved ones.

C. G. Jung's observation (cited in Martin, 1966), "That which youth found and had to find outside of itself, in the second half of life must be found within," has become increasingly true for me in my personal journey of aging. Disciplined meditation and prayer have taken on freshness and are experienced as energizing and renewing. Priorities in lifestyle and use of time have been altered and rearranged. All of this is happening in the midst of my own continuous aging process. But with a difference. I am learning what Viktor Frankl has stressed concerning the need to keep the door open between immanence and transcendence.

My spirituality, however, does not exist in some holy haze of isolation, but in relationship and connectiveness, especially with my family and faith community. Special and unique family rituals, for example, have been introduced and have evolved into symbolic and supportive ways of coping with transitions and crises in a universe that is saturated with a blessed ambiguity. The humor and craziness that at times characterize family festive occasions also keep us human and affectionately bonded at many levels, included the spiritual.

The meaning of time and its passing has changed for me. Time past is now more valued. Viktor Frankl maintains "nothing and nobody can deprive us of what we have safely delivered and deposited in the past." For me, the passing of time is now not erosion but accumulation. The baggage of memories and experiences I now carry on my journey is more complete and full but, surprisingly, not burdensome. I find myself engaged in more reflection and teasing out of meanings of my life from the "storehouse of the past." A configuration, a mosaic of meanings, begins to take shape and leads me forward into the present and to the very precipice of the future. I have discovered that my basic faith in an Ultimate Being who has brought me to the present can be trusted as I face the uncertain and shadowy future.

My journey of aging has more recently taken on a quality that I find somewhat puzzling but intriguing. It is a subtle but discernible movement toward androgyny, and it has some complementary parallels in my wife, JoAnne. It has its roots, as I can now more readily detect, in earlier stage of my life, but it was often blocked or stifled by more repressive roles and prescribed patterns. This melding of masculine and feminine sensitivities has broadened my perception of and response to life as androgynous qualities have emerged and express themselves more spontaneously. It seems that this phenomenon is related to a more holistic expression and formation of my more authentic humanness that includes the spiritual dimension, and I will be interested to continue to track it in the unfolding years of my adult life.

A physician friend of mine contends that there are at least two times in life when persons ought to be required to go off on a retreat and reflect on the meaning of their lives. One, he suggests, is when we choose our vocation; the other is in older adulthood as we get closer to retirement and experience more poignantly the narrowing boundaries of our lives. I have not yet reached the stage of retirement, but I have begun to experience more and more the narrowing boundaries. In my spiritual journey of aging, I have also come to know myself as an indissoluble amalgam of shadow and light, angelic and demonic, in the paradoxical unity of contraries that constitute my essential humanness. As I age, I have become more fully aware of a centripetal spiritual energy that centers and grounds my life and prevails over the centrifugal divisive forces that are *ever* present, working to spin out and scatter the fragments of my life. It is this power or dimension, rooted in a trust in an Ultimate Being, that enables me to live life at every stage of the life cycle *sub specie aeternitatis,* under the aspect of eternity.

NOTE

Reprinted with permission from *Generations, 17*(2), pp. 27–28, 1993. Copyright The American Society on Aging, San Francisco, CA.

REFERENCE

Martin, B. (1966). *If God does not die.* Richmond, VA: John Knox Press.

PART III

Effects of Religious Beliefs and Spiritual Practices on Meanings of Time and Aging

The Influence of Spiritual Beliefs and Practices on the Relation Between Time and Aging

Robert C. Atchley

This chapter is about the influence of spiritual beliefs and practices on the experience of time as people age. To deal effectively with this complex topic, we must look briefly at several meanings of time and why the experience of chronological time might accelerate with age. Then we can examine spiritual beliefs about time and look at practices that might affect perceptions of time. Finally, we can consider how spiritual beliefs and practices might mediate the relationship between age and the experience of time.

Life is too short. This common saying is seldom uttered by young people; it is used by middle-aged and older people to indicate that time is precious and we cannot afford to waste it, especially on interpersonal conflicts or frustrating activities. But the experience of time depends on the context, which includes age, spiritual beliefs, and spiritual practices.

Experiential time can be fast or slow; it is relative. As Albert Einstein said, "When you sit with a nice girl for two hours, you think it's only a minute. But when you sit on a hot stove for a minute, you think it's two hours. That's relativity" (Safransky, 1990). The subjective nature of experienced time does not mean that it is not affected by social and cultural influences. Indeed, like most personal mental constructs, the meaning of time is conditioned by social norms and expectations.

Historical time stretches back at least 5,000 years in the written record, and future time looks forward as far as the mind can project, but this sense of the word *year* is very different from the meaning we attach to a calendar year because we can experience the passing of a calendar year whereas we cannot experience a millennium. Unless we transcend our own potential lifetime in our view of the future, we cannot think about the needs of future generations. Being able to think in panoramic time is thus an important human skill.

We are all tied to the various biological clocks within our bodies that influence the processes of senescence. We experience the effects of these biological clocks, such as gradual stiffening of joints in later adulthood, but these clocks operate outside our consciousness and therefore outside our experience.

By contrast, we are constantly made aware of chronological time because it is used to order our lives. Unlike preliterate societies, which tended to use very rough measures of time, based mostly on movement of the sun, phases of the moon, change of seasons, and annual cycles of animal and plant life, modern and postmodern societies are fixated on chronological time. Most of us carry devices strapped to our wrists that allow us to know the chronological time reasonably precisely. We use technology to keep our room temperature constant across the seasons and to light our environments at all hours of the day and night, which allows us to ignore the natural rhythms of daylight and darkness. Our lives are scheduled by a time to arise, a time to go to work, time schedules at work, times to eat, times for prayer, times for recreation, and time for sleep. Constructing an ideal lifestyle in today's world could be expected to include a daily routine tied to the clock. Clock time is used so extensively to organize our many activities that few people can get by without a time planning device such as a detailed calendar. Computer software sold today often includes programs for detailed chronological time scheduling.

In addition to hourly, daily, seasonal, and annual cycles of time, the cultural life course sets forth general chronological age ranges at which we are expected to go through transitions from one life stage to another. Thus, most people enter middle age sometime around age 40, later adulthood around age 60, and old age around 80. These cultural life stages are composite pictures of lifestyles and values that are expected of persons in a particular life stage. Most people go through the various life-stage transitions on schedule chronologically.

Despite the heavy emphasis on chronological time in our culture, most people are very aware that our perceptions of the speed of time's passing are not mechanistic but depend very much on what we are experiencing during a given span of chronological time.

The conventional wisdom has it that, with advancing age, time is experienced as accelerating, to the point that by age 90 the years seem to go by rapidly. Most aging individuals report that this generally fits their experience. Possible explanations for this phenomenon are several. First, as people are freed from child rearing and employment, they may be liberated from the tyranny of the clock. As a result, they may no longer be intensely sensitive to the passage of time; they may not pay as much attention to time. Second, it is possible that the activities that engage elders are more susceptible to what Csikszentmihalyi (1993) calls *flow*. Flow activities engage a person's attention to such a large extent that time perception is lost. Afterwards, the individual may feel that time has passed very rapidly, but while in the experience of flow, the person has no sense of the speed of time's passing. Elders often report that when they engage in activities while alone they experience the loss of time perception and self-consciousness that characterize conventional consciousness (Mannell, 1993). Third, as people grow older, accomplishing routine tasks may take longer, and what once was a comfortable daily routine may now seem a time-pressured one. These all seem plausible explanations for why time is perceived to pass more quickly as age increases.

However, there is also evidence that both belief and behavior can influence perceptions. What we *believe* to be true, we are more apt to *perceive* to be true and vice versa. For example, if we believe that sane people can experience visions, then we may be more likely to interpret an experience of an angel as a vision rather than as a hallucination. Likewise, if we continue to practice in an area of life, our perceptions can be influenced by what we learn from our practice. For example, musicians must learn a complex process of creating rhythm and timing in music. As they continue to practice, their experiences of both producing rhythm and listening to rhythm can change over time. Young musicians often seem to be trying to create the greatest possible number of notes for a given time period, whereas older musicians often pay more attention to the beauty available by alternating periods of sound and silence into simpler, more elegant rhythms (Simonton, 1989).

Studies of how aging might influence the experience of time have thus far ignored the spiritual aspects of being human. However, it is likely that both spiritual beliefs about time and spiritual practices over time influence the relation between aging and the experience of time.

Spiritual here refers to beliefs, practices, and experiences that loosely revolve around an inner domain of human experience. Spiritual experience includes sensory and psychological input but extends to include transcendent ways of knowing as well. Many elders are able to grow spiritually within their customary religious traditions; others reject the faith of their youth to develop new, less structured, and less hierarchical faith communities. Some eventually come back to their original faith tradition more gently as their contemplative understanding deepens. In the mystical texts of Hinduism, Buddhism, Judaism, Christianity, and Islam, meditation or contemplative prayer is a central method in growing closer to the Absolute, the Void, Yahweh, Christ, or Allah. Such contemplative understanding allows old texts and doctrines to be seen in new ways, and elders can participate in their religious communities while at the same time detaching themselves psychologically from what they see as contradictory and paradoxical religious dogma.

To develop understanding of how aging interacts with the experience of time and how this relationship may be mediated by spiritual beliefs and practices requires concepts about the many relationships among aging, spirituality, and time. This chapter illustrates how this might be done by:

- Selectively reviewing beliefs about the meaning of time in various spiritual traditions

- Discussing the relationship between various spiritual practices and the experience of time
- Looking at how spiritual beliefs and practices might mediate the relationship between aging and the experience of time.

BELIEFS ABOUT TIME

Important beliefs about time include beliefs about whether there is a continuation of personal consciousness after death, whether elders are obligated to take a panoramic view of time to lead the society into the future, whether life stages are related to inner spiritual growth, and whether inner spiritual growth changes the experience of time. Does spiritual growth include a timeless state of consciousness in which the experience of time does not exist? Does spiritual growth require focus on transcendent experience, present-moment awareness, or both? How does the focus of awareness affect experiences of time?

Belief in a personal afterlife is characteristic of many religious belief systems, and belief in a personal afterlife means that the life span of one's human body is but a tiny fraction of the time available. This belief downplays the importance of the current lifetime. Likewise, belief in an afterlife in another life form through reincarnation minimizes the importance of getting it right within one lifetime. By contrast, some religions contend that this is it, you only go around once, and time in the current lifetime is more important than for those who believe in eternal life in some form. If people believe in one lifetime, then approaching the end of that lifetime can produce much more powerful spiritual growth as well as despair at lack of growth. For Erikson and Erikson (1998), for example, perceiving that there is not enough time left to perfect the self is an important motive for letting go of perfectionism and being able to integrate the ideal self with the real self, with its range of good and bad qualities and history. Of course, even people who believe in an afterlife may face an existential crisis when physical death becomes real to them if they have not converted their belief into the certainty of faith.

Young and middle-aged adults are often expected to focus their attention on relatively short-range goals, such as getting a formal education, maintaining a connection with the economy, selecting a life partner and rearing children, and contributing their energies to the community. Leaders of business, government, and voluntary organizations develop 5-year plans, not hundred-year plans. But Rabbi Zalman Schacter-Shalomi, in the book *From Age-ing to Sage-ing* (Schacter-Shalomi & Miller, 1995), makes the point that elders are uniquely qualified to take the long view. Child launching and retirement, a long span of experienced historical time, with its many changes, and feelings of generativity about the welfare of grandchildren and great-grandchildren are interests that motivate elders to be concerned about what sort of world we will be leaving for our offspring over the next hundred years. To Schacter-Shalomi, this perspective leads to more concern over the welfare of the planet Earth, especially its environmental, intercultural, and political integrity. Elders traditionally played this role, but in the process of modernization this role was transferred to "experts," who often do not look at issues from a panoramic time perspective. *Spiritual Eldering* is the expression Schacter-Shalomi uses to indicate that recovering the role of elder in postmodern societies requires a level of spiritual development on the part of elders before they can have the transcendent attitudes and panoramic view of time required to play the role of spiritual elder.

A panoramic view of time is an important characteristic that differentiates those who are capable of spiritual eldering from those who are merely old. In the panoramic view, the span of time is vast, including geological eons. As elders confront questions of meaning and probe deeper into their consciousness, their time perspective can shift to include their relatedness to time in its cosmic dimensions (Schacter-Shalomi & Miller, 1995). As elders develop spiritually and experience union with the timeless divine ground of being, their perspective on time shifts away from chronological time pressures.

Many faith traditions relate spiritual development to stages of the life course. For example, the Hindu conception of life stages includes a householder stage and a renunciate stage. In the householder stage, people use their concern with family and vocation to motivate an inner spiritual journey involving meditation, not as an escape from reality but as a way of seeing ultimate truth in their everyday lives. In the renunciate stage, which traditionally begins with the birth of the first grandson, people do not drop out of life to become recluses. Instead, they become so focused on the Absolute within themselves that they gain a transcendent perspective that allows them to see themselves and their world in a very different way, a way in which time is fully understood as a human creation. From an experiential point of view, time is in you, you are not in time.

This basic Hindu philosophical position was used by Tornstam (1994) to develop his theory of gerotranscendence. He posited that advanced aging increases interest in contemplation, which in turn produces a shift in perspective that dramatically reduces the importance of chronological time. Thus, one might argue that the loosening of social constraints that occurs in later adulthood and old age allows contemplative understanding to blossom into transcendence, with a dramatic effect on the experience of time. Note that these are *concepts* of the relation between aging, life stage, spirituality, and the experience of time.

Cole (1992) provided an insightful portrait of how biblical ideas from the Jewish and Christian perspectives shaped early American Protestant conceptions of the relation between life stages and spiritual development. Old age was seen as the culmination of a spiritual journey of life. Elders, through their lifelong struggle to understand and carry out the will of God, were more developed spiritually compared with the young. That is, experience across time was assumed to be a necessary element of spiritual insight. Elders were expected to set a moral and social example for the young. Early American religion had high expectations of elders, including dignified behavior and appearance and continued social contribution. These ideas are very much a part of the life course expectations in American churches today.

But these ideas of spiritual growth over time compete with a view that the effects of aging—whether aging means growing decrepitude and incapacity or continued vitality—are largely under the individual's moral control. And the evangelical view of salvation as immediately wiping away sin means that the experience of elders is downplayed. The notion of respect for elders remains, but a sense that elders by virtue of their experience of contemplation and struggle can be spiritually advanced is often missing (Cole, 1992).

Concepts of time, and therefore aging, as being needed for spiritual growth can be a sometime thing, depending on the directions of cultural change. In the year 2000, religious idea structures are again becoming more open to the image of spiritual growth with aging. This trend is no doubt related to more cultural emphasis on the positive aspects of aging in the 1990s. It is also probably related to the greater attention in popular culture and gerontology research to the voices of experience, to the journals and oral histories produced by elders themselves, which often contain commentaries about how extended life experience relates to spiritual insight.

Most religious traditions also contain beliefs about the effects of transcendence and present-moment awareness on the experience of time. For example, although the major concepts of Jewish, Christian, and Islamic traditions are all rooted in a personified conception of God, there are within each of these traditions mystical, experiential concepts of God, not as person-like but as very mysterious and only very incompletely capable of being apprehended by the verbal mind. For instance, in *The Cloud of Unknowing* (Johnston, 1996), perhaps the first Christian meditation guide to have been originally written in the English language, the anonymous author likens God to a "cloud of unknowing" that can only be approached by assuming an open stance of bare being. The cloud of unknowing is within the experiencer, not something external, but to even sense the cloud of unknowing, the meditator must leave worldly concerns, including time, behind in a "cloud of forgetting." This conception of God is very similar to the Hindu conception of the Absolute, which was described by St. Bonaventure as "a sphere, whose center is everywhere and whose circumference is nowhere" (quoted in Wilber, 1996, p. 135). Eternal God or Absolute is not characterized by infinite time but by an absence of time. Thus, if people connect with the experience of God or the Absolute within themselves, they transcend time as well as the other aspects of a phenomenal world bound by concepts such as time and space. As Wilber (1996, p. 137) put it, "The Absolute can be present in its entirety at every point in time only if [the Absolute] is itself timeless." This same general perspective is contained in the Buddhist concept of nothingness, which is less an absence or void than no-thing-ness; not this, not that, but an entirety in which ideas such as subject/object, time, and space do not apply.

To experience "the ground of being," Huxley's (1941) term for the ultimate principle that forms the eternal context for spiritual experience, thus requires that we transcend conventional consciousness. A major obstacle to transcendence is being distracted by worldly concerns. Although it may be possible by strength of will to develop the skill needed to be "in the world but not of it" early in life, transcendence is thought to be more common in later life, for reasons mentioned above.

Paradoxically, aging is also thought to make possible a greater capacity to be in the present. Although stereotypes hold that elders dwell excessively in the past, research has shown that healthy elders living in the community experience a balance of thoughts and experiences from the past, present, and future. Indeed, the proportion of elders who have the capacity to patiently attend to the present with what the Buddhists call bare attention is much greater than the proportion of young and middle-aged adults who have a similar capacity. Present-moment awareness is also a form of timelessness, in the sense that the present moment, not the passage of time, is of the essence.

SPIRITUAL PRACTICES AND THE EXPERIENCE OF TIME

Various religious traditions contain rituals that are designed to break the hold of the everyday world on consciousness. For instance, the Jewish concept of the Sabbath is more than just a day of rest; it is a time for renewing one's relationship with God. The Muslim practice of daily prayer creates five opportunities each day—on arising, at midday, in midafternoon, at sunset, and when retiring for the evening—to focus attention on the divine. Catholic monastic traditions schedule breaks for prayer and contemplation seven times each day: at daybreak, around 9 a.m., at noon, at 3 p.m., about 6 p.m., in the early evening, and at midnight. Most meditation-based traditions encourage practitioners to have a specific time for meditation each day to make a habit of meditation. These rituals all use concepts of time to create pauses in the swirl of worldly activities, pauses during which attention can be focused on ultimate concerns.

The discipline of regular spiritual practice over time creates a rhythm of connection with the ground of being, and this rhythm can become a self-sustaining system in the sense that, in all their variety, the experiences that come from spiritual practice become an end in themselves. Over time, contemplative prayer and meditation may become less means to an end and become more ends in themselves, and in most cases this occurs over an extended period of time.

Meditation is a central spiritual practice in many spiritual traditions. Unfortunately, the word *meditation* often evokes a stereotype of people dressed in flowing robes and sitting in the lotus position. People confuse the outer appearance for the inner intention. In fact, there are many different meditation methods, and individuals may use different meditation methods, depending on their immediate needs. How various meditation methods influence the experience of time varies greatly. For example, the Transcendental Meditation technique uses meditation on a mantra—subvocal sounds that have been found to focus attention—to induce a transcendent state of consciousness that is completely beyond sensory and verbal experience. In this state, the meditator loses track of time completely. On the other hand, Buddhist mindfulness meditation involves paying close attention to sensations of breathing, which focuses attention on simply being rather than on what the body or the mind may be doing. In the beginning, mindfulness meditators often experience the passage of time as excruciatingly slow. But after years of daily meditation and intensive meditation retreats, practitioners tend to "give up on time." As conscious being becomes a larger and larger part of the mindfulness meditation experience, which takes time, time often matters less during meditation.

Prayer is also a central spiritual practice for most faith traditions. Prayer can be classified into ritual prayer, petitionary prayer, and meditative prayer. Ritual prayer repeated over and over for countless repetitions can have transcendental effects, carrying the practitioner out of conventional consciousness and into greater sensitivity to the divine. Ritual prayer can also induce a devotional attitude toward God or serve as a reminder of important religious or spiritual ideas. Petitionary prayer asks something of God. Meditative prayer has little form. The practitioner simply "waits upon the Lord." The point is to be present, open, attuned to messages from God, yet not expecting any specific experience. Peacock and Paloma (1991) found that younger adults were much more likely to engage in ritual and petitionary prayer compared with older adults, and older adults were much more likely to engage in meditative prayer compared with younger adults. In a 20-year longitudinal study of adults who were age 70 and over, I found that the incidence of meditative prayer increased substantially with age.

Meditation and prayer are spiritual practices that tend to work mostly with the mind and basic consciousness. However, movement disciplines such as T'ai Chi or dance, music, and other arts can also be important spiritual practices. As spiritual practices, expressive disciplines can invoke flow (Csikszentmihalyi, 1993), which is experienced as an intense and effortless concentration wherein there is no experience of time. Thus, as spiritual practices, these activities can require intense attention to the present moment; they can also transcend time.

SPIRITUAL BELIEFS AND PRACTICES, AGING, ADULT DEVELOPMENT, AND THE EXPERIENCE OF TIME

Virtually none of the studies of age changes in perception of the speed of time passage have been able to look at individual differences that might be attributable to spiritual beliefs and practices because these studies did not assess individual spiritual beliefs and practices. This section looks at some possibilities that might be useful for future inquiry.

How might spiritual beliefs and practices mediate the relation between aging and the experience of time? First, such mediation might occur as a result of the effects of spiritual beliefs and practices on the potential causes of altered time perception with age.

For example, some perceptions of a speed-up in time with age may be a result of paying less attention to time through overhabituation or the experience of flow. If overhabituation is a cause of the speed-up in time perception with age, then mindfulness practice could be expected to offset any tendency toward overhabituation and speeded-up time perception. The practice of mindfulness meditation involves intense awareness of the details of the present. Mindfulness is the opposite of overhabituation, and in mindfulness people perceive their environment more intensely than in conventional consciousness. In a state of mindfulness, people are intensely focused on the present moment and not preoccupied with time.

People who engage in ritual prayer for long periods each day or who spend much of their time in contemplation might be unlikely to perceive the pace of time as important. This would be especially likely in those whose practices emphasize *being* rather than *doing*. To the extent that spiritual practice induces an experience of flow, people who spend hours each day in ritual prayer may be in a very pleasant state during this time but still be left with the question, "where did the time go."

To the extent that spiritual practices promote an experience of losing oneself in the activity, spiritual practices take the practitioner to a world unbounded by time. Not all practices that produce the sense of flow are spiritual, but most spiritual practices have the potential for flow. Of course, to be able to ignore time, people must be free to some extent from social time constraints.

If perceiving time as passing quickly is a function of paying less attention to time, then later life offers many opportunities to free life's schedules from "the tyranny of the clock." Retired people often report that they experience a much more relaxed pace and more freedom from time pressures compared with when they were working. People who have launched their children into adulthood often experience a dramatic increase in "free time."

Where the spiritual journey may be involved here is in influencing what people do with the time freed by retirement and the empty nest. Those who use this time for contemplative reading, meditation, prayer, or devotions are choosing a lifestyle that emphasizes an inner journey in a region of consciousness in which time is less relevant. For example, a man in his eighties reported to me, "You become free of time when you realize that time is in you, not you in time."

On the other hand, those who use the time freed by retirement and child launching to become more involved in a path of service may find that they have substituted one set of time-based obligations for another. But time pressures are subjective, and those who have been on a contemplative spiritual path for many years may be able to engage in service without feeling the pressures of time because they take a mindful approach to service, which promotes realistic expectations of what can be accomplished and a let-be attitude toward time.

If aging causes people to slow down, yet people want to continue in their customary lifestyle, then aging may cause an increase in time pressure and a sense that time is speeding up. Many older people drastically simplify their lifestyles to balance their capabilities with their expectations. The spiritual journey can have an effect here by altering a person's sense of priorities. As people grow spiritually, they tend to take a transpersonal view of life. They often deemphasize their social and materialistic goals in favor of more enduring inner qualities such as altruism and generativity.

Beliefs can also mediate the relationship between time and aging. If people believe that their fundamental being is timeless, then death is less fearsome and there is little reason to feel that time is running out, which could be expected to reduce the sense that time is speeding up. On the other hand, if people believe that death is final and that time is finite, then as they get older they may begin to see time as a scarce resource and to see it as passing faster.

If people believe in a personal afterlife, then time is irrelevant in that their life is eternal. However, if they believe that eternity will be spent either in Heaven or Hell and that what they do in this life determines which, then they may have a heightened sense that time is running out and that time is passing ever more quickly.

If people believe that transcendence and enlightenment are possible, then they may experience these states. People who have transcended their purely personal concerns are unlikely to be concerned about the pace at which time passes, regardless of their chronological age.

These various possibilities by no means exhaust the potential ways that spiritual beliefs and practices might mediate the relationship between aging and the perception of time. They do illustrate a complex web of possibility. As we continue to ask the types of questions raised in this book, we will continue to find that spiritual beliefs and practices have important influences.

I have found it very useful to think about human beings as interactive systems in which bodily systems, knowledge, mental capacities, coping styles, lifestyles, and social environments interact in complex ways and evolve by incorporating feedback from experience (Atchley, 1999). From the point of view of continuity theory, physical, psychological, and social characteristics are basic structures and processes. Beliefs and practices of individuals are imbedded in a culture and society, and change in the individual or in the culture or society can change beliefs or practices. But changing beliefs or practices can also affect physical, psychological, or social characteristics, and widespread individual changes in belief or practice can change culture and social arrangements.

Given that there is a multitude of specific elements subsumed under the labels of beliefs, practices, aging, and adult development, the number of potential interactions is astronomical. Even if we limit ourselves to the experience of time as it is affected by physical, psychological, and social aging, and adult development—especially spiritual development, the number of dimensions to explore is mind boggling.

REFERENCES

Atchley, R. C. (1999). *Continuity and adaptation in aging: Creating positive experiences.* Baltimore: Johns Hopkins University Press.

Cole, T. R. (1992). *The journey of life: A cultural history of aging in America.* New York: Cambridge University Press.

Cszikszentmihalyi, M. (1993). *The evolving self: A psychology for the new millennium.* New York: HarperCollins.

Erikson, E. H., & Erikson, J. M. (1998). *Life cycle completed.* New York: Norton.

Huxley, A. (1941). Introduction. In S. Prabhavananda & C. Isherwood, *The song of God: Bhagavad-Gita* (pp. 11–22). New York: Penguin.

Johnston, W. (Ed.). (1996). *The cloud of unknowing.* New York: Image.

Mannell, R. C. (1993). High-investment activity and life satisfaction among older adults: Committed, serious leisure, and flow activities. In J. R. Kelly (Ed.), *Activity and aging* (pp. 125–145). Newbury Park, CA: Sage.

Peacock, J. R., & Paloma, M. M. (1991). *Religiosity and life satisfaction across the life course.* Paper presented at the annual meeting of the Society for the Scientific Study of Religion, November, Pittsburgh, PA.

Safransky, S. (1990). *Sunbeams: A book of quotations.* Berkeley, CA: North Atlantic Books.

Schacter-Shalomi, Z., & Miller, R. S. (1995). *From age-ing to sage-ing: A profound new vision of growing older.* New York: Warner.

Simonton, D. K. (1989). The swan song phenomenon: Last-works effects for 172 classical composers. *Psychology and Aging, 41,* 42–47.

Tornstam, L. (1994). Gerotranscendence: A theoretical and empirical exploration. In L. E. Thomas & S. A. Eisenhandler (Eds.), *Aging and the religious dimension* (pp. 203–229). New York: Auburn House.

Wilber, K. (1996). *Eye to eye: The quest for a new paradigm* (3rd ed.). Boston: Shambhala.

CHAPTER 10

Discovering the Spirit in the Rhythm of Time

Marita Grudzen and James P. Oberle

Over the course of history, human beings have discovered many pathways to the spiritual realities in their lives. In past ages, there was more immediate access to the Spirit in the ordinary activities of everyday life. Seen as an active force in Nature and human events, the Spirit gave meaning to human life. With the spiritual realm intimately interwoven with material existence, the *rhythm of time* connected with the *rhythm of nature*. The seasons of the year—winter, spring, summer, and fall—reinforced the sacredness of everyday life. The winter created space for going deep within the cave of the soul for it was a time of inward introspection. The spring was a period of germination; it was the time to plant the seeds of spiritual insights that would become fertile through the daily care and observation of the months in which new realities could grow strong. The summer months witnessed the actual formation of new life in a visible form and removed any foreign objects that would inhibit or degrade the full maturation of the soul's enlightenment. In the fall, humanity realized the fruits of its labor and partook of the earth's bounty in a sensual and spiritual feast.

Today, postmodern culture has radically separated human experience from the movement of the Spirit through time. In this paper, we analyze the reasons for this separation and discuss the ways spiritual practices can heal the divide between the spiritual and the material worlds. First, we provide a brief account of how time has been conceived since the ancient days when the world's major religions came into being. We believe that human constructions of time originated in religious worldviews that sanctified the times of human life unfolding from birth to death. As human cultures evolved, however, connections to the realm of the Spirit as expressed in the natural cycles of life were broken. We analyze the spiritual consequences of the dawning of the industrial age and the mounting losses of support for contemplation that have continued into the present age of information and its "new economy." Next we consider how today's overscheduled persons can recover contemplative time. Adults of all ages are discovering their deep and profound need to integrate spiritual practices into daily life. We review a number of these practices and focus especially on the ancient practice of walking a labyrinth. These spiritual practices can deepen human understanding and acceptance of life's seasons and thus place the experience of aging in a spiritual context. We conclude by suggesting that as we age, we are challenged to transcend the bonds of measured time and explore the realm of timelessness and eternity.

TIME IN RELIGIOUS HISTORY

The concept and the measurement of time have evolved through the centuries. The very first reflections on time by our primordial ancestors were simply thoughts about light and darkness. It is unlikely that there was any sense of quantity or quality in their original thought processes. Gradually these reflections included a predominant cyclical dimension. The cycles that they would have perceived were the phases of the moon and the movement of the stars. Additionally, the seasonal cycles would have been noticed. Since our earliest ancestors were hunters and gatherers, the growing season or cycle became an important part of their consciousness. We also know that ancient peoples felt a strong connection between the female fertility cycle and the fertility of the earth. The earth became known as "Mother Earth" or "Mother Nature."

About 5,000 years ago, time began to be divided into days, lunar months, and years. The creation story in the Book of Genesis is an excellent example of this early division of time. While it is unlikely that the creation day is a 24-hour period, we know that in the story, God creates day and night. This is the most basic division known among people of ancient civilizations. Also, God creates for 6 days and rests on the 7th day. This reflection was important for a liturgical cycle that began to evolve. This liturgical cycle was further influenced by the seasonal cycle because the Israelite people had special obligations at the beginning and ending of the harvest season. Once Israel possessed the land, the feast of Passover was celebrated. This was calculated from the phases or cycles of the moon. It was at this point that the quantity of time became a reality.

It was also at this point that chronological history began to emerge. Time was measured from the moment when God entered the course of human history. A time line was established to coincide with the biblical accounts of creation of human history and God's redemption of the Israelite people. The birth of Jesus the Christ became the significant dividing line in the linear account of history as told by the biblical writers of the New Testament. After the New Testament period, time was divided between the so-called Old and New Covenants.

With the merger of Greek and Roman civilizations and the further emergence of linear concepts of time, classical writers began to divide history into chronological epochs or large intervals of time. Later, with the development of the chronograph, discrete intervals of time were measured (for more detail, see chapter 2). This instrument allowed us to measure time in seconds, minutes, and hours. For those who needed even more precise measurements, we were able to subdivide the seconds into tenths, hundreds, and thousands.

Thus, there were now two major measurements of time: the cyclical and chronological concepts of time. These measurements are critical for all of our reflections on the concept of time. It is interesting to note that while Western cultures have focused on chronological or linear time, Asian, African, Native American, and Latin cultures have opted more for a cyclical model. To balance these competing foci we have the concepts of liturgical/ritual time and rhythms of time. In each of these there is a mixture of cycles as well as linear progress.

Another view of time derives from the Greek term, *kairos*, which was originally associated with Christianity (see chapter 13). The many references to *kairotic* time in the New Testament convey the notion of the fullness of time. Thus, many passages state that when the time was ripe, God acted. Alternatively, when time is complete, there is a fullness of time. Finally, *kairos* refers to peak moments in time—"time outside of time"—when time stands still or when hours go by and it seems like only minutes. This is the mystical experience when time has meaning but no measurement. These are the moments when we are harmonized with the world and time expands to its fullest extension.

The Eastern concept that is closely aligned with *kairos* is the Buddhist understanding of mindfulness. If we are mindful, then we are fully present. We live in the eternal now, and we do not have to deal with laments (lost time in the past), nor do we focus exclusively on the future (wasting time in excessive planning). Rather, we live in the present moment. We allow that moment to have its fullness, and we are not stressed. There is never stress in the present because one can always do what one is presently doing.

Once events or cycles of time were established, the three monotheistic religions began to sanctify time. The 7-day week became the norm into which the sanctification was structured. (It is interesting to note that when governments tried to suppress religious movements, they often tried to change the weekly cycle. Some had a 10-day cycle as a method of eliminating the religious day of rest.) Each of the major religions selected a day. For the Jewish people it was Saturday; Christians selected Sunday to commemorate the Resurrection; and Muslims have Friday as their sacred day.

Within the week each of these religions also have sanctified times during the day. At a minimum the Jew was to offer morning prayers and evening sacrifice. In countries that are predominantly Muslim, "callers" remind people of the times for prayer. The day has five times of prayer. For the Muslims living away from the "callers," there are guide books published based on latitude and longitude and the exact movements of the sun that remind them of the appropriate times for prayer.

The Christian community based its early times for prayer on the Jewish cycle. However, once Christianity became an established movement, and once monasticism came into existence (third century A.D.), a much more elaborate system of prayer times emerged. To sanctify the entire day, the monks (men and women) prayed at eight different times. The longest period occurred at Vigils (2 or 3 a.m.). This was a "night" hour, an hour of anticipation. It was done in the very early morning to consecrate the day. It was also done during the darkness so that one would not be distracted by things that could be easily seen. Thus, one could focus exclusively on divine things.

Other moments for prayer included Lauds, morning prayer (6:00 a.m.), Prime (7:00), Terce (9:00), Sext (12:00), and None (3 p.m.). The day was concluded with Vespers, evening prayer (6:00 p.m.), and Compline (8:00 p.m.). Currently, there are many different modifications of this. The primary hours are morning and evening prayer. Each prayer moment focuses on different psalms and different readings from the Bible. Frequently, the psalms or the readings call the prayer's attention to light and darkness, the heat of the day or the cool of the evening. They allow the natural rhythms of the day to be reinforced in prayer.

From these days and weeks, each of the major religions also built in cycles of fasting and feasting as well as long-term cycles for sabbatical and jubilee. All of this is done so that the believers can recall God's action in their lives and be thankful for God's abiding presence.

THE LOSS OF CONTEMPLATIVE TIME

Enormous social and spiritual changes occurred as humans moved from a more agricultural type of civilization to industrial development and then to the fast-paced technological changes in the twentieth century. The passing of the agricultural age began to accelerate in the United States at the end of the nineteenth century as people embraced the Industrial Revolution, which had swept through England during the prior century. The Industrial Age witnessed the growth of urban life and the movement of peoples from rural areas into the urban industrial centers of the United States.

The rhythms of urban life were quite different from those of the agricultural sectors of the country that lived within the seasonal qualities of Nature. The timetables of work and leisure were governed more by the pace of the factory rather than that of the farm. The sense of connection to Nature began to unravel as the machine age dawned. Early in the century, the automobile and airplane were invented. These two innovations were revolutionary in that they not only greatly quickened the pace of travel between locations, but they also began to disconnect us from reverence for "mother earth" and her deeper mysteries. Twentieth century "progress" focused on mastery of the earth rather than appreciation of her inner Spirit.

As we moved into the age of mass production, our sense of time became compressed to fit the scope of the journey. Time was no longer rooted in the daily sunrise and sunset but rather the call of the factory whistle and the auto, bus, or train that took men and women to work in the nation's industrial centers. The invention of the electric light bulb was another step in the revolution away from Nature's rhythms of sunrise and sunset to the rhythm of the electrified city whose life now began to consciously function throughout the day and night. Soon factories were operating three shifts: the normal day shift from early morning to late afternoon; the afternoon or swing shift, which worked from late afternoon to about midnight; the night shift began around midnight and ended with the new work day starting again about 7:00 or 8:00 a.m. We now had a 24-hour day, with many people's lives running completely opposite to Nature's rhythms. The Second World War also further magnified these time changes as most factories were running 24 hours per day to feed into the industrial war effort.

By the end of the Second World War, the sense of rhythmic time had clearly shifted in the United States away from its agricultural past to the 24-hour day of industrial production. To accommodate the need of returning servicemen for new homes and job opportunities, the United States subsidized the development of a suburban housing boom. This development further separated men and women from their connection to Nature's time for most workers had to commute from a suburban location to an urban center for their employment. The ancient connections of home, family, work, and Nature were growing ever more loose as life became more complex and governed by the rhythms of the modern corporation and needs of the nation-state to maintain industrial productivity.

The religious sphere was relegated to a time totally separated from daily work life. The local church or synagogue became another phenomenon of suburban life and was usually limited to a Saturday or Sunday obligation. The Spirit had effectively lost its deep connectivity to most of modern life.

The modern world of industrial capitalism had its own inherent logic and philosophy. Multinational corporations now controlled most of the time available to modern men and women who lived in the American metropolis. They provided a variety of material benefits to their workers, but they, in return, had to give their devotion and time to this new patriarchal structure. Just as the medieval Church had demanded obedience of its priests and bishops, so did the new multinational corporation demand a similar loyalty from its technical workers and managers. The Church and Corporation both required a willingness to surrender much of one's life and time to a benevolent despot who gave out rewards to those who most closely followed institutional directives and policy.

The rhythm of the modern corporation was quite different from the rhythms of Nature, on which most of the ancient wisdom traditions built their sense of the Sacred. The American secular culture now seemed to dominate most of modern life. Time for secular America and the Corporation was horizontal time. It was based primarily on a concept of time as a servant of progressive advancement in the spheres of technology and economy. It lost the sense of transcendence, which characterized earlier civilizations that saw time as the window to eternity. Time was now seen only as an opportunity to enhance one's personal well being through whatever means a modern society could provide. Time no longer had the transparency present in earlier cultures and civilizations.

Every part of the day had to be scheduled, and Americans increasingly lost the true meaning of leisure as the time to do nothing. American corporate culture responded to this by inventing the entertainment industry to fill up "free" time. This became another component for a "modern" society that indirectly controls even the "free time" of its citizens. Popular culture is a commercial component of capitalistic society, which partakes of the same requirements as other sectors in the economy.

Economic time—productive time—is utilitarian and instrumental in its focus. In contrast, real leisure time is contemplative in its focus and does not attempt to "possess" or "manipulate" the object of its contemplation. This meditative posture for a human being is one that opens the deeper regions of the soul to "see" the Transcendent in the midst of the ordinary and the customary.

During the Cold War period the United States focused its attention on the nuclear arms race and the space race. Time took on the connotation of a "race." We had to win this "race," so we poured enormous resources into this contest. Obviously, time became even more of an instrumental commodity that had to serve our purpose of competing with our communist adversary. The modern corporation aligned itself with the American military establishment to create what was often called the "U.S. Military-Industrial Complex." Two companies in Northern California that became an integral part of this complex were Lockheed Missile and Space and FMC Corporation. This sector of the economy took on some of the characteristics of a Crusade. Just at the medieval popes called on faithful Catholics to conquer the Infidel and win back the Holy Land, so did the President of the United States call on our citizens to win back space exploration from the Russians and also win the race for technological superiority by developing a new generation of superior weaponry.

During the last two or three decades of the twentieth century a further revolution in time occurred. Just as earlier technological developments had created a new understanding of humans' place in Nature, so did these new developments change people's understanding of their own control over many aspects of time. The discovery of the microchip led to the computer revolution, which is commonly called the "Information Age." One of the leading pioneers in this revolution was the Intel Corporation, which developed some of the earliest commercial applications of the microprocessor in the early 1970s. The microprocessor allowed for ever faster rates of computation and data manipulation. The microprocessor became the key component in the personal computer that spread throughout the United States over the remainder of the century at ever lower prices. The computer/electronics revolution, which took place over a period of about 20 years, does not compare with the futuristic revolution brought about by the proliferation of the Internet and cellular technologies over the last decade of the century. These technologies have had a profound impact on our understanding of time. They have changed our understanding of the workplace, the home, and our ability to understand time as a utilitarian component of our consciousness.

The technological revolution now underway has spawned the "New Economy," which has transformed our national economies into one global economy. The workplace is now considered to be the whole globe, where we interact with colleagues throughout the earth. The division between home and work is quickly disappearing as more and more people telecommute. Virtual corporations are becoming ever more common, and most knowledge workers find themselves to be an ever more mobile commodity with little long-term commitment to a particular company. The knowledge worker is often working 50 or 60 hours per week just to keep pace in a technological competition with workers around the globe to develop the latest and fastest new technological improvements for the new Internet and digital economy. Very few people even understand all the implications of the "New Economy," so they feel that it is literally running ahead of them. Time seems to be beyond our control. We now feel that we are outdated within a matter of months rather a period of years.

This kind of psychology has huge implications for our understanding of Spirit in that we have lost touch with some of the fundamental dimensions of time in our race for technological superiority. There is a growing sense of *impermanence* that pervades the new social and cultural context of our era. In previous eras men and women could feel a greater sense of stability for they usually worked at one or two jobs for the greater part of their lives.

In the "New Economy" many jobs and even many companies become obsolete within a 5- to 10-year time span. Knowledge workers must continually educate themselves to the latest technical advances or they soon will be left behind in the race for global technological superiority. Time pressure leads to high levels of personal stress. Men and women who work in this fast-paced world have difficulty balancing their personal lives with their work lives. Often there is a serious imbalance, which can lead to marital stress and family dysfunction. Many observers of the Internet generation are suggesting that new forms of psychological addiction are emerging as a result of the stresses placed on the individual in this emerging economy. There is often a growing sense of anonymity, which can lead to feelings of isolation and separation from the larger community. Individuals replace real human interaction with e-mail and chat rooms. Electronic commerce can become another way to remove oneself from direct contact with real people in a real physical community. We can now envision a future in which most of our daily functions occur within the "cocoon" of our sanitized technical environment: sitting in front of a computer screen or our Web TV. We no longer have to rub shoulder to shoulder with the amalgam of people who frequent the old "village square."

In the midst of this new cultural reality, we realize the need to regain our sense of identity through a conscious slowing of our pace of living. One author suggests that we learn to *stop and listen* to the still, small voice within ourselves (Kundtz, 1998). Stopping can be a way to regain one's footing on the terrain of life. We often feel that our lives are consumed by the constant challenges placed before us in our daily lives. We might ask ourselves what would happen if we just *stopped doing* for a few days and learned how to *be and live* within a more contemplative frame of reference. When we stop our daily routine, we are forced to look within ourselves for a deeper level of meaning and reflect on the inner life of our soul. When we are preoccupied with external demands on our time, we literally can feel that we do not belong to ourselves. We can feel that our external environment controls our being.

Through stopping and reflecting, we can regain a sense of connection to our soul rhythms, which often work at a totally different pace than the rhythms of our externally oriented life demands. The function of stopping is not just to cease activity. It is meant to help us *focus* our attention on the interior life, which is rooted in Spirit.

RECOVERING CONTEMPLATIVE TIME

The act of stopping is the first step on the road to recovery. Just as 12-step programs call persons to a change of consciousness, so does stopping create the context for change. What kind of changes can come out of stopping? Perhaps the most important change is the intent to live a more *authentic life.*

In the Christian tradition, the act of remembering or *anamnesis* (memorial) is the fundamental way Christians know their identity as followers of Christ. They remember the Passion, Death, and Resurrection of Christ in the memorial or *anamnesis* of the Eucharist. In a similar manner we need to remember our own life history and the "stepping stones" of our life. In the journal method of personal spiritual growth popularized by Ira Progoff, the writer is asked to reflect on the critical moments or "turning points" in spiritual life. Through this process we gain access to the deeper spiritual well that characterizes the movements of our soul. Historically we have spoken of a spiritual calling that comes from the center of one's soul. We can begin to hear this call more clearly when we stop to listen. Our listening allows us to review the key facets of our life experience and determine what is really most important and revitalizing at this stage in our life journey.

There are few people in our modern society who do not experience the need for renewal at key stages in their lives. The renewal can take many forms, but it usually involves some change of direction. We often are speeding along on the highway of life without too much thought about why we are on such a fast track. The act of stopping allows us time to survey the landscape around us and within us. We can also look back on what internal and external forces have brought us to this specific moment. We realize who the important people are in our life that have fed us along life's journey and helped us become fuller and deeper persons. We can take time to look to the future and determine what qualities seem absent from our life that are necessary for our future growth. We can now visualize a better and more optimum state of mental, physical, and spiritual health as we project a new image of ourselves onto the playing field of life.

St. Ignatius of Loyola often incorporated visualization into his Spiritual Exercises. We must also take time to visualize what is the inner core of our heart's desire. We can only find this core of truth through silent reflection over an extended period of time.

David Kundtz (1998) uses an artful phrase, "a Grinding Halt," in his book *Stopping*. Often we are forced to stop our customary lives for a time because of events beyond our control—for example, a death in one's family, a divorce or separation, a career change, or a protracted illness. These events unsettle the established routines of our life and make us pause to examine what is actually happening in our lives. We often find that there is some glaring imbalance, which strikes us almost immediately after we take some time for reflection.

A time of crisis can awaken us to the reality of what has or has not occurred in our spiritual journey. We can *consult* with others who have known us over a long time period to ask their help in a period of *reassessment.* It may require an act of humility to accept the truth of one's present moment, but that is all we really have, and it is still precious. The Zen masters have all told us that the first step to enlightenment is to learn how to be with ourselves just as we are. This is the fundamental truth from which we can begin anew our spiritual journey. Any other state of mind is at least one step removed from the actuality of our present consciousness. We need to learn the art of acceptance and actually be grateful for the tragedy and comedy within our life drama. Often a seeming tragedy can lead us to great spiritual insight and personal transformation.

Through a period of slowing down and watching the rhythms of nature, we begin to realize that we are an amazing part of God's creation. We cannot deny the wonder that is present in our simple acts of physical existence: breathing, eating, playing, walking, and talking. By this process of watching ourselves, we take the pressure of daily events literally "off of our backs" and breathe a big sigh of relief. We realize that life goes on no matter what we do or don't do. Life is bigger and more wondrous than anything that we might do to confuse or upset its balance. When we take the time to "do no-thing," we actually learn how "to be" or learn that we are "being." We must learn how to "just be."

This simple act is very difficult for someone who is a high achieving person. It runs counter to many cultural assumptions about how we achieve happiness and fulfillment. We presume that happiness comes when we are most busy and occupied with many tasks. The great wisdom traditions seem to indicate something quite different. Happiness or enlightenment only comes as a gift to those who are psychologically empty of any need for immediate accomplishment or gratification. We do not need to be a monk, priest, or even a devout and pious soul; we need to learn how to let go of expectations and demands on others and ourselves. When our soul is peaceful and centered, we project this peace and tranquility out into the world and discover our personal bliss.

Many of us fear solitude and the movement of our soul into realms that seem beyond rational control. We have forgotten the wisdom of our ancestors who went down into caves to experience the true mystery of their lives. In the southern part of France, at Lascaux, we have only recently discovered some of the earliest forms of pictorial representation in the history of the human species. These men and women felt a need to descend down into the earth to depict their understanding of the cosmos. This can be seen as a metaphor for our own time. We need to descend into the cave of our own consciousness to discover our place in the cosmos just as our ancestors did. They saw the seamless unity of all life. We have difficulty grasping such unity within our technological civilization. We can use our creative imagination just they used their imagination to depict our new understanding of our place in Nature.

We have a new creation story given to us by modern science, which can be understood as the manifestation of the Spirit in Matter. The Jesuit paleontologist Pierre Teilhard de Chardin did not see any opposition between the new creation story and that of the unfolding of Spirit in time. In fact, Teilhard understood time as the literal unfolding of Spirit into matter through evolutionary processes. Teilhard saw the material world as a "divine milieu." He took issue with a perception of the world as a purely secular phenomenon. Rather, he saw the world as the manifestation or epiphany of the divine. Many accused Teilhard of pantheism, but he would claim that he really was a panentheist, that is, he saw the divine active in all creation but not completely identified with it.

Teilhard's mysticism resonates with many of the discoveries that have become commonplace in the twentieth century. It is possible to see the Internet as a kind of concrete manifestation of Teilhard's concept of the "Noosphere," that is, the "thinking envelope" that encircles the planet earth. At the time Teilhard developed his vision, there was not even a hint of the discovery of this new global communications network. He foresaw, however, a time when human beings could consciously connect with one another in a new way that would bring the human race ever closer to each other and transcend the tribal and national identities that characterized the species up until the twentieth century (Teilard de Chardin, 1959, 1971).

WALKING THE LABYRINTH

Today, many scholars and spiritual seekers are finding ways to access the Spirit through very ancient spiritual practices. One of those practices that has emerged very strongly in recent years is the labyrinth. A labyrinth is a sevenfold circular path that moves from the edge of the circle to the center and then back again to the outer edge (Figure 10.1). It is a path that allows persons to symbolize their spiritual journey as a movement from the "edges" of life to the "center" of life. Usually a person will walk this path in a slow and meditative manner and take some time for thoughtful meditation and reflection at the center of the labyrinth. As one moves to the center of the circle, there is a conscious letting go of life's problems and preoccupations.

The first recorded labyrinth was found on the island of Crete and the oldest surviving labyrinth is located in Sardinia and dates from about 2500 B.C.E. There are the remains of a seven-circuit labyrinth located on Mt. Knossos in Crete. The Greek historian Herodotus is the first person to use the term "labyrinth" in his writing in about 489 B.C.E. Most scholars believe that the labyrinth's spiral configuration is

FIGURE 10.1   The labyrinth at Mercy Center, Burlingame, California.

drawn from the presence of the spiral in Nature and that the labyrinth has a connection to Nature mysticism. The labyrinth became a ritual for helping human beings feel the presence of the divine manifested in the whole cosmos (Artress, 1995).

In Arizona and the American Southwest, the Hopi tribe used a form of the labyrinth in their religious culture as other native peoples in the Americas used similar religious symbols based on the lunar calendar. Native peoples did not separate their lives into the sacred and the secular. Daily life activities such as walking, sleeping, and cohabiting were part of their nature mysticism. It would seem that the labyrinth was particularly suited for helping ancient peoples understand the movement of their lives as a progression toward the center of the divine mystery. By moving in a circular path, they imitated the cycles of Nature that move from death to life and back again in an eternal cycle of death and rebirth. They could pass from temporal time to eternal time when they walked the labyrinth. This movement from "numbered" time to infinite timelessness occurs when a person deeply enters the labyrinth process.

One of the most famous labyrinths in Europe is found at Chartres Cathedral, which was built on an earlier pre-Christian site a few miles west of Paris and became an important place of pilgrimage for the medieval world. This labyrinth formed the model for the labyrinths at Grace Cathedral in San Francisco that represent the epicenter of the modern labyrinth movement—an effort to encourage the spiritual discipline of labyrinth walking throughout the world.

Some who walk the labyrinth model their journey on the classical threefold spiritual path of the life of the Spirit: the path into the center is the time of *purgation* or emptying of self and letting go of temporal concerns; the time in the center is the period of *illumination* where the pilgrim experiences new clarity, insight, and contemplative quiet; the path outward is the path of *union* for the seeker has found new ways to integrate the Spirit with other dimensions of earthly life and bring the presence of Spirit into daily activities. The natural rhythm of walking helps to embody this spiritual awareness as we proceed out into our daily life.

There are several approaches to walking the labyrinth. Some prefer to walk the labyrinth in silence, whereas others use an image or words as a kind of mantra. Many people take off their shoes and walk the labyrinth in bare feet to symbolize reverence and humility.

Taking time to prepare is important, for the walking is meant to bring us into awareness of the presence of God in our lives, a presence often obscured by the pace of our lives. It is important to walk slowly through the labyrinth to allow the deeper presence of God to penetrate. There is no right or wrong way to experience the labyrinth and each person will have a different understanding of its impact. However, the almost universal experience of those who make this pilgrimage is the immediate realization of a new sense of the divine in the midst of temporal life.

We often speak of the labyrinth as "sacred geometry." It has a kind of mathematical precision in that you must follow the path exactly to make it to the center. If you deviate from the path, you find yourself "lost" on the journey through life. The labyrinth also serves then as a metaphor for one's spiritual path. We all need such a path but it can take many different forms. Persons of any religious background can deepen their spiritual journey by walking the labyrinth, for it transcends any religious tradition. The key, of course, is finding one's path. The labyrinth makes us aware that there is a path waiting for us. We only need to discover one that is suitable for us.

Spiritual practices such as the labyrinth help to us transcend our focused and limited way of seeing reality to one that is more inclusive of the transcendent dimension of human existence. We do not have to seek out these archetypal realities; they are always present to us. We need only allow ourselves the timely opportunity to experience them more deeply. The labyrinth is particularly suited for slowing down the pace of life in a gradual manner. In it, we move from the temporal to eternal dimensions through a process that physically embodies what is occurring on a spiritual level.

CONCLUSION

Perhaps the greatest challenge one faces when reflecting on the reality of time is that it is both internal and external, both visible and invisible. For the modern person, this causes great difficulty, for we have been "programmed" to focus only on the external, the visible, the measurable. Yet, that part of our life is often the least significant. Echoing Plato, we believe that it is the world of ideas that is critical if we are to adjust our concept of time so that in aging we might become more deeply acquainted with the spiritual realities once so apparent to our ancestors. While we often rely on appearances, we also recognize they show us very little. They cannot show consciousness of spirit, soul, history, or love. Appearance can be an illusion; at its best it is only a fraction of reality.

Persons in our culture have been very comfortable in looking at reality from a quantifiable perspective. We want to measure length, depth, and width. All of these are external to the self, and we have convinced ourselves that this is what is real. We have been conditioned to believe that ultimate truth is external to the person. Ideas had to become actualized in physical space before they could be considered real. Therefore the only things that were real where those that existed in measurable units.

The great tragedy with this approach is that when time is limited to chronology, humanity seeks solutions to the problem of time outside of the self in the "real" world. The problem of time is expressed in a number of ways, ranging from the perceived "lack" of time to deeply rooted fears of time's passage and the inevitability of aging and death. However, the material world of appearances cannot ultimately resolve this problem, and this is why from the beginning of history people have turned to spiritual practices and religious beliefs to try to comprehend time.

We believe that humanity's truest self lies in the realm of Spirit that is not constrained by time. We need to be open to this reality if we are to accomplish any good. What is outside of time is free from opposites and free from contradiction. The greatest reality exists not in the future but outside of time—outside of the illusion of time. God creates timelessly and outside of time. We come to the fullness of time by adjusting our perspective and by living—and aging—in the now. We can do this by realizing that eternity is not a quantity of time but rather a quality of time.

As we grow older, we repeatedly encounter the problems posed by mere chronological time. We are challenged to rethink our relationship to a temporal reality defined so narrowly. This can be understood as a form of repentance. Once we change the way we think about timeless nature of our truest self, we can come to a more complete understanding of time and thus experience its fullness. Another way of stating this is to say that as we age, we are invited to become mystics, be captured by the Spirit, and discover the rhythm of God's eternal time.

REFERENCES

Artress, L. (1995). *Walking a sacred path: Rediscovering the labyrinth as a spiritual tool.* New York: Riverhead.

Kundtz, D. (1998). *Stopping: How to be still when you have to keep going.* Berkeley, CA: Conari Press.

Teilard de Chardin, P. (1959). *The phenomenon of man* (B. Wall, Trans.). New York: Harper.

Teilard de Chardin, P. (1971). *Christianity and evolution* (R. Hague, Trans.). New York: Harcourt Brace Jovanovich.

CHAPTER 11

The Contemplative Context of Time

Elizabeth Oates Schuster

> It will be at our peril if we put all our faith in the measurable, and dishonour that which lies beyond statement.
> —Florida Scott-Maxwell

The time has come to redefine the term "quality of life" as it relates to the experiences of those who are in the latter stages of life. Too often individuals who work with older adults are expected to make certain that the clients and residents they serve are active, busy, and outwardly engaged. The extent and degree of active engagement is typically used as a measurement of quality of life. I have observed this process first hand when spending time in continuum-of-care settings. I have seen the well-planned activity calendars and the effort that goes into coming up with activities that are meaningful, creative, and interesting (no easy task). In fact, I can speak first hand on this subject as I spent 5 years as an educational program director in a senior center.

This is all well and good. People want to participate in life; they want to reach out to one another, to interact, to accomplish important goals, and to lead vital and active lives. Yet, one of the many lessons I learned while growing up with my grandfather as one of my primary caregivers and during the 3 years I studied a group of writers (average age 88) living in a nursing home was the importance of paying attention to the inner life.

As we grow old, our pace naturally slows and there is time for reflecting on what our lives have been all about; for contemplating the meaning of life. As we enter into our later years, it becomes apparent that our bodies need to slow down. We begin to let go of many things that were of great importance to us a few years earlier. Our focus turns away from the external world as the opportunity to become fully engaged in the process of reverie and introspection presents itself (Atchley, 1993). It is at this time that we become more acquainted with who we are, what our lives have been about, what we have contributed, and what more we want to accomplish before we take our leave of this good Earth. At this stage of life we have the time, the quiet, and the solitude available to us. These moments of silence can provide profound insights into the meaning of life. This is not to say that the very old totally disengage from the world. In fact, the opposite is true. If individuals choose to consciously and meditatively explore their inner worlds, chances are their last years of life will take on greater meaning and their relationships with themselves, with their loved ones, and with the world will become deeper and richer.

Ram Dass (1998), a former Harvard professor and well-known teacher and lecturer on Eastern and Western spirituality, provided an alternative viewpoint on the quality of life when he wrote, "Paradoxically, in the period before death, the quality of life can be heightened even though our bodies are failing" (p. 163). How can this be? It all depends on how you define quality of life. Activity Theory is often used by professionals and academics as a means of justifying the tendency to equate a busy, active life to a quality life. According to Moody (1998), the theory argues that the more active we are, the more satisfied with life we are. Here, the emphasis is on doing. In fact, the theory asserts that our identity is determined by what we do. Yet, when we are close to dying, we are not *doing* much of anything, are we? So how can Ram Dass assert that the quality of our lives may actually reach new heights when we are doing less or even nothing at all?

There's the catch. At this point in our lives we are active, but we are busy *being* rather than doing. For a good portion of our lives, we focus our attention and energies on the external world. We are involved in making something of ourselves, of obtaining material possessions, playing a multitude of roles, raising a family, progressing up the promotional ladder. We are Active with a capital A. Yet, around the middle of life, there is a natural tendency to turn our attention and focus inwards. Some people consciously respond to this urge to more deeply explore their inner worlds, while others choose to go on as if nothing is changing, and the voice inside that is asking to be noticed is ignored or not even heard. Most of us fall somewhere in between, where we hear the call to pay attention to the inner life and find ourselves spending perhaps a little more time staring out a window, gazing at a tree in full flower, and then, with a sudden jolt, come "back to reality" with the realization that we were simply being. During this time, no thoughts invade our reveries; there is a sense of nothingness. And yet, at the same time, there is a feeling of oneness, of connectedness, and of a calm and peaceful presence, as though we are sitting with a good friend in silence. No words are necessary or even possible. At these times we are the observer, and the more we quiet ourselves the more in touch we become with the inner transformations that may be expressed as a reconciliation, leading to state of unification and completion. Metzner (1998) referred to this mystical exploration of inner space as the "inexpressible experiences of transformation" (p. 9). Inexpressible in that we cannot name the unnamable. Rather than naming or labeling, there is a knowing, a remembering. We discover that everything we need to know is within.

The state of completion and what Thich Nhat Hanh (1998a, 1998b) referred to as the order of inner being is akin to what is known as the state of self-actualization. Maslow (1968) described this ever-evolving state as an integration and unity through the actualization of talents and potential. Moody (1997) expanded on this description with the following insights:

> Those who attain self-actualization . . . are at peace with themselves, yet they also have their eye upon the star. Self-actualized persons have an unbiased perception of reality and a healthy acceptance of themselves and others. They love freely, give gladly, tolerate fully, but

> at the same time maintain a discrete sense of privacy and detachment. They particularly avoid blind conformity and identification with the herd. (p. 278)

Note that one of the primary features of self-actualization is a balance between being engaged in loving and giving, and yet, at the same time, seeking privacy and autonomy. There is not a conscious effort to attain balance, a willingness to serve, and privacy; these attributes automatically emerge when the person is in the state of self-actualization.

A result of this natural state of being is a detachment of oneself from the outer world. How does this play out in a setting where quality of life is determined by the level of engagement and involvement in-group activity? The person's behavior who is actively engaged in the state of self-actualization may be misinterpreted as being an act of unhealthy withdrawal, when, in fact, the reality is the opposite. Atchley (1993) observed, "solitude [is] not a negative, vegetative state, but rather an opportunity for focused thought and absorption" (p. 483). While the person may not appear to be actively engaged with her or his world, there may be a great deal of activity occurring deeply within as the person finds himself or herself in a naturally occurring meditative state. In correspondence, Armin Grams (April 17, 1999) wrote, "meditation is an intense activity; salutary contemplation and reverie require substantial expenditures of energy, but . . . energy of quite a different sort than that usually associated with activity theory." The sort of energy that is expended is unlike the energy of doing, which tends to eventually run out, ending in entropy. The energy released during inner work is Self-renewing (the capital S in Self denoting the higher Self).

So while there is activity, transformation takes place deep within the psyche. And, unlike external activity, the productivity is not measured by a material artifact or some other physical representation. In fact, productivity is not a valid measurement when it comes to inner work. Instead, as the person glides along on the inner paths of awareness and consciously immerses herself into the transformative process of self-actualization, she experiences what Metzner (1998) envisioned as a gradual unfolding from deep within, like "the opening of a flower (compared to the opening of a *chakra*), and the growth of a tree or butterfly (compared to the psychic growth of a person)" (p. 16). It is a state of evolving, of being. No picture is painted; no attendance in a group activity is accounted for; there is no doing. This intrinsic transformation instead is valued for what it is: the evolution of the soul.

At this point, I believe our understanding of the experience of spirituality and inner world transformations in late life would deepen by having an opportunity to learn from a remarkable individual, Fanchette Stewart, who also happens to be my teacher, my mentor, my spiritual guide, and my very dear friend (see Figure 11.1). Fanchette was born in Liege, Belgium in 1926 and lived in occupied Belgium through World War II. Her father was a mystic and had a profound influence on her own spiritual beliefs and practice. According to Fanchette, her father was, "a champion of justice." She continues, "The influence that my Papa had on my world-view is quite great, because of the essence of his convictions, which he lived

FIGURE 11.1   Fanchette Stewart.

daily. He was a member of the Belgian resistance all through World War II and demonstrated that one should be able to die for one's convictions but never kill. Statements such as: 'Nothing is as it appears to be—seek always the reality behind the appearances,' and 'Question, question everything—without questioning one develops no inner convictions,' were guiding posts in my upbringing. He welcomed my questions and would talk about everything without judgments, frequently sharing with me what he had derived from his own mistakes. He allowed and encouraged my reading profound works at an early age and discussed them with me."

"My Papa was a great admirer of Leo Tolstoy's *Civil Disobedience and Non-Violence.* Mahatma Gandhi was his revered model of a successful life, and he also admired Rabindranah Tagore. Those were also among my early teachers. He was a deeply spiritual man, vehemently opposed to 'organized religions,' which he saw as divisive and petty, based on ego and not on spirit. He respected and loved esoteric Christianity and the Sufis of Islamic mysticism and remained all of his life a student of holy works in all great traditions because they teach us that love is supreme."

Fanchette graduated from the Lycee Leoni de Waha and attended the Polyglotte Institute majoring in Languages and was soon hired as an interpreter by the United States armed forces to work at the 06014 Depot in Liege. After attending the University of Liege, she met her husband to be, and they were married in 1946. In July of that year, at age 19, Fanchette arrived in Lubock, Texas and soon enrolled at Texas Technological College where she taught French and German. In 1963 she moved to Norman, Oklahoma. At that time there was a Kellogg Foundation at the University of Oklahoma, and, according to Fanchette, it was "a real Mecca for those who, like myself, were pursuing studies in psychology." At the Kellogg Foundation she and her colleagues were able to study with visiting professors including Erich Fromm, Abraham Maslow, Rollo May, Carl Rogers, and many more.

Eventually the Stewart family moved to Ann Arbor, Michigan where the Institute of Transactional Analysis was located. After completing the courses at the institute, Fanchette taught living skills and self-awareness classes in various locations in Michigan and Ohio. The family moved to Coldwater, Michigan in 1986 and Fanchette began to organize self-awareness, meditation, and spiritual living classes at the local prison and other locales throughout the community. She has this to say about the prison program: "We currently have many ongoing groups, and I find it most rewarding. Our small Prison-Ashram project is truly inspiring for all who are involved."

Fanchette was brought up with a deep respect for Eastern philosophies, such as Hinduism and Buddhism. As noted above, early in her life, the writers and teachers who most influenced her spiritual growth included Tolstoy, Gandhi, and Tagore. More recently, Fanchette has studied the teachings of Thich Naht Hanh, His Holiness the Dalai Lama, Frances Horn, Jae Jah Noh, and Elizabeth Kubler-Ross, among others. She has been practicing meditation for the last 40 years.

The following are Fanchette Stewart's thoughts about spirituality in late life that she shared with me during several conversations over the past year. As a 72-year-old woman who has devoted a good deal of her life to inner exploration and service, she has many gems of wisdom to offer those who wish to listen. She speaks in a wonderfully deep, robust voice that is accented by her first language, French. It is not atypical for Fanchette to slip into her mother tongue when she is making an important point; is excited, happy, angry; or if she simply wants to get your attention.

Being a spiritual being and knowing it from childhood on, is a great asset. I grew up with someone [her father] who repeated day in and day out, "Remember, *nothing* is as it appears, always seek the reality behind the appearances." And, you know, that reality is invisible. That's why I always use the example with my classes, that when you look in the mirror, you see your instrument, you see your body, you see your tool, but you are that which is doing the looking. And you don't see that. That energy you don't *see*. And *that* is reality.

My first spiritual experience was when I was 6 years old. I was at school and one little boy younger than me had to go pee, and it was the third time the lunch lady sends me with him to the bathroom. So I am getting vexed. So I sit him down, I yank his pants down, and angrily sit him on the pot—I can see myself—and I say in French, "You are not going to get up until you have done something!" Not kind, not nice at all, and of course he starts crying. And I become aware of a skirt, and it's green and there are two lovely feet, and I think "Oh, boy! Oh, mon dieu!" She is looking at me with a very stern expression and I know instantly I am in deep trouble. I take him off the pot, I put his pants back on and I take him by the hand and I go back to the lunchroom and I ask the lunch lady, "Who's the lady in green?" The poor woman says, "There is nobody else here, I am the only woman here." I tell I tell her what happened and she says, "Oh."

When Daddy comes home I relate to him the story, and he says, "Ahh! Your guardian one!" I say, "She's beautiful," and he responds, "Yes, she taught you a lesson." Never use force. I mean I *knew* that, never to be forgotten again! Here you see the advantage of going to a father who did not marginalize, who did not ridicule, who was open and ready, and had a spiritual explanation.

That was the first time. The second time was about a year later at Christmas time. I knew that there was not a Saint Nicolas but I knocked myself out pretending there was so my parents would not know that I knew. I walked around exclaiming, "Merci, Saint Nicolas, merci!" and suddenly, there she stood [my guardian], and big tears were coming down her face, and I knew she was crying for me.

So from the beginning it was a conscious decision to be aware of being a spiritual being. We are all on a journey, but it was, from childhood on, a conscious knowledge of being on a journey. Because of my spiritual upbringing when I was a child on the edge of starvation I *knew* that I was going to get something to eat, and it came, always. When we didn't have coal, we needed coal, I *knew* somebody was going to give me coal, and they did. I had no idea who or how, but they did. The perspective of your life is entirely different when you come from an observing point, versus—like so many people—feeling that life is happening to you. There is a sense of being an observer as well as a participant.

[This perspective results in the belief that] growing old is unimportant. World War II[1] and my father gave me clues: The impermanence of life, the total unimportance of things, of accumulating things,

---

[1]In a later conversation Fanchette quoted Thich Naht Hanh's (1998a) remembrances of growing up in time of war and the lessons suffering offers: "I grew up in a time of war. There was destruction all around—children, adults, values, a whole country. As a young person, I suffered a lot. Once the door of awareness is opened, you cannot close it. The wounds of war in me are still not healed. There are nights I lie awake and embrace my people, my country, and the whole planet with mindful breathing.

Without suffering, you cannot grow. Without suffering, you cannot get the peace and joy you deserve. Please don't run away from your suffering. Embrace it, and cherish it. Go to the Buddha, sit with him, and show him your pain. He will look at you with loving kindness, compassion, and mindfulness and show you ways to embrace your suffering and look deeply into it. With understanding and compassion, you will be able to heal the wounds in you heart, and the wounds of the world" (p. 5).

because, after all, there was our house one minute and the next minute it was gone. These things taught me as a child some very deep truths as to what is important in life and what isn't. Obviously, what *is* important is life itself, and loved ones, and everyone. It is a sense of belonging to everything. And so the process of "aging" is something that is natural.

I remember one time with my mother, I was in the process of making a rather unkind comment about a young woman who was about 20 and I was about 16. The comment had nothing to do with appearance of either me or her, it had to do with her behavior. Mother said, "Be very careful, in a twinkle of an eye, you will be as she is, and, in a twinkle of an eye, you will be as I am." So that really early aging was described as being not a problem, and that's why I say I am so very grateful I did not grow up in this country.

Here is an example of what I mean. I was at a country club in Atchison, Texas and I was 35 or 36 at the time. I was listening to two women, who were 27 or 28 and talking about being "on the shelf," and I remember laughing uproariously, because, to me, it was such a stupid concept! I mean, here they were the picture of vitality, and they considered themselves to be on the shelf!

I get the feeling that in this society aging is dreaded. I didn't get that when I was growing up in Belgium. Aging is just a part of life. It's an opportunity to learn. For example, when I had my accident [at age 64 Fanchette was hit by a car while crossing the street and was in trauma care and rehabilitation for more than a year], I had the opportunity to experience life from a wheelchair, which I had never done before, and that was tremendous. I learned so many things, and this knowledge I would have never have if the accident had not happened.

So I have remained opened to all of life's experiences without judging. It was taught to me that judging was the curse of mankind. And so there was always that real sincere effort at not passing judgment. When one is free from the urge to compare and to judge then there is much greater ability to be in the moment, because comparing obviously entails looking back at the past, it's a judgment. So when we don't have that urge, we can truly be living in the moment.

By being open to all that life has to offer, the enthusiasm for the gift of life keeps increasing. And I am the recipient of that, I am not aware of doing it. The gift comes from the indwelling entity, the spiritual being, I don't care what you call it, it is what we are; a spiritual being having an experience in the body. Fanchette is a manifestation of the spiritual being at this point in time. That's why I refer to it as a state of grace.

At this point in our conversation I made the statement to Fanchette that our society tends to regard aging as a process that is primarily a physical decline of the body and it means, to many people, that my body is getting older and is a burden, a weight. I asked her to comment on this because to me it seems that Fanchette is experiencing the opposite sensation, a lightness of being.

Fanchette responded, "I think it has been a wonderful body, it has served me well. It's a beloved tool. Through it I can love, through it I can be. It has always been my contention that if we were graced enough to bring up our children to be aware, to not speak of the reality of something, but the *realities,* then they have an advantage. Because they are not *just* a body, and a mind, and a spirit. They are *primarily* a spirit and all of these gifts are unto them. So they *look* at the world differently, they *look* at living differently."

"Fanchette," I asked, "how is your experience different from other older adults you know?"

"It is different because so many people are so limited in their minds. I feel free, and they feel their body is stiff and they resent it, they can't move like they did. Well, who in the hell can? It's just that there are so many things that they deplore, and they seem to forget that they are still alive, they still have the chance to learn, they are still able to enjoy, and they are not letting themselves. I have obviously a different concept compared to most of what is real and isn't.

"From the inside out I have not experienced aging. I do not have an internal sense of growing old. I know the body is getting older, and that's ok. I have an internal sense of being me. Everything is transformation."

I asked Fanchette if she could speak about those transformations. "I am meditating less. I think because I am more in a steady state of meditation. It's not meditation *per se,* it's being aware of the breath, the mantra, mindfulness of everything, absolutely everything. This is a mindful decision. But I think it has everything to do with what is real and what isn't. It's being aware that most of what is there for us to see, to taste, is there for our pleasure, but its very ephemeral, it's not going to last. This leads to the acceptance that you are not going to last either. That's what makes it so precious, the fact that you are in a body and you're kicking, and you are able to be, it's just wonderful! And you know it's finite. If you have this sense of what is real and what isn't you are consciously and knowingly preparing for death. But it's not morbid and it's not somber, it's just going from what you know to something different. Hopefully consciously."

"Can you share with me what the term 'quality of life' means to you?" I asked.

"When I look at the journey, it's been such a thrill. Yes, it has had its difficulties. Of course! Those are the lessons. But, I look at it and think, 'By God, it can't be, 72 years old, this is ridiculous! Maybe 50 to 55, whatever 55 is, I don't know.' But there is no sense of a period of time; it's like a circle. Eventually one comes to a point in the circle and then one pops out, and we call that death. I look at the journey and it's not linear, I have no sense of being a long time. It is a sense of timelessness."

I mentioned to Fanchette that many people in our society seem to equate aging with death and morbidity and fear. In response, she described her feelings about death with sounds. She said, "There's a certain amount of 'EEK!' and certain amount of 'HUBBAH HUB-BAH HUBBAH!' " Then she offered a message to those who are preparing for death. "Cultivate joy. Do not go about being petty and judgmental and all of that crap. When I came to this country, death was in the closet. It was not considered good manners to speak about death in a formal situation. People who grow old with dread are at a severe disadvantage. They think that is the end of them. I know that who I am goes on forever; we are forever. The indwelling entity goes on. There is a real mixture of anxiety—will I do it like my father—totally conscious? I envy that, I want that, I want to be worthy of that. I want to be able to go the same peaceful, caring, compassion-ate way he did. By being concerned about my mother, her well-being, telling her now is the time, he prepared her. That's something that I look forward to."

"Fanchette, will you talk about the teachers who most influenced your life?"

"Abraham Maslow, David Bohm, there is no one who meant more to me than Maslow. Many years ago, a friend who was a psychologist was studying perception and he asked me to participate in his study. I shared with him that for many years I had had this sense of being right on the edge of knowing and then it would slip away. And he said, 'Ah! I know just the book for you to read,' and it was Maslow's *Toward a Psychology of Being* (1968). I read it and I immediately sent off a letter to Maslow. [Serendipitously], it was shortly after that he came to Oklahoma as a guest professor so I met him and went to his classes. In his writing and teaching he explained what was happening using the hierarchy of need, and he attributed it to the evolutionary force in human kind; that you grow, you go for a while, and then you reach a plateau and rest, and then grow some more. You keep what you gained before but you constantly break through to a new cloud. And he said that the moment of peak experience is when you have all the answers to all the questions you ever had, and then of course, when you return to the body, they're gone.[2] This explained for me what I was experiencing when I had that sense of knowing everything I wanted to know but I could not retain it, because that was another dimension from where I was living. I never had the sense of something unusual was happening. I had a sense of a click-click in my head, that this is important, and then there would be some information, and then I would be back not knowing like I had been before, and that's still going on. Maslow gave me the key of ultra lucidity."

"How has that understanding helped you along the spiritual path?" I asked.

"I accepted what was taking place as normal. My sense is when I die I will get a hold of the knowledge and keep it, because I won't be a prisoner in my body anymore."

"Can you talk for a minute about letting go?" I asked.

"That's something we must practice every day, and we can do this by giving our most cherished possessions to people we love. Because eventually we give up everything including our bodies. We need to learn by the time we are 60 that accumulating material things is a myth, that we are not going to take anything with us. I want to fly free."

"Can you speak for a moment about loss?"

"When you have losses in the body it makes what you are still able to do that more precious. When we experience loss and become

---

[2]Moody (1998) wrote, "Peak experiences, according to Maslow, are our healthiest moments. They are those times when we feel the most alive, the most tuned in and balanced—moments when we are clear, free, unencumbered, living at our optimum potential, the best we've ever been" (p. 278).

dependent on another we are giving that person the privilege of being needed. When I was in the hospital flat on my back for 4 months I was deeply grateful but also felt that I could give and take, and that's why they were so loving and so attentive."

Before we concluded our conversation I asked Fanchette to tell a story she shared with me several years ago about an experience that occurred on April 19, 1990. "Suddenly, I was aware of not having any idea whatsoever of who or what I was, and at the same time the perception of hearing a high pitch scream and having the sense in my mind that, 'Oh, that's my ego.' From then on I have known I have a name, Fanchette, and I answer to it but that is not who I am. And I have no idea of who or what I am. None whatsoever! I have been obviously working towards it."

"How does that reconcile with what you talked about, that I am body, mind, and spirit but most of all spirit?"

"I have a body, I have a mind, but that is not who I am. I know I am not what we associate with names, personality, and so forth. It's very liberating. I mean it's not gone, [the ego] it keeps creeping back, but at that moment, it was a sense of total and utter freedom."

"Fanchette, will you sum up your ideas on the experience of spirituality as it relates to aging?"

"To me it is the steadfastness of joy. There have been problems, and some people thought they were very serious problems. I want to emphasize joy because our world is sadly missing it. Joy is health, you know, it has a direct influence on an individual's health and well-being. Joy is just there, it's always been there, and I love it there. It is a sense of bubbling happiness. I used to say fun. But, Allen (Fanchette's husband) in his wisdom said, 'You mean joy, you have the joy of being.' There is the awe, there is the wonder, and it is all joy.

"We are here to manifest who we are, we are here to create Heaven on Earth. So we cannot differentiate between the spirit and the physical self, the body, they are all one thing. What animates the body is the spirit, when the spirit flies off you have a corpse, and it's not much good to anybody!

"Here are my final thoughts: Let go of judgment, cultivate joy, be thankful, love all—knowing that it is all you. Practice letting go daily those things that hold great value and meaning. During our lives, we do not work to determine what kind of older person we will be. Elders work hard at becoming wise through practicing meditation, giving, and simply being. An elder is a guide, a teacher, a guru. And, we teach nothing that we are not living. To be an elder demands that an individual lives who she or he is. An elder's life is an expression of who they truly are.

"Above all, in preparing for successful aging, there must be that dimension of acceptance of the process. You cannot age successfully and resent the process. And that's already true in your twenties! Successful aging in the spiritual sense is being happy."

Our perception of the aging process is deeply affected by the beliefs we choose to embrace. Fanchette grew up in the midst of war and great struggle. Yet her father, who was a mystic, brought a perspective to these life experiences that stretched the boundaries we tend to impose on our lives. Rather than speaking of one reality—that which is visible and measurable—Fanchette's father and other teachers opened her mind to the possibility of multiple realities, unseen, yet profoundly present and felt.

If, as we age, we consciously and mindfully choose a way of being that accepts and practices a belief that we are more than our bodies and minds, and, in fact, that we are primarily spirit and the body is merely a tool for the spirit to relate to the world, then the experience of growing old, as we see from Fanchette's example, is very different, and it may be argued, in many ways more natural. In nature, the process of birth, growth, decline, and death is simply seen as that which is. Nature does not judge the processes of life and dying as being good or bad. The physical being is not meant to last, and the letting go of the body with grace comes naturally if one accepts that the body or even the mind is only part of what life is all about. Coming to a place where the spirit is invited to express itself through the personality is also what life is all about.

Old age is a good time to do the work of letting go and exploring the inner world. In a talk on aging and change Ram Dass (1992) noted that aging works to the spiritual advantage. This is a time when our hearing and vision goes, and we might not be able to move around as easily as when we were younger. In his talk, Ram Dass exclaimed, "This is the ideal time to meditate! Isn't this the optimal time to sit down and shut up and to really listen inward? And yet, we treat it as a failing." As the functions of the body decline, we tend to focus on what we have lost rather than on the message the body is giving us; slow it down, listen inwardly. The body seems to be saying, "Follow my lead, don't resist!" By paying attention to the lessons the body is expressing and through resting silently, we begin to notice that other activity is occurring, not within the body or the mind, but deeper. This quieting process comes naturally as we move into the final stages of life and toward death, and, as Ram Dass notes, "the way in which we relate to death is a function of how much we are identified with that which dies." In other words, how we perceive the last phase of our lives is deeply affected by how attached we are to the body and all of its troubles.

In the talk on aging and change Ram Dass (1992) often used the metaphor of cultivation. He encouraged us to cultivate a sense of wonderment and joy, while at the same time discouraging the denial of the aging process. This denial is in fact an attachment to the body and personality, and these two aspects of our being are aging. Yet, as Fanchette and Ram Dass stress, that the reality is that who we are has no age. The spirit, or indwelling entity, or higher Self—whatever you choose to call it—does not age, does not grow old and die. It simply is. It is timeless. We are timeless.

To consciously choose to be in touch with this aspect of our being is the most important work of life and particularly of the second half of life. Barbara Myerhoff's book, *Number Our Days* (1978) tells the story of elderly Jews living in southern California who face incredible problems including poverty, inadequate housing, and physical danger. The story captures the great dignity and inner strength these individuals brought to each and every struggle. It is a rare documentation of the power of the human spirit. In the book, Heschel, one of the older Jewish men, talked about pain being "an avenue to the soul" (p. 197). He continues:

> So when pain comes, I am patient. I shut up, active silence . . . I call the pain out. After you go through this you discover you got choices. You become whole. This is the task of our life. I want to live this kind of life, so I can be alive every minute. I want to know when I am awake, I'm altogether awake. (p. 197)

Here, Heschel conveys what Ram Dass also asserts, that old age is a time to be silent and practice active listening. To become friends with all aspects of our being, including the body, and yes, even the pain. The choice to do so must be a conscious one.

This process of conscious choice is sometimes perceived as being part of the process of becoming an elder. Rabbi Schachter-Shalomi

(1995) defined elders this way: "Elders go through a conscious and deliberate growth, becoming sages who are capable of guiding their families and communities with hard-earned wisdom" (p. 16). Like Ram Dass and Heschel, Schachter-Shalomi also noted that to become an elder we must slow down and learn to be quiet.

Unfortunately, the typical administrative goals for most gerontological and geriatric programs do not include encouraging the client or resident to actively choose silence or quietness and to settle into inward reflection. Often, the expression of spiritual values and spiritual work is left to whomever has been designated as the pastoral counselor or religious staff. This practice denies the reality that inner work does not begin when in walks the spiritual staff and stops when counseling is completed. Instead, "spirituality should be understood as a soulful quest, path or journey" (Miller, 1999, p. 39).

So how do we know when someone is doing inner work, is seeking the inner path and not withdrawing into a state of depression and isolation? The first piece of advice is to simply ask! Also, as Fanchette and others have noted, if one is involved in inner exploration there will be a sense of unity, of completeness, or a movement toward completeness. Myerhoff (1978) wrote about Jacob who, through his autobiographical writing, explored the questions "What has it all meant?" and "Why was I here?" As a way of conveying the importance of writing as a means of making sense of one's life, Myerhoff quoted Olney (1973) who wrote *Metaphors of Self: The Meaning of Autobiography*: "Through autobiography man creates by the very act of seeking, that order he would have . . . [looking for] a oneness of self, an integrity or internal harmony that holds together the multiplicity and continual transformation of being" (p. 221). Look for this sense of oneness, the integrity and connectedness with all that is. The person will be very present, right there with the moment. There will be a state of grace and harmony and peace.

If an individual who serves the old is interested in encouraging, accepting, and acknowledging the reality of spiritual activity and its role in late life growth and change, then he or she needs to be willing *to be* with the individual who is moving along this path. How well we connect with persons who are on a spiritual quest is determined by our own state of being. By reading books like this one that share insights on spiritual aging; by practicing meditation; and by cultivating an openness to the wonders, joys, and lessons the inner world offers, we are preparing ourselves to sit with elders and to know them as they are. Our goal is to connect with the indwelling entity and to become one with the spiritual being. This practice will also directly influence the way we grow old, and it will move us from the state of believing (mind) to a state of knowing (heart).

Boerstler's (1982) tiny but profound book titled, *Letting Go: A Holistic and Meditative Approach to Living and Dying,* provides guidance and understanding on how to be with someone when he or she is experiencing inner transformations that are inherent in the living and dying processes. It is not surprising that mediation and breathing are the focus of his work. Boerstler noted that: "Meditation is the most profound means of 'letting go' . . . sharing the breath of another person during this transformation of consciousness is a most sacred experience . . . it is said that breath connects all life to consciousness." Miller (1999) expressed a similar idea when he wrote that the spirit is the "animating force, the energy of life . . . the breath of life and of inspiration" (p. 39). Through meditation and breathing we are able to connect first with our own spiritual energy, and then with the timeless, ageless being within each and every person our lives touch.

On a final note, as persons move along on the spiritual journey, they do so not with a sense of withdrawal and isolation. In fact, the opposite is true. As we seek to explore the inner depths and make contact with the higher Self there comes an acceptance of one another, an inner unity. There is a completeness, a wholeness, and an inner spaciousness that makes room for all of humanity and all of life.

In closing, I would like to return to the quote from Florida Scott-Maxwell's book, *The Measure of My Days* (1968) that appears at the beginning of this chapter. It reads, "It will be at our peril if we put all our faith in the measurable, and dishonour that which lies beyond statement" (p. 64). When we insist on using measurable outcomes, visible, concrete outcomes to determine the quality of life, we do a great disservice to the old in our society. For it is the immeasurable quality of the spirit that is the true essence of life. It is our responsibility and our privilege to open ourselves to this basic truth. Through practice we will come to know the elders in our lives as they are, and this knowing, while immeasurable, is priceless.

REFERENCES

Atchley, R. C. (1993). Spiritual development and wisdom: A vedantic perspective. In R. Kastenbaum (Eds.), *Encyclopedia of adult development* (pp. 479–483). Phoenix: The Oryx Press.

Boerstler, R. W. (1982). *Letting go: A holistic and meditative approach to living and dying.* Watertown, MA: Associates in Thanatology.

Maslow, A. (1968). *Toward a psychology of being.* Princeton, NJ: Van Nostrand Reinhold.

Metzner, R. (1998). *The unfolding self: Varieties of transformative experience.* Novato, CA: Origin Press.

Miller, M. E. (1999). Religious and ethical strivings in the later years: Three paths to spiritual maturity and integrity. In L. E. Thomas & S. A. Eisenhandler (Eds.), *Religion, belief, and spirituality in late life* (pp. 35–58). New York: Springer.

Moody, H. R. (1998). *Aging: Concepts and controversies.* Thousand Oaks, CA: Pine Forge Press.

Moody, H. R., & Carroll, D. (1997). *The five stages of the soul.* New York: Doubleday.

Myerhoff, B. (1978). *Number our days.* New York: Simon and Schuster.

Olney, J. (1973). *Metaphors of self: The meaning of autobiography.* Princeton, NJ: Princeton University Press.

Ram Dass (speaker). (1992). *Aging and change.* (Cassette Recording No. 1/ 1, Omega Conference on Aging). San Anselmo, CA: Hanuman Foundation Tape Library.

Ram Dass (1998). "Being" in the moment. In E. J. Rosen (Ed.), *Experiencing the soul: Before birth, during life, and after death* (pp. 157–168). Carlsbad, CA: Hay House.

Schachter-Shalomi, Z., & Miller, R. S. (1995). *From age-ing to sage-ing: A vision of growing older.* New York: Warner Books.

Scott-Maxwell, F. (1968). *The measure of my days.* New York: Viking Penguin.

Thich Naht Hanh (1998a). *The heart of the Buddha's teaching.* Berkeley, CA: Parallax Press.

Thich Naht Hanh (1998b). *Interbeing: Fourteen guidelines for engaged Buddhism.* Berkeley, CA: Parallax Press.

CHAPTER 12

The Job Hypothesis: Gerotranscendence and Life Satisfaction Among Elderly Turkish Muslims

L. Eugene Thomas

The first time I became aware of Lars Tornstam's work was in a 1992 Forum article in *The Gerontologist* in which he questioned the cultural assumptions that have found their way into our gerontological theories. In particular, he called attention to the almost religious fervor with which the Disengagement theory was attacked by most gerontologists and suggested that their animosity reflects the valorization of goals of productivity, effectiveness, and independence that pervade our culture and have seeped into our social science theories. In the article he went on to suggest, partly tongue in cheek, that we play with the thought that unproductivity, ineffectiveness, and dependency be considered as guiding values for our treatment of the elderly (Tornstam, 1992).

I was intrigued when Tornstam made reference to his concept of gerotranscendence in which he sought to develop a theory from the perspective of the elderly themselves, without placing our own theoretical caps on their heads. For a number of years I had been working on the question of optimal personality development with age, and had come to the conclusion that there seemed to be a more contemplative quality among those elderly persons who were aging well. Although one did not dare breathe the word "disengagement" in gerontological circles, it was clear that the Activity theory of successful aging was seriously flawed. The theory of gerotranscendence offered a way of avoiding a choice between the horns of the dilemma of Activity versus Disengagement theories.

Lars and I struck up a correspondence and ended up doing collaborative cross-cultural research on the theory of gerotranscendence. In particular, we wanted to determine the applicability of the theory in as many different cultural settings as possible and with groups known to hold allegiance to cultural goals differing from that of mainstream society.

My own research has taken me to Turkey, as I sought to gain a cross-cultural perspective on this topic. Rather than attempting to test the applicability of the gerotranscendence theory to Turkish culture in general, in this paper I would like to examine an interesting subhypothesis that emerged as I conducted my research over the course of a year. I have titled this formulation the Job Hypothesis.

In the prologue to the Book of Job, one of the most interesting in the Hebrew Bible, we learn two important facts about Job: he is a devout man, and he is very wealthy. With Oriental hyperbole, we are told that he had 7,000 sheep, 3,000 camels, 500 yoke of oxen, 500 she-asses, and very many servants. He also had seven sons and three daughters, who apparently got along very well and shared family feasts and celebrations on a regular basis.

Then the scene shifts to the higher regions, where God and Satan were having a conversation. When the Lord pointed out to Satan how righteous his servant Job was, Satan observed that given all the wealth the Lord had bestowed on him, there was little wonder that Job was religious. Satan then threw down a challenge to the Lord, "Put forth thy hand now and touch all that he has, and he will curse thee to thy face" (Job 1:9, Revised Standard Version). This we might dub the "Satan Hypothesis" of life satisfaction, that is, that high life satisfaction is contingent on physical comfort, social support, good health, and so forth.

Thereafter, a series of disasters struck Job, in which he successively lost his sheep, his camels, his oxen, and even his sons and daughters. As if that were not enough, Job was afflicted with loathsome sores, and became a laughing stock of society. With this Satan apparently won the bet, because Job, although not cursing God, defended his righteousness before scoffing friends and accused God of perpetrating injustice against him. Not only that, but Job showed every evidence of having low life satisfaction, if we compare his comments to our current gerontic criteria:

"Let the day perish wherein I was born, and the night which said, 'a man child is conceived.' Let that day be darkness" (3:3–4). This would be an instance of regret for the past on the life satisfaction scale.

"For my sighing comes as my bread, and my groanings are poured out like water" (3:24). This serves as an expression of low mood tone.

"I am not at ease, nor am I quiet; I have no rest, but trouble comes" (3:26). He does not take pleasure in everyday events.

Here is a man with very low life satisfaction by any measure we might use. On the other hand, one would gather that before his misfortune he was high in life satisfaction. So one might conclude that life satisfaction is dependent on health and worldly wealth, and as these decrease, life satisfaction decreases. It might be noted that much of the current research on the correlates of life satisfaction fall in line with the formulation of the Satan Hypothesis.

But the story of Job does not end there. After many chapters of lamentations by Job and reproaches by his friends, a strange thing happened. We are told that the Lord finally answered Job out of the whirlwind. There follows the magnificent passages when the Lord questioned Job:

"Where were you when I laid the foundations of the earth? . . . when the morning stars sang together and all the sons of God shouted for joy?" (38:4,7).

"Have you commanded the morning since your days began, and caused the dawn to know its place, that it might take hold of the skirts of the earth, and the wicked be shaken out of it?" (38:12–13).

As a result of this experience Job affirmed, "I had heard of thee by hearing of the ear, but now my eyes see thee" (42:5). After this theophany, Job was a changed man, no longer complaining about his hardships and losses. The extent to which his life was changed by this experience is suggested by the fact that the Lord blessed Job and restored his fortune twofold: 14,000 sheep, 6,000 camels, 1,000 she-asses, and so forth. Again, one can assume that this is Oriental hyperbole, by which the writer meant to say that Job's life was transformed by this experience, and thereafter he lived a long and contented life.

The Job Hypothesis suggests that without a sense of the transcendent, Satan was right: losses in old age lead to low life satisfaction. With a sense of the transcendent, or shall we say the gerotranscendent, life satisfaction will remain high, whether a person retains his health and possessions or suffers the losses of Job. In an idealized prediction of the hypothesis, we would expect to find persons high in both gerotranscendence and life satisfaction as well as persons low in both gerotranscendence and life satisfaction. According to the idealized model, we would not expect to find people with high life satisfaction if they were low in gerotranscendence, nor would we expect to find persons high in gerotranscendence but low in life satisfaction.

THE DATA COLLECTION PROCESS

I conducted this research in Turkey, a predominately Muslim country that is rapidly modernizing, with a secular government and a Western orientation. Turkey was of particular interest because it is the home of a number of Sufi religious orders. Sufism is the mystical branch of Islam, and I was interested to learn how persons of this orientation handle the challenges of aging. Also, as a comparison, I interviewed elderly persons who were not particularly religious. For both groups, I selected persons who were viewed in their community as being especially mature. I did not define for my informants what I meant by maturity, but asked them to go by the standards of the community to which the person belonged. This method of sample selection by lay nomination is similar to the method used by Baltes and his colleagues in their Berlin wisdom studies (Baltes, Staudinger, Maercker, & Smith, 1995), except that I did not limit my sample to public figures as they did.

For the interviews, I employed a research assistant who was knowledgeable of the religious community and who served as an interpreter for Turkish-speaking respondents. In open-ended interviews, I explored their present situation and attitudes, as well as past experiences that led them to where they are now. Since the concept of gerotranscendence was a major focus of this study, questions that tapped the different dimensions of the theory were incorporated into the interview. These questions were developed in collaboration with Lars Tornstam and a member of his research team, Fereshteh Ahmadi, who spent 10 days working with me in Turkey, taking part in several interviews, engaging in participant observation, and helping to develop procedures for coding interview protocols for gerotranscendence.

Two or more interviews were conducted with each informant, and where possible I observed respondents in interaction with family members and others. Following the strategy of grounded theory (Glaser & Strauss, 1967), interview tapes were transcribed verbatim upon completion, and field notes on participant observation were recorded throughout the duration of the research.

Again, in the tradition of grounded theory, interviewing continued until pattern saturation was reached, that is, subsequent interviews did not produce new categories (Strauss & Corbin, 1990). This research strategy provides in-depth information on a relatively small number of respondents. Specifically, I conducted interviews and participant observation with 19 informants in Ankara and with 13 persons in Istanbul. Contact was established with and informal interviews and observations made with several other persons who were not included in the sample because of age (only persons 65 and older were included) or because, for various reasons, complete interviews could not be conducted.

Of the entire sample, 15 were chosen who were devoutly practicing the Muslim religion. Four of this number were shaikhs, that is, spiritual leaders of Sufi tarikats (two each from the Naqshibendi and Kadiri Orders), and an additional eight who were identified with the Sufi tradition. The religious group was predominately male (14 of 15). Most of these interviews were conducted in Turkish (13 of 15). Although I made special effort to find elderly women who were considered spiritually mature and religious, informants were unable to come up with names. It was not clear whether this was due to an inadequate sampling net or whether it reflects the state of religious identification in this population.

Seventeen individuals were interviewed for the nonreligious sample: eight women and nine men. Members of this group, being more Westernized, were more likely to speak English, and almost half of the interviews (eight) were conducted in English, with occasional assistance from the research assistant. Individuals in this group ranged in age from 69 to 87, with an average age of 78.4; the average age for the religious group was 78.6, ranging from 66 to 83. The groups differed somewhat on educational level; all of the secular sample had a college education, with five attaining graduate degrees. Ten of the 15 religious individuals were college graduates, with four of them holding advanced degrees. Of the remaining members of the religious sample, four had only grade school education, and one had completed high school. It should be noted that the educational level of both groups is considerably higher than the average for Turkey (and the United States for that matter), reflecting the elite nature of these samples, selected from persons regarded in their community as being mature.

CODING, EXCERPTS, AND INSIGHTS

Interview transcripts were coded for eight dimensions posited by the gerotranscendence theory (Tornstam, 1996): (1) unitive cosmology; (2) self-understanding; (3) decrease in self-centeredness; (4) everyday wisdom; (5) meaning and importance of relationships; (6) mystery dimension of life; (7) view of own mortality; and (8) attitude toward material assets. Table 12.1 gives the relevant elements of these dimensions. Each interview protocol was rated on all of these dimensions independently by two scorers, utilizing a 5-point Likert scale. Rater agreement of 80% or higher was achieved for the overall sample, and scoring disagreements were resolved by means of consultation.

Likewise, a coding scale was devised for measuring life satisfaction from a global reading of the interviews, in which the five dimensions of the concept (Neugarten, Havighurst, & Tobin, 1961) were rated: (1) zest vs. apathy; (2) resolution and fortitude; (3) congruence between desired and achieved goals; (4) positive self-concept; and (5) mood tone. As with the gerotranscendence coding, each interview was coded independently by two raters on a 5-point Likert scale,

TABLE 12.1 Dimensions of Gerotranscendence

Dimension	Description
Unitive cosmology	Sense of greater connection with earlier generations Borders between past and present decreased Transcending barriers (e.g., spiritual communication) Diminished boundaries between self and others
Self-under-standing	Awareness of one's good and bad qualities Questioning previous conceptions of self
Decrease in self-centeredness	Sensitive to the needs and feelings of others Increase in altruism and concern for safety Ambitions and goals less self-centered
Everyday wisdom	Practical wisdom and understanding of the human condition Less ideological, more pragmatic More tolerant of human foibles
Meaning and importance of relationships	Transcends conventional socially defined relationships Less superficial relationships with others Less feeling of competitiveness Need for solitude
Mystery dimension of life	Aware that there is more to life than rational knowledge Sense of the "numinous" dimension of the world
View of own mortality	Not afraid of death, *AND* View of life as continuing beyond death New way of looking at life and death
Attitude toward material assets	Little concern with material assets Real happiness based on immaterial assets Material assets seen as a means (e.g., help others) not as an end in themselves

with rater agreement of 85% or higher; disagreements were worked out through consultation between raters.

There was clear evidence of gerotranscendence in some, but far from all, of our respondents. In fact, almost half of the respondents, including three who were nominated as being very religious, were found to be almost totally lacking in gerotranscendence. Only 5 of the 32 respondents were found to exhibit the full range of gerotranscendence. Interestingly, one of these was not nominated as being religious, while two of the remaining four were Sufi shaikhs.

To give a feeling for the quality of gerotranscendence found along the nonreligious, it might be beneficial to turn to the interview with Mr. Derinsu, an 82-year-old retired diplomat, who scored at the top of both the gerotranscendence scale and the life satisfaction measure. It was interesting that in spite of his obvious spiritual interest, his outward appearance of secularism led him to being nominated for the nonreligious group.

An indication of his level of life satisfaction, along with his awareness of the transcendent, is suggested by his response to the question: "What is your biggest regret, looking back on your life?"

> I don't have any regrets. I always thank God for his help; I believe in Him wholeheartedly. And God for me—I am a pantheist. I see God everywhere. When I look at the beautiful flower, I feel my heart trembling, saying, "How did You create these things?" I believe in Him wholeheartedly.

When I asked him if there had been any change in the way he looks at himself with age, he replied:

> Well, first of all, with age I become more tolerant. People criticize youth for their music, their behavior. At their age perhaps I was doing the same thing. My elders were criticizing me, but I accept them as they are.

Later, in response to the question, "Have your relationships with people changed?" his response was:

> Yes. As I said, it has been sweetened by years. I used to get angry at a thing, a statement. But today I don't get angry any more. . . . And I learned keeping quiet. [Silence (chuckling).] This is one of the blessings of age. You don't disturb yourself, and you don't disturb others either.

More typical of the quality of gerotranscendence found among the respondents were responses of persons like Shaikh Acar and Mr. Ortakara, both of whom were highly religious. Mr. Ortakara lives with his third wife. His first wife died leaving him childless, and his second wife and young daughter were killed in a car accident. He has turned over his wholesale grocery business to his two nephews, who look on him as their father. When he is not at the mosque, Mr. Ortakara spends his days at the business, entertaining a parade of friends and family members who come by to consult with him or just to spend time with him. What was remarkable about Mr. Ortakara was his infectious zest for life and concern for other people, despite the fact that he is almost blind from glaucoma. The following excerpts give a feel for his transcendent view of reality and how it is reflected in his life.

I.   What regrets do you have for the past?

O.   I would change nothing in my past. Because I believe that this life is provisional and temporary. The second life is forever.

I.   How often do you think of death?

O.   I never forget about death.

I.   Are you afraid of death?

O.   I am never afraid of death. Wholeheartedly I want to meet God as soon as possible. Nowadays everything has been delegated to my brother's sons. Everything is in strong hands now, so I have nothing to worry about. I am expecting to join Allah.

I.   Have you had any special prayers answered?

O.   Actually, all of them are. I never wish for anything for myself. I don't pray for my own well-being, but for all mankind on earth. Not just Muslims, but for members of other religions also. For the safety and happiness of mankind. Also for the happiness of the creatures, the plants and animals, all of them.

I.   Has your relationship with your family changed over the years?

O.   My nephews are like very close friends. And the wives of my nephews, they are also good friends with me. Whenever they have difficulty, instead of consulting their husbands, they consult me.

Mr. Ortakara has only a grade school education and is basically self-taught, although he did have a Sufi shaikh who was his mentor in the early years. By contrast, Shaikh Acar was trained in medicine, with a specialty in psychiatry. Despite educational differences, they share a similar transcendent view of the world, colored by their Muslim upbringing and culture, but distinct in many respects. In the cases of Sh. Acar and Mr. Ortakara, their beliefs and attitudes were grounded in their own experience, particularly the transforming experiences they had while on pilgrimage to Mecca. For instance, when I asked Sh. Acar if going on pilgrimage when he was 37 had an impact on his life, he replied:

O. Yes, to be in Mecca is a turning point. The pilgrimage is to approach God with love. In ordinary life the approach to God is through knowledge. But in Mecca, when you perform pilgrimage, you approach with spiritual love.

I. You said last time that going to Mecca was like a time tunnel. Could you explain a little what you meant by that?

O. Hajj is a kind of space tunnel. The entrance of the spirit into the space tunnel is Mecca. You pass over the threshold, you pass over complete worlds into another world. The spirits of all human creatures, Prophet Adam to the end of the world, all these spirits are there, especially on Mt. Arafat.

I. Did you experience this yourself at Mt. Arafat?

O. Yes. There is great mercy of God in that place. Despite many difficulties, the spirit is anxious to go there. I have been to Mecca many times, but only two times for myself, and the rest as a representative for others.

The importance of service to others was a recurrent theme in the interviews of Sh. Acar and Mr. Ortakara, as it was among others exhibiting high gerotranscendence. For Sh. Acar, however, it was a mission in life. When he completed his residency in psychiatry over 30 years ago, he opened what he calls his "office" in a poor section of Ankara. From this storefront center he has worked with what we would call street people, more particularly, the mentally ill, providing them with food, and a sympathetic ear.

When I asked Sh. Acar what his greatest accomplishment was, he replied without hesitating:

> Service to mankind. If a man serves other people, it can be considered beneficial to mankind. Great spiritual revelations that some people claim to have, they are not as important as giving service.

Five persons exhibiting the highest level of gerotranscendence also exhibited the highest level of life satisfaction. To say that they were happy, although true, does not do justice to the qualities they displayed. A more accurate description would be to say that they radiated a remarkable sense of contentment with their lives and a keen appreciation for life at the present moment. Significantly, other people seemed to pick up these qualities and to be attracted to them. What was especially remarkable was the interest and attention they were given by close family members. For example, while Mr. Ortakara and I were talking, his grandson (actually, his nephew's son) came into the room. He just beamed as Mr. Ortakara hugged him and gave him a kiss on each cheek. Later when I asked how he recognized his grandson, with his loss of vision, he chuckled and replied, "He smells better than the most beautiful flowers."

High life satisfaction, however, was not limited to those high on gerotranscendence. Although more dispersed on the life satisfaction measure, with some displaying low satisfaction, many who were low on gerotranscendence displayed high zest for life, satisfaction with their past accomplishments, and acceptance of their past without regret. For example, Mrs. Kutrulu, a spry 86-year-old, has lived alone since her husband died over 40 years ago. She recounted how her husband and mother died within a period of 6 months. When I allowed as how that must have been a hard time for her, she replied:

> Well, I think maybe I was realistic. Of course I was sad. But I accepted it, because there was no other thing to do (chuckling). And I tried to help them as far as I could.

As she described her present life it was clear that this realistic acceptance of whatever came along still prevailed. Although she saw her accomplishments as modest, she harbored no regrets about the past and continued to find pleasure in her daily routine.

From the beginning of the interview, she made it clear that she did not subscribe to any religious beliefs, which she pretty much held in contempt. She went on to explain that she had no belief in life after death, and viewed death as "a chemical matter." When I asked her if she had ever felt herself in the presence of a power greater than herself, that lifted her out of herself, she chuckled, and replied:

> I don't ever think so. I hope I don't have something like that. I don't like to have higher than myself.

Mrs. Kutrulu was not typical of my informants, however. Most of those in the sample, even persons who were otherwise the most secular, and who were not practicing Muslims, still believed in the basic tenets of the faith, including the existence of God, life after death, and so forth. For instance, Mr. Ozkok, an 86-year-old former member of Parliament and a staunch Kemalist (i.e., believer in the secular state established by Ataturk), holds these basic Muslim beliefs, although he does not perform daily prayers, fast during the month of Ramadan, and so forth. He feels strongly that the Islamic religion needs to be reformed, and said that he quit going to mosque for prayer when the call to worship was changed back to Arabic, from the Turkish that had been imposed by Ataturk in the early days of the Republic.

But, like Mrs. Kutrulu, Mr. Ozkok was at the top of the life satisfaction measure. As a member of Parliament, and since, he has devoted his life to fighting for social justice, and working for causes still commands most of his time. When I asked him if he has changed much over the years, he replied,

O.	I entered into politics at a young age, and I was very aggressive all the time. I always fought for the things I thought good. And I still continue to do it, for the things that are good. I write articles for magazines, and I criticize the existing politics. My struggling life still continues.

I.	Do you have a pretty firm sense of identity; that is, who you are now?

O.	To be very active, is my identity. To work very hard. And to try to impose my ideas on others.

Despite this driven desire to be active, Mr. Ozkok is clearly high in life satisfaction at the present time. This is probably due to the fact that, although he is 86 years old, he is able to remain active in numerous projects and causes, planning his days a week in advance, attending some meeting or affair several times a week, reading two newspapers everyday, watching television news, and so forth. It was clear that he took pleasure in all of these activities. Being a relatively nonintrospective man, he holds little regret for past decisions and feels satisfied with what he has accomplished in his life.

Not all of those in the sample who were low on gerotranscendence were as high in life satisfaction as Mrs. Kutrulu and Mr. Ozkok, however. Mr. Erkat, now very active in his religious practice, spends more time ruminating on the past than either of them. He still regrets the way he neglected his first wife and what he perceives as his contribution to her death, which occurred over a quarter of a century ago. Rather than being pleased with his clear memory of the past, he observed:

> I picked up everything in my memory, and it is a garbage box. I realize that I learned many things when I was younger, but not what I should have. If I could go back 50 years, I could have learned more basic things and more positive things, instead of using my mind as a garbage can.

There were also nonreligious persons with low scores on both gerotranscendence and life satisfaction. Mrs. Remzi, a young 76 years old, lives with her husband in a very comfortable flat in the embassy section of Ankara. They are both in good health and socialize with a group of friends who they had known before retirement. Both she and her husband have advanced degrees and taught at the college level, and both had been successful in their careers. In fact, Mrs. Remzi served as dean of her college for several years.

Despite what outwardly would appear an almost idyllic retirement life, Mrs. Remzi has begun to think about death during the past 2 years and dreads being left alone should her husband die before her. At one point I asked her:

I. When you get up in the morning, what do you most look forward to?
O. That's why I say it is rather boring these years, because I have nothing serious to accomplish. Reading books. Going outside, just to be in a crowd with people. I go to the cinema alone because my husband won't go.
I. Do you have anyone you confide in about your personal thoughts and feelings?
O. Yeah, I'm confiding in you now.
I. You are, indeed, and I appreciate it.

Earlier she had told about a time during the military coup in the 1970s, while she was dean of her college, when she and other professionals were arrested and kept in prison for 9 months. As she told about this experience, her face lit up, as she relived the excitement of the period, concluding:

> That was the cream of my life. I never dreamed that something like that existed. I enjoyed it because I was in there with young teachers. And politicians. All educated people. You became conscious; you knew more about your country, knew more about everything that you just passed over before, without noticing.

Later, when I asked her what the title would be if a book were written about her life, she replied:

O. "Portrait of a professional woman between 1920 and 1972." From the time I was born, until the time of imprisonment.
I. Did your life end then?
O. No [quickly]. But it did, in a way. I have so much free time. I don't start anything new. I should.

Actually, Mrs. Remzi's low level of life satisfaction (she was rated 2 on the 5-point scale) is unusual for this sample. Only two other respondents were scored at the 2 level on the life satisfaction measure, and only one person scored at the lowest level; all the rest were rated at 3 or higher. The woman who rated lowest in the sample, an 80-year-old professional woman, had lost her husband a little over a year ago and was suffering from several degenerative diseases. It should be noted that she was also at the lowest level on the gerotranscendence measure.

DISCUSSION

The fact that persons high in gerotranscendence were also found to be high in life satisfaction can be explained from several different perspectives. At the most obvious level, a transcendent view of life enables persons to place their lives, and whatever suffering they encounter, in a larger and meaningful context. For persons holding traditional Muslim religious beliefs, for example, suffering is seen as the will of God, which the devout are expected to accept as part of their spiritual path. A firm belief in life after death, of which the present life is seen as only a temporary prelude, further enables them to look on misfortune and adversity with equanimity.

But even persons who do not hold orthodox Muslim beliefs, or any religious beliefs for that matter, seem to be able to find meaning in suffering. Viktor Frankl, in his reflections on life in Nazi concentration camps, and his subsequent work with troubled individuals as a psychiatrist, has observed that finding meaning in what happens in one's life is of central importance. Quoting Nietzsche (not exactly noted for his orthodox religious beliefs), he observes, "He who has a *why* to live for can bear with almost any *how*" (1963, p. 121).

Further, the beliefs associated with a transcendent world view—decreased competitiveness, a sense of relatedness to others—might well add to an individual's level of life satisfaction, irrespective of religious beliefs. In a study conducted over 30 years ago, Clark and Anderson (1967) looked at the beliefs and attitudes of a sample of persons living in the San Francisco area who had a history of mental problems and compared them with a sample of elderly persons who were living successfully in the community. They found that the hospitalized group still subscribed to the dominant cultural value orientations of achievement, individualism, and future orientation. By contrast, those successfully residing in the community tended to embrace value orientations that were given only secondary importance in society: cooperation, collegiality, and present time orientation.

It should be noted that these latter values are in several respects similar to the dimensions identified by Tornstam as indicators of gerotranscendence. It is interesting to consider that in the Anderson and Clark study their community sample was not particularly religious. In fact, they note that their community sample was, "an amazingly secularized group of people" (1967, p. 395). They found that less than half attended religious services regularly, and only a third of this group were "reasonably assured of immortality" (p. 338), suggesting that they had different reasons for accepting secondary cultural value orientations than because of their religious beliefs.

It should be remembered, however, that Tornstam's theory does not assume that gerotranscendence is necessarily connected with religion. He posits that it is a naturally occurring phenomenon with age, subject, of course, to cultural influences in the way it is manifested and interpreted. Essentially, the central characteristic of gerotranscendence, Tornstam claims, is that it is a move toward a new "meta-theoretical paradigm" (1989, p. 58), whereby the individual views the world through different cognitive lenses. This may or may not be manifested in religious identification and participation, according to Tornstam. Clark and Anderson's findings are on the whole compatible with the findings of this study, although they did not explore this level of meta-theoretical paradigmatic cognition in their study.

In our sample of nontranscenders we found little evidence of the secondary cultural values that Clark and Anderson speak of, that is, less competitiveness and individualism. In fact, part of the reason for their being scored low on gerotranscendence was the fact that they did not display these qualities to any significant degree. The question arises, then, as to how some of them could be high on life satisfaction, while still holding dominant cultural value orientations.

Reinhold Niebuhr said somewhere that the only alternative to Christianity was Stoicism. Translating this to a less sectarian formulation, Stoicism might serve the same function as gerotranscendence: as a buffer against life's inevitable losses and disappointments. Taking a rough definition of Stoicism as, "living the totally rational, harmonious life, indifferent to pleasure and pain" (Hahm, 1997, p. 520), this was not found to be a commonly held view among the respondents in this study. The one person who clearly seemed to fit that category was Mrs. Kutrulu, mentioned earlier, whose philosophy of handling misfortune was to be "realistic," as when her husband and mother died within 6 months of each other, "because," she said, "there was no other thing to do." Later in the interview, she gave a similar response when asked if she thought about death often:

> No. I saw my mother and my brother when they died. I don't fear death. I know that it will happen, and I accept the reality.

At 86 Mrs. Kutrulu is keenly aware that she could die at any time, and having no close relatives left, has made arrangements with a burial society for her funeral. In the face of this, she still exhibited high life satisfaction, coming out at near the top of the scale.

Far more typical was the attitude of Mr. Ozkok, mentioned earlier, whose sense of identity was "to be very active . . . To work very hard."

This attitude, which is far removed from Stoicism, pervaded Mr. Ozkok's interviews. For example, when I asked him if he had developed a philosophy for handling pain, he replied:

> In order not to be defeated by pain and suffering, I do not want to lie down. Instead, I was to be more active as I get older.

In the same vein, Mr. Payaslioglu, a vigorous 71-year old who still holds a part-time job to supplement his retirement income, gave a telling response to the question, "What do you most dread?"

> To be an invalid. This is the thing that I dread the most. So that's why I am trying. I look young for my age, and am still active. This because I try to FIGHT, expand the youth, push back the old age, as much as you can.

Interestingly, while Mr. Payaslioglu is moderately high in his level of life satisfaction at age 71, Mr. Ozkok is at the top of the life satisfaction measure at age 86, suggesting the staying power of their counterphobic approach to life.

The word "counterphobic" is a clinical term that refers to a defense mechanism adopted by an individual by means of which he or she handles a fear by attacking it head-on. In the case of Mr. Ozkok and Mr. Payaslioglu, their high level of activity definitely appears to be an effective mechanism in maintaining a high level of life satisfaction. But the term "defense mechanism" usually carries an implication of brittleness, of glossing over underlying problems. Whether these persons will remain at such a high level of life satisfaction when they are no longer able to lead active lives remains to be seen, as they face the inevitable losses and diminishments of old age.

From the present cross-sectional study, there is other evidence to suggest that their level of life satisfaction might well decline should illness or some misfortune curtail their high level of activity. An examination of the four persons in the sample rated as being lowest in life satisfaction—two men aged 69 and 92, and two women aged 73 and 80—suggests that current stressful life events have contributed to their present low life satisfaction. There are strong suggestions that three of these four would have been high on life satisfaction had they been interviewed at an earlier point in their lives. Actually,

I had a conversation with one of them 2 years earlier, when I was in Turkey arranging for the research. Mrs. Yavuzer, who was then 78, was still teaching at the university, and lived with her husband in an elegant apartment overlooking the Bosporous. At the time her husband, although not in good health, was a cheerful companion, and helped anchor her busy life. From outward appearance it is reasonable to infer that her life satisfaction was quite high at the time. When I interviewed her 2 years later, her husband had died the previous spring, her health was failing, and her activity level was severely restricted. By then she was living a very isolated and depressed life, which was reflected in her very low score on the life satisfaction measure.

Of the remaining three persons rated low in life satisfaction, two others appeared to have dropped in satisfaction due to negative circumstances: one from isolation imposed by failing eyesight, and the other because of having to give up his home and move into smaller quarters away from his friends. Only one of the three, Mrs. Sahinkaya, seemed to have led a relatively unhappy life, even before her husband's stroke and her daughter's marital problems. But these are only speculative reconstructions. Trying to determine earlier life satisfaction from cross-sectional interview data must remain tentative. Only longitudinal research can give us firm data on the issue.

CONCLUSION

These data can be seen to provide support for the central claim of the postulated Job Hypothesis. High levels of gerotranscendence were found to be associated with high levels of life satisfaction, with no respondents being rated with high gerotranscendence and low life satisfaction. Like Job, they had come to know God, or the transcendent, from first hand experience, not from second hand hearsay knowledge. This change in their view of ultimate reality was reflected in their personal lives in important ways, such that they were able to find meaning in losses and misfortune that might have led to despair, and like Job were experiencing a high level of contentment and satisfaction in their later years.

There were some in the sample who displayed low levels of both gerotranscendence and life satisfaction. When they were faced with far less than Job's proverbial losses of 3,000 camels, 500 yokes of oxen, and 500 she-asses, these individuals failed to find meaning in their lot, and fell into despair, much like the early Job. This phenomenon provides support for the Satan Hypothesis, that is, Satan's assertion that if Job lost all the comforts God had bestowed on him, he would curse his fate and despair of life.

But persons exhibiting low gerotranscendence and high life satisfaction provide a potential challenge to both the Job Hypothesis and the Satan Hypothesis. According to the theory of gerotranscendence, persons who have a low sense of gerotranscendence can be high in life satisfaction only as long as they face no major loses and misfortunes. Likewise, these persons present a potential challenge to the Satan Hypothesis, which holds that high life satisfaction is possible only so long as one has physical comfort and social support. The question arises for both theories: is it really true that the nine persons who displayed high life satisfaction and low gerotranscendence have not experienced significant misfortune and losses?

Although we only have self-reports to go on, the evidence would seem to point to a negative answer to the question. Among those who displayed high life satisfaction, despite being low in gerotranscendence, there were instances of loss of spouse, health problems, financial limitations, and so forth, which might well have undermined their level of life satisfaction. As noted above, there are other approaches to life that might allow individuals to handle such losses without falling into despair. The Stoic stance, exhibited by at least one respondent, appears to provide a sufficient buffer against the inevitable losses of old age to allow a high level of life satisfaction. The prospect, at least in the case of Mrs. Kutrulu would seem to be that her "realistic" approach will take her through whatever hardships she undergoes in the future.

More common was the stance that we termed the "counterphobic" strategy, whereby the individual maintains a high level of professed life satisfaction by remaining constantly active. The question arises as to whether this strategy, although effective for a time, might prove to be limited, given the inevitable losses and physical insults of aging. Although based on retrospective data from respondents who are presently low in life satisfaction, there was the suggestion that those who were found to have low levels of both gerotranscendence and life satisfaction may represent the eventual fate of those whose counterphobic strategies permit them to have a high level of life satisfaction now. But longitudinal data would be necessary to address the issue more directly.

In conclusion, it can be said that these data provide at least partial support for the Job Hypothesis. Like Job after his experience with the Divine, persons who have a transcendental view of the world were found to be uniformly high in life satisfaction. The fact that there were persons high in life satisfaction who were low on gerotranscendence can be made to fit into theory only if we assume that all such persons have not suffered adversities up to this time, a view that does not seem to fit the data. Likewise, such an assumption would be required to salvage the Satan Hypothesis. Further, the Satan Hypothesis is presented with an additional challenge by those persons whose transcendent view of reality enables them, like the later Job, to live a contented life in their old age. Perhaps our current gerontic theories of successful aging stand in need of a bit of revision in light of these findings.

If a conclusion is to be drawn concerning the theory of gerotranscendence, it would be that this study provides overall support of the theory, but raises questions about possible generalizations (though not posited by Tornstam) that some enthusiasts may imply concerning the theory. Specifically, the fact that there is strong support for the claim that gerotranscendence is positively related to life satisfaction does not necessarily mean that a gerotranscendent view of the world is necessary for there to be high life satisfaction, even in times of adversity. Human personality seems to be too complex and subjective judgment of well-being too idiosyncratic to allow us to predict outcomes such as this with any degree of certainty.

REFERENCES

Baltes, P., Staudinger, U., Maercker, A., & Smith, J. (1995). People nominated as wise: A comparative study of wisdom-related knowledge. *Psychology and Aging, 10,* 155–156.

Clark, M., & Anderson, B. (1967). *Culture and aging: An anthropological study of older Americans.* Springfield, IL: Charles Thomas.

Frankl, V. (1963). *Man's search for meaning: An introduction to logotherapy.* New York: Washington Square Press.

Glaser, B., & Strauss, A. (1967). *The discovery of grounded theory*. Chicago: Aldine.

Hahm, D. (1997). The Stoa and stoicism. In D. J. Zeyl (Ed.), *Encyclopedia of classical philosophy* (pp. 527–537). Westport, CT: Greenwood Press.

Neugarten, B., Havighurst, R., & Tobin, S. (1961). The measurement of life satisfaction. *Journal of Gerontology, 16*, 134–143.

Strauss, A., & Corbin, J. (1990). *Basics of qualitative research*. Newbury Park, CA: Sage.

Tornstam, L. (1989). Gero-transcendence: A reformulation of the disengagement theory. *Aging, 1*, 55–63

Tornstam, L. (1992). The quo vadis of gerontology: On the scientific paradigm of gerontology. *The Gerontologist, 32*, 318–326.

Tornstam, L. (1996). Gerotranscendence—A theory about maturing into old age. *Journal of Aging and Identity, 1*, 37–49.

CHAPTER 13

Chronos to *Kairos*: Christian Perspectives on Time and Aging

Susan H. McFadden and Jane M. Thibault

> Now after John was arrested, Jesus came to Galilee, proclaiming the good news of God, and saying, "The time is fulfilled, and the kingdom of God has come near; repent, and believe in the good news."
>
> —Mark 1:14–15

In his elegant description of the spiritual dimension of his experience of aging (see chapter 8), Mel Kimble wrote about the meaning he derived from the "salvific symbols and rites" of his faith tradition, especially during the difficult days when he was recovering from malignant melanoma. Perhaps because he was writing in a secular publication, he did not name the faith tradition that had "shaped and altered [his] life at all levels." In this chapter, we reflect on that faith tradition—Christianity—and the perspectives it offers on time and aging. Unlike Mel Kimble, we are neither ordained nor educated in theology. However, as women who share his Christian faith, we have knelt with him at the communion rail, and, through our own work, study, and life experiences, we have come to appreciate how the narratives, symbols, and rituals of this faith give meaning to time. We approach this task with humility because we understand that Christianity has many forms and faces; as White, middle-class, middle-aged women who usually identify ourselves as a Congregationalist-UCC (SHM) and a Catholic/Methodist (JMT), we cannot possibly speak for all of them.

Mel Kimble stated in his essay that with the passing of years, he was learning the difference between the measured, linear *chronos* and the meaning-filled time of *kairos*. Of the two transliterated Greek words, *chronos* is most familiar to us, especially with the proliferation of multiple ways of parsing time technologically, intellectually, and experientially. *Kairos* is the Greek word used in the Gospels and the Pauline letters to refer to the fulfillment of time as, for example, expressed in the quote from Mark at the beginning of this essay. *Kairos* has multiple meanings and expressions in Christianity that refer both to the individual and to the work of the faith community. Adding to the complexity and mystery of these ways of speaking about time, there is no dichotomy between *chronos* and *kairos*. People do not escape from *chronos* time when they embrace the promise of the fulfillment of time by identifying with Jesus's call to love God and other persons, and in so doing, "stop" time experientially. Mystical experiences and self-transcending acts of love for others occur when the sun is at a certain position in the sky and the earth is in a particular point in its rotation around the sun.

Our effort to address the relation between aging and Christian meanings of time begins with a more detailed consideration of *kairos* in terms of its theological, personal, and collective meanings for aging persons. We turn next to a comparison of *chronos* and *kairos* in the lived experience of contemporary middle-aged and older adults. Finally, we move from a psychosocial perspective on Christian beliefs about time and aging to an ecclesiological discussion that focuses on implications for Christian faith communities seeking to support *kairos* experiences in the lives of elders and to speak prophetically to a society that often views aging strictly from the perspective of *chronos*.

MEANINGS OF *KAIROS*

Theological Perspectives

In the most general sense, *kairos* refers to time that is replete with meaning. According to the Christian scriptures, Jesus taught that meaningful time is already here, that the realm of God is at hand—existing in the present time—when people accept his promise of grace and forgiveness and respond with acts of love. Paradoxically, he also pointed to the coming of the fullness of God's realm in the future, emphasizing equally its "not-yet-ness."

Christianity is both a historical religion and an eschatological religion. It is historical in that it claims that God's actions occur within human history. From the covenant made with Abraham and the giving of the Law as witnessed in the Hebrew Testament to the birth, death, and resurrection of Jesus Christ, Christians believe that God's love for humanity has been expressed directly in the lives of human beings bound by time in the regular rising and setting of the sun and the revolutions of the earth around the sun.

The eschatological aspect of Christianity looks to the future when, as promised by Jesus, human history as we know it—with all its acts of injustice and cruelty—ends, and God's rule of love triumphs in all human hearts (Russell, 1966). The *eschaton,* or final day, is doubly expressed in human life. For individual believers, it means, in Mel Kimble's words, the "ultimate destiny," when in death they become united with the eternal. For humanity stretching out unknown numbers of generations in the future, the *eschaton* will arrive when all persons love God with heart, mind, and soul and love others as they love themselves. Even though to a skeptical world it may appear that such a day will never arrive—that time can never be fulfilled—Christian hope rests in the promise that humans can repent and reject their former ways of injustice and cruelty and live into the future according to the model set by Jesus. The notion of fulfilled time, or *kairos,* describes a present moment that includes both past and future and provides a stark contrast to the neutrality of *chronos.*

Roman Catholic theologian David Tracy observed that this distinction between *kairos* and *chronos* has important implications for older persons, stating that the naïve view of *chronos* creates both intellectual and existential problems in addressing the aging process.

> This 'everyday' model of time can really provide no legitimate human meaning to the process of aging but only to any given and really fictitious moment in the process. [It] cannot illuminate how either the past or the future can function meaningfully for any present moment since every moment is not merely distinguished but radically separated from prior and successive moments. (Tracy, 1975, p. 123)

Writing about aging and meaning in the Christian tradition, ethicist Stephen Post employed Augustinian language and stated that older people can find meaning "from a retrospective critique of the pride, sloth, avarice, and sensuality of earlier years" (1992, p. 138). In the present moment, Christians find meaning "through faith in the continuing reality of a merciful and just God, through hope in everlasting life, through acts of authentic other-regarding love, and through a continued interior search for the peaceful presence of God within the soul" (p. 131).

Experiential Dimensions of *Kairos*

In her study of the sources of meaning in late life, *The Ageless Self,* Sharon Kaufman (1986) validates these perspectives. Instead of succumbing to a mechanistic view of development as merely the accumulation of years defined according to *chronos*, Kaufman perceives aging as "continual creation of the self through the ongoing interpretation of past experience, structural factors, values, and current context" (p. 151). She cites the case of Ben, one of her interviewees, who when asked if he felt his age, 74, responded that he did not identify with his chronological age, and that he felt the same as he did when much younger. Ben's primary value in his earlier years was his religious affiliation; it alone continued to give his life meaning in providing him with personal history, sustenance for the present, and hope for the future. Ben stated:

> The older I get, and the less I'm able to do for people, the less use I'll be to them. I'll be narrowed down to the time when I will be

alone and helpless except for whatever visitors choose to come, which I know won't be very many. So, if I didn't have that final resource (religion), life would look very bleak to me. . . . I don't see how people can get along, why they aren't driven to great sadness by the fact that people are going to desert them. . . . I would call on my religious aids, on the parish priest, and I would expect him to reinforce my hopes about the next life. (p. 157)

From her in-depth interviews of elders, Kaufman learned that the development of personal identity is a continuous process of experiencing events in a cultural context, which then requires the person to reflect on these experiences to integrate them into the present life through "continuous restructuring" (p. 150). This process of continuous restructuring "allows individuals to maintain a feeling of unity about themselves and a sense of connection with the parts of their pasts they consider relevant to who they are at present" (p. 150) and who they expect or wish to become in the future, even if that future exists after death.

Not all of the persons interviewed by Kaufman resembled Ben in terms of having religion occupy—as William James famously stated—"the hot place in a man's consciousness, the group of ideas to which he devotes himself, and from which he works, . . . *the habitual center of his personal energy* (1902/1961, p. 165). The continuous restructuring process of which Kaufman wrote may occur strictly as a psychological response to developmental contingencies with no reference to the sacred. On the other hand, for some individuals, this process occurs within the context of religious beliefs and spiritual awareness. For example, Cheryl Learn's phenomenological study of older women's spirituality revealed that "re-creating the self" is an important component of spiritual growth. Learn identified two aspects of this process of re-creating the self that served spiritual development: integrating the past and cultivating the present (Learn, 1996, p. 85). However, Learn did not connect her descriptions of spirituality to any specific religious beliefs. If she had, she might have observed that for Christians, hopeful anticipation of the future is an essential component in the creation of a meaningful sense of time.

When Mel Kimble learned that he had malignant melanoma, he reexamined the "mosaic of meanings" in his life. The mosaic included the recall of personal experiences of the past as well as his trust in God's presence as he faced the "uncertain and shadowy future." This sense of trust and hope in the future, despite the contingencies of human life, emerged from his Christian perspective on time as *kairos.* During the long months of his recovery, Mel Kimble "[made] the most of the time (*kairos*)" (Colossians 4:5) and lived in grateful response to God's grace.

To make the most of the time (or to "redeem" the time, as the King James Version has it) means to devote oneself to loving God and other persons—to draw the promised realm of God into the present. Whether experiencing a life crisis like Mel Kimble's cancer or simply life's ordinariness, the conscious process of viewing time as *kairos*—time with spiritual meanings—can shape the ways persons love God, other persons, and themselves. For example, writing in a popular magazine, *Spirituality & Health,* Mary Ann Brussat (2000) described how one day she was riding the train and observed an elderly couple struggling to remove their luggage from the overhead rack. Instead of rushing ahead to leave the train, she offered assistance and said to them "I'm in no hurry." Brussat reminds us that this simple phrase can become a significant spiritual practice, for it is not only a way of showing love to others, but it is also an act of humility in that one does not set oneself apart from others. Saying "I'm in no hurry" is a way of "making the most of the time" we have in this life.

Kairos and Collective Action

In the twentieth century, some theologians, church leaders, and laity came to view *kairos* in a larger sense, beyond the domain of believers' choices to accept grace and fulfill the promises and challenges of the Gospel individually. An early expression of this sense of *kairos* as calling for collective action came from Germany in 1934, when theologian Karl Barth led a group of Christians in the preparation of "The Barmen Declaration." This document asserted that Christian faith and hope lay in the Word of God and not in the Nazi Party. In that *kairos* moment, Barth and his colleagues clearly defined the crisis and called on the faithful to resist the evil. In the 1970s and 1980s, expressions of this interpretation of *kairos* came through the liberation theology associated primarily with the efforts of Roman

Catholic priests, nuns, and laypeople working in Central and South America to enable poor, indigenous people to resist the oppression of wealthy landowners and corrupt governments.

Liberation theology proclaims a sense of urgency about the present historical moment and the possibilities for collective action to bring justice and mercy to a hurting world. Writing about *kairos* in this sense, Robert McAfee Brown stated that although Christians have a dismal, 2000-year-old history of disagreeing about just about every significant aspect of human life, sometimes the need for action is so stark, so dramatic, that "the privilege of amiable disagreement must be superseded by clear-cut decisions" (1990, p. 7). *Kairos Documents* written in the 1980s by groups of Christians in South Africa, Korea, the Phillippines, Namibia, El Salvador, Guatemala, and Nicaragua spoke plainly and powerfully about the need to overturn the repressive status quo in these and other countries. Liberation from the evil regime of apartheid did come to South Africa, a result in part of the resistance of Christians (although Brown would be swift to point out that, as in Hitler's Germany, some South African Christians embraced the evil). The *Kairos Documents* are grounded in the clear and unequivocal teachings of Jesus about the poor; they name the sources of oppression in colonialism, imperialism, and civil war; they warn of continued suffering unless the moment is seized for change; and they joyously declare the bold hope of Christians for the realm of God to move closer to our times.

But what does the poverty of peasants in Chiapas or the suffering of the people of war ravaged Sierra Leone have to do with the question of meaning, time, and aging? We suggest that the *kairos* moment of urgency can come veiled in wealth as well as in poverty, in relative peacefulness as well as in war. Prosperity and peace may make the urgency of the moment more difficult to apprehend, but nevertheless one can part the veil and discern that this time of growing awareness of increasing numbers of older persons invites reappraisal of the ways persons have become captive to *chronos,* fearful about their own aging, and blind to the needs of older persons in their communities. Examination of the implications of the "longevity revolution" is one way of collectively "making the most of the time," which currently raises so many moral and spiritual challenges for adults of all ages.

Although many older Americans are fairly comfortable in a financial sense, still poverty oppresses many other old people, particularly racial and ethnic minorities, and especially women in these groups. Even among wealthy elders, one can find extreme despair and loneliness. Jesus repeatedly showed how God is on the side of the poor and the persecuted. In our times, this would include the old woman moaning in a filthy nursing home bed and the homeless old man contemplating suicide. And although Jesus clearly proclaimed the responsibilities of the rich, nonetheless, he would undoubtedly feel compassion for the wealthy widow who lacks nothing in her life except meaning because she cannot locate meaning in an aged and frail body that contradicts cultural norms of beauty. Jesus would also have a message of compassion and hope for the selfish old man who has plenty of money but, with no sense of meaning in his life, daily dilutes his despair with alcohol.

Many religious congregations (including Jewish and other faith traditions) have begun to respond to this *kairos* moment of an aging society. They provide numerous services to older persons, give support to caregivers, and teach the young to not fear aging and the old. What has generally been missing, however, has been concerted, cooperative action to change the social attitudes and public policies that exacerbate the suffering of older persons. Robert McAfee Brown would argue that many of these congregations have succumbed to "the middle class luxury of feeling immobilized by complexity" (1990, p. 12). Granted, effecting social and political change is enormously complex. However, "if the Church is truly to be an agent of God's grace, if it is to proclaim the good news of God's unconditional love and manifest itself as a caring community, then it must join together with all persons of good will to advocate justice for the elderly by means of just laws justly enforced" (Heinecken, 1981, p. 88).

Before the *kairos* potential in this historical moment of an aging society can be realized, Christian belief proclaims that first there must be repentance as shown in the quote from Mark. What sin must be confessed? The *Kairos Documents* named idolatry as the major locus of sin—the worship of false gods—"from imperialism and colonialism to racism and the love of money, the last of which becomes a pervasive idol clothing itself in many forms" (Brown, 1990, p. 12). In connection with the themes of this paper, we next examine the idolatries of *chronos* as experienced by middle-aged and older persons. As we explain, often these idolatries are connected to the worship of wealth, as evidenced in the phrase "time is money." Wealth can be broadly understood to include not only money and possessions, but also the hoarded accumulation of status and power, beauty and fitness, and even knowledge and expertise.

CHRONOS AND *KAIROS* IN MIDDLE AND LATE ADULTHOOD

The Challenges of Midlife

It is almost a cliché these days to talk about how middle-aged people feel oppressed by their schedules. But how can an oppressor also be the object of veneration, of idolatry? For some persons, complaints about life "in the fast lane" support a self-image of productivity and importance. These are the individuals who boast of rarely taking a vacation and of always being "connected." The "24/7" life of the early twenty-first century, in which the world marketplace operates 24 hours a day, 7 days a week, has become identified not only with stress and sleep deprivation, but also with the rapid accumulation of great wealth and status. We live in a society that cannot tolerate the psychophysical feeling of boredom or "down-time," so we respond by engaging in increasingly stimulating entertainment (e.g., extreme sports) and by extending and intensifying work hours and increasing output. Thus, while many persons feel oppressed by *chronos,* they also embrace their oppression because of the great material rewards they gain from it and the physiological sensation of excitement. References to the old story of Mephistopheles' sale of his soul are absent from the business pages, but nonetheless, the image remains powerful as people sacrifice their health, relationships, and spiritual well-being to the idol of time. This is a *chronos* in which each moment is filled and "multi-tasked"; it is not a *kairos* that is fulfilled in terms of commitment to love and justice for all persons.

Theologian Thomas Oden once identified what he called "idolatrous anxiety" (1969, p. 181) in a book on the structure of human awareness of time and being. This anxiety prevents people from living into the future with trust in God. One can hear strains of "idolatrous anxiety" in the plaints of persons who feel entrapped by their schedules and helpless to make changes in life priorities. Given its source in hard work and material success, two virtues of our times, combined with the addiction to "adrenaline rush," some persons may be *unwilling* to make significant changes in their lives to reduce anxiety rather than *unable* to do so.

In one of his most comforting, often cited, and equally often ignored sayings, Jesus preached that people should not worry about tomorrow, what they would eat, drink, and wear, but rather they should trust God who loves them and in gratitude for that love, strive to imitate it (Matthew 6:25–34). This view of living in the fullness of the present is not the same as defending against anxiety by living in a frenzy of narcissistic self-indulgence. Psychologist of religion Paul Pruyser once described the latter as "thoughtless addiction to the present produced by infantile pleasure-seeking" (1968, p. 249) and stated that it results from allegiance to *chronos* in which each moment is disconnected from every other moment. The individual who lives like this feels no responsibility or accountability for either the past or the future. In a paper written the year before he died, Pruyser returned to this theme in reflections on ways of maintaining hope in adversity. He noted that a healthy sense of time would affirm St. Augustine's statement about the "three presents: 'a present of things past, a present of things present, and a present of things future' " (Pruyser, 1987, p. 469). This healthy approach to time produces the kind of mature hope that enables persons "to approach reality as something-in-formation, something-in-process" (p. 469). In other words, it is a way of living in terms of *kairos*, not *chronos.*

In the proliferation of books and programs aimed at helping overworked, overscheduled middle aged persons reduce and regulate stress, some are beginning to suggest the importance of paying attention to spiritual matters. Although sometimes this spirituality seems to serve narcissistic ends ("how can my spirituality make me feel better?") and reinforce the idolatry of *chronos* ("the 60-second spiritual workout"), nevertheless there is a growing desire among many persons to approach issues of spiritual practice and religious faith with seriousness and humility and without expectations of a "quick fix" (see examples in chapters 9 and 10).

Although the literature on stress clearly associates it with increased risk of mortality from problems ranging from cardiovascular disease to immune system dysfunction, ironically, the existential dread of death is sometimes an unconscious motivator of the very behaviors that increase the risk of mortality. People defend themselves against this dread by denying death. Sometimes denial takes the form of idolizing *chronos* by filling up every moment in every day with activity; sometimes the denial comes in the guise of pursuit of the spiritual stress relievers. In Christian terms, however, the freedom of *kairos* means liberation from the anxiety about death that produces this denial. As Mel Kimble stated, the personal experience of *kairos* points to his "ultimate destiny." This "ultimate destiny" has been variously described through Christianity's history and even today there is considerable disagreement among believers about the "afterlife." Although some Christians maintain very literal understandings of life eternal, others assert the hope of St. Paul: "Now I know only in part; then I will know fully, even as I have been fully known" (I Corinthians 13:12). The conviction that drove away the dread of death for Paul was that God, who had been present with him at his birth, would be present with him at the hour of his death.

The Challenges of Later Life

Although older persons are generally thought to have less anxiety about death than middle-aged persons, this assumption may be one of those "accepted truths" in gerontology that with closer scrutiny, turns out to be very complex, reflecting the statistical blurring of individual differences. In their book reporting on interviews with the elderly parents of children enrolled in the Berkeley Guidance Study, Erikson, Erikson, and Kivnick (1986) detailed a number of conversations in which older adults spoke frankly about their sense of a foreshortened future. Some admitted fears about death and what might lie on the other side; others focused their concerns on the possibility of suffering in dying. Still others expressed no worry at all about the future and impending death. The authors did not note whether there were religious differences among these persons, and empirical research on the relation between religiosity and death anxiety has yielded mixed results (Thorson, 1998).

Just as older persons are not immune to anxieties about death, they are also not immune to the tangles of time that ensnare the middle-aged. Again, it is almost a cliché for retired persons to assert proudly that they "have never been busier." Retirement offers older adults the gift of liberation from overscheduled lives, and yet some persons have so embraced cultural ideals linking productivity and human value that they cannot give up their idol. Christianity bears some responsibility for these attitudes for through the centuries, church leaders have warned that "idle hands are the work of the devil." According to the sociologist, Max Weber (1930), this attitude became institutionalized in the West as the Protestant view of the obligations of this world increasingly supported the capitalist economic structure of Europe. Because of the waning respect for old age since the industrial revolution (Cole, 1992), it is not surprising that older adults—particularly those in the "young-old" category— persist in attaching value to their lives through their productivity and use of time.

We offer this critique with caution, recognizing that persons' interpretations of how they "use" and "spend" time are subjective. What we might view as a defense against mortality through overscheduled lives that have no space for spiritual reflection, others might defend as living the Gospel in service to others. In Christianity, even the oldest person is required to love God and the neighbor. Whether one is worshipping *chronos* through overwork or imitating Christ through sacrificial love of others may finally be discerned only by that individual and God.

Any discussion of time, activity, and old age must recognize that not all older persons control their own schedules by living independently. Rabbi Dayle Friedman has written eloquently about the burden of time experienced in the nursing home, where life revolves around the *chronos* imposed by the structure and needs of the organization. Regardless of age, persons have the psychological need to look forward to small pleasures. Experience of the present moment is enhanced if some future source of enjoyment can be anticipated. But, for many nursing home residents, one day is like the next and this monotony of time paralyzes the soul (Friedman, 1995). However, as Friedman notes in her description of the ways the religious observances of Judaism can meaningfully order time in institutions, religious practices and beliefs can offer even the frailest nursing home resident a sense of fulfilled time, of *kairos*. Carefully designed worship services that are sensitive to the needs of residents, along with other forms of religious outreach like the encouragement of prayer, can bring a new meaning to time in the nursing home.

In its celebration of the liturgical year, Christianity combines *chronos* with *kairos* and provides the adult living in the nursing home with the promise of "something new" all humans need. J. Roy Stiles, a Catholic pastor in Louisville, Kentucky, calls nursing home residents "Advent People," those who are waiting for their birth into full union with Christ at death. Instead of a place to while away the time in boredom and discomfort until the end of life, when perceived in this way the nursing home becomes a place of active preparation offering time to look forward with the most intense expectation. All the trappings of *chronos* time are stripped away, and the nursing home becomes akin to a monastery. However, for nursing home residents to realize the spiritual potentials in their predicaments, persons in the religious community outside the nursing home must become committed to meeting the pastoral and spiritual needs of institutionalized elders, including those with dementia.

INSTITUTIONAL RESPONSES TO THE PROBLEM OF TIME IN MIDDLE AND LATER LIFE

Spiritual Formation

Nursing homes rarely offer spiritual formation programs, and often in local congregations such programs are oriented toward adolescents and young adults. The older adults of the congregation may instead become the volunteer force in the kitchen, office, and grounds, with less and less spiritual influence, primarily because "a good church" is often thought to be one with children and young families. Churches need to recognize their own corporate sin of abusing older persons' willingness to work long hours in support of institutional programs. Formerly, women of all ages were the core of church volunteers; today, with the majority of younger women in the work force, unable to attend to congregational needs, both male and female elders are filling in the gap. Thus, elders often do the more physical and administrative "hidden" work while their life-learned wisdom and spiritual expertise goes largely untapped and unnurtured.

We believe it is the responsibility of churches not only to warn of the dangers older people risk in not paying attention to the way they experience time, but also to teach elders how to reflect on their experiences and incorporate them into their understanding of the meaning and spiritual significance of their lives. Formal programs of life review can be added to adult education offerings and spiritual formation programs to facilitate such reflection. Encouragement of meditative and contemplative prayer and the teaching of these practices will provide people of all ages the opportunity to experience *kairos.*

Recovery of Sabbath

The growing feeling that something important is missing from their lives has led some persons to reexamine the meaning of Sabbath. Among Christians, both Catholic and Protestant, there is an expressed longing for the ways that celebration of the Sabbath enables an individual to recover a sense of *kairos,* and to replace material pursuits with spiritual ones, if only for a day. In these times, so strictly ordered by the clock and calendar, Christians are looking to the practices of Judaism to see how they, too, might set aside time to visit what Rabbi Abraham Joshua Heschel (1997) called the "island of stillness":

> In the tempestuous ocean of time and toil there are islands of stillness where man may enter a harbor and reclaim his dignity.
> The island is the seventh day, the Sabbath, a day of detachment from things, instruments and practical affairs as well as of attachment to the spirit. (p. 35)

Like the books on spirituality and health with which they share shelf-space in bookstores, recently published books on Sabbath for Christians vary in quality, with some treating Sabbath observance as just another therapeutic tool in the armamentarium of stress-reducers. Some persons wish to recover Sabbath on an individual basis, sensing the need for spiritual focus but at the same time, they may feel alienated from the religious institutions that provide Sabbath ritual. Many Christian congregations are responding to the longing for the "island of stillness" by welcoming and educating those who know little about the liturgy of Sunday services and even less about the theology that stands behind the liturgy.

Why do people need what the old hymns call "Sabbath rest"? Heschel's metaphor of respite from the "tempestuous ocean of time and toil" is clearly one reason. Respite can be obtained in a number of ways by eliminating the activities that consume time and energy in the rest of the week—working, using the computer, shopping—and making time for meditation, being with friends and family, and enjoying the beauty of this world. When Sabbath includes the ritual of corporate worship, an even broader redefinition of time occurs. Barbara Myerhoff echoed this idea in her reflections on the meaning and significance of religious rituals. She wrote, "ritual alters our ordinary sense of time, repudiating meaningless change and discontinuity by emphasizing regularity, precedent, and order" (1984, p. 324). Even though *chronos* is always a part of life, and even guides certain religious practices such as "praying the hours" or moving through the liturgical calendar, nevertheless, ritual provides a portal into the realm of *kairos.*

The sacramentality of Catholicism, especially the Eucharist celebrated in the Mass, offers the faithful an entry point into sacred time. Every time they gather, believers "re-create, re-present, and re-enact" the last meal that Jesus shared with his disciples (Cunningham, 1985, p. 36). When they do this, they transcend clock-time and become ritually connected with all believers before them who have shared words and acts of the sacrament. Catholicism, says Cunningham, "has many eyes: It looks back in time to assess its fidelity to the things which have been handed to it, i.e., its tradition; it looks beyond time to the eternal present which is God; it looks to the future from its own present for the promised Kingdom" (p. 38).

Within Protestantism, one finds considerable variability in terms of how often the sacrament of Holy Communion is celebrated and how the ritual is interpreted. Today, even as a number of mainline Protestant denominations seek to recover the holiness of Sabbath, some churches that traditionally had focused more on interpretation of the Word (e.g., in sermons) are beginning to devote more attention to sacrament and liturgy. Other Protestant denominations, like the Lutheran Church to which Mel Kimble has belonged all his life, have always retained the Eucharist as central to worship.

Besides offering the opportunity to step away from the daily demands of *chronos*, regular worship in Christian churches orients believers within the liturgical year, as mentioned earlier with regard to the nursing home experience. The year begins with the season of Advent, when the faithful assess their world's desperate needs for salvation and await the celebration of the incarnation. Following the season of Christmas comes the time of Lent, a period of self-examination and sometimes, of sacrifice. After the grief over the crucifixion and the joy of the resurrection at Eastertide, Christians celebrate the season of Pentecost in memory and celebration of the way God's spirit has drawn believers together in the church since apostolic times. This cycle of seasons has repeated for two millennia in Christianity.

As aging people worship on a regular basis, they may increasingly reflect on their lives within the context of the liturgical year. For example, although people are always a year older with the coming of each Christmas and Easter season, nonetheless the circularity of the liturgical year sheds a different light on time. By hearing the words of scripture announcing the birth of Jesus or the empty tomb year after year, Christians are called to evaluate their lives not in a linear way according to how much they have gained (or lost) with the years, but in a devotional way by contemplating how close they have moved to living the commandment to love God and others. This yearly activity of reassessment enables Christians to "continuously restructure" their understanding of life experiences and thus promotes further spiritual development.

Ideally, in worship persons create a community where age, race, gender, class, sexual orientation, and all the other identifiers that separate and divide them in the secular world no longer matter. Of course, this is not an ideal world, and sadly, many who claim to be Christian still find unloving ways to exclude others. Nevertheless, on occasion we have witnessed joyful and reverent worship that unites feeble old people holding canes and oxygen tanks with pierced and tattooed young people; African Americans shouting alleluia with prim White matrons in hats; wealthy businessmen in expensive suits with homeless men in rags. In those *kairos* moments, the "body of Christ" becomes vibrantly real.

Naming the Idols

In addition to educating people of all ages about spiritual formation and the practice of Sabbath, Christian congregations need also to examine the social attitudes and public policies that support the idolization of *chronos*. This is the part of Christian witness that often makes believers and nonbelievers most uncomfortable, for it extends the witness of the Church beyond institutional walls. We understand the controversy generated by the writings of liberation theologians who have insisted that Christians have a responsibility to name the sin that corrupts society and prayerfully seek God's direction in bringing about change. Unfortunately, but understandably, many Christians who marched for peace and civil rights in the twentieth century developed distaste for political action when they witnessed the "culture wars" produced by religious fundamentalists asserting their positions on abortion, the theory of evolution, and other flash-point issues. Nevertheless, we suggest that now may be the time for witnessing to the social and political implications of the Christian perspective on the meaning of time and aging. We have already discussed in an earlier section how Christians are called to work to bring the rule of God to fruition through acts of justice and mercy, and we have suggested that in our times, this includes promoting well-being among all old persons. Regarding the moral implications of the discussion of time and aging, we now identify three significant issues.

The first concerns the idolatry of *chronos* in terms of Americans' work lives that leave little room for enjoyment of family, friends, and for spiritual development. Sociologist Arlie Hochschild has eloquently documented this problem in two significant books. In the first, *The Second Shift* (1989), she examined the demands on women, particularly mothers, who work full time and return home to another 8 hours of child care and housework, often with little assistance from their husbands. A more recent book, *The Time Bind* (1997) identified the seductions of work, and argued that many individuals experience the structure of work as preferable to the emotional uncertainties pervading family life. Therefore, they may willingly work long hours, especially when that work is amply compensated. In addition to studies like these, many public policy analysts have noted other characteristics of American work life that sap the spirit, exhaust people physically, and leave them alienated from important relationships. These include lack of support for family leave when children are born or adopted or when elders need care, forced overtime, and limited vacation time.

What would happen if Christians refused to support the social structures and political policies that prevent people from taking Sabbath time and living fully in adulthood? What would happen if they declared the spiritual costs of materialism? What would happen if religious people stood up to the emerging "24/7" ethos of cyberculture and condemned its theft of time for spiritual practices as well as its blindness to the fact that many people of the world still struggle for the basics of life and have no need for computers? What would happen if Christians could agree on tactics to promote social and political changes that would support the creation of more meaningful time for young as well as middle-aged and older persons regardless of their economic circumstances?

A second moral problem shaped by contemporary views of time is ageism itself. Negative stereotypes about older people persist, and even though one sees more older faces in the media, they tend to be White, middle-class, and healthy. Cosmetic surgery is a booming business as more middle aged and older people become persuaded that youthful appearance must be obtained regardless of the costs. Older women continue to be the object of social disparagement, especially in regard to appearance. Thus many more women than men experience aging as "a veritable trauma" (Woodward, 1999, p. xix). Wealthy women suffer from this trauma because they have the time and resources to support the pursuit of the accoutrements of youth. Poor women experience the trauma of aging in inadequate housing and with an accumulation of chronic health problems exacerbated by lack of access to good medical care. Often their families have been ravaged by poverty, drugs, crime, and other social ills, leaving them with few resources but sometimes with the added obligation to care for grandchildren and even great-grandchildren.

Could it be that now is the time—a *kairos* moment—for prayerful reflection about ageism and its implications for persons of all ages, classes, and races? Is this the time to declare that human value has nothing to do with age and transcends mere appearance and social circumstances? What would happen if we named the idols and then sought to replace them with humble obedience the call to love others and seek justice for all?

This leads to the third moral problem raised by examining time and aging from a Christian ethical perspective: life extension. Stephen Post speaks eloquently about this and notes that the Christian acceptance of life as a "dialectic of decline and redemption" (1992, p. 144) has both individual and social implications. Christians accept that death is part of life and that expensive life-prolonging practices may be refused when persons and their families recognize that they will not restore quality to life. Moreover, Post writes that Christian commitment to love and justice requires the examination of how such practices affect the social order by reducing the resources needed to promote health and well-being generally. He comments on "idolatrous medical progress that is simultaneously social regress" and asks, "How many urban ghettos are a virtual wasteland except for the tower of some awesome hospital structure through which the homeless and oppressed will never pass?" (p. 144).

Do Christians in this time of prosperity have the moral will and courage to declare their belief that the mortal body need not be kept alive at tremendous costs to others? Is this an issue about which congregations might engage in prayerful study followed by witness to political and corporate power structures?

CONCLUSION

Augustine questioned, "What is time then? If nobody asks me, I know: but if I were desirous to explain it to one that should ask me, plainly I know not" (cited in Melloh, 1990, p. 773). Russell (1966) has stated, "there is no 'official' theory of time, defined in creeds or universally agreed upon by Christians" (p. 59). There is also no "theology of aging" set aside from basic Christian theological affirmations (Heinecken, 1981). Nevertheless, examination of fundamental Christian beliefs and practices points toward a countercultural view of time and aging. Time is not merely a series of meaningless, disconnected moments, but rather it can be filled with the memory of God's redeeming work in Jesus's birth, death, and resurrection and anticipation of the ultimate realization of his teachings about love of God and love of others. The acceptance of time as *kairos* can provide individuals with a new sense of meaning about life and aging, and it can provide their religious institutions with a focus for moral action.

In the last section of this essay, we posed a number of difficult and controversial questions. We recognize that many religious persons and congregations understand the ethical implications of the idolatry of *chronos* and have identified the urgent issues raised here. They are studying how to live their faith more fully and they are expressing this through political and social action within their communities.

Many persons engaged in these activities are older individuals who understand their service as a fundamental expression of their religious faith. Even those whose lives are extremely constrained by suffering often continue to "[make] the most of the time" through acts of devotion in loving God and other persons. Their embrace of *kairos* should be more widely noted and studied for they are indeed exemplars of spiritual development. We have no doubt that these elders can be found not only among Christians, but also among Jews, Buddhists, Moslems, Hindus, and so forth. Although we have examined the distinction between *chronos* and *kairos* from a Christian perspective, this is an approach to thinking about time that persons from other faith traditions also encounter in various forms. Studies of how persons of different religious faiths understand time could provide much-needed insights into alternative models of aging and inspire collective action to "redeem the time" and hasten the realization of the way of love for all persons—young and old.

REFERENCES

Brown, R. M. (Ed.). (1990). *Kairos: Three prophetic challenges to the church.* Grand Rapids, MI: William B. Eerdmans.

Brussat, M. A. (2000, Summer). No hurries: Effortless acts of a spiritual life. *Spirituality & Health,* 18.

Cole, T. R. (1992). *The journey of life: A cultural history of aging in America.* New York: Cambridge University Press.

Cunningham, L. S. (1985). *The Catholic experience: Space, time, silence, prayer, sacraments, story, persons, catholicity, community, and expectations.* New York: Crossroad.

Erikson, E. H., Erikson, J. M., & Kivnick, H. Q. (1986). *Vital involvement in old age: The experience of old age in our time.* New York: Norton.

Friedman, D. A. (1995). Spiritual challenges of nursing home life. In M. A. Kimble, S. H. McFadden, J. W. Ellor, & J. J. Seeber (Eds.), *Aging, spirituality, and religion: A handbook* (pp. 362–373). Minneapolis: Fortress.

Heinecken, M. J. (1981). Christian theology and aging: Basic affirmations. In W. M. Clements (Ed.), *Ministry with the aging* (pp. 76–90). San Francisco: Harper & Row.

Heschel, A. J. (1997). *I asked for wonder: A spiritual anthology.* New York: Crossroad.

Hochschild, A. R. (1989). *The second shift: Working parents and the revolution at home.* New York: Viking.

Hochschild, A. R. (1997). *The time bind: When work becomes home and home becomes work.* New York: Metropolitan Books.

James, W. (1961). *The varieties of religious experience.* New York: Collier. (Original work published 1902)

Kaufman, S. R. (1986). *The ageless self: Sources of meaning in late life.* Madison, WI: University of Wisconsin Press.

Learn, C. D. (1996). *Older women's experience of spirituality: Crafting the quilt.* New York: Garland.

Melloh, J. A. (1990). Theology of liturgical time. In P. E. Fink (Ed.), *The new dictionary of sacramental workship* (p. 773). Collegeville, MN: Liturgical Press.

Myerhoff, B. (1984). Rites and signs of ripening: The intertwining of ritual, time, and growing older. In D. I. Kertzer & J. Keith (Eds.), *Age and anthropological theory* (pp. 305–330). Ithaca, NY: Cornell University Press.

Oden, T. (1969). *The structure of awareness.* Nashville, TN: Abingdon Press.

Post, S. G. (1992). Aging and meaning: The Christian tradition. In T. R. Cole, D. D. Van Tassel, & R. Kastenbaum (Eds.), *Handbook of humanities and aging.* New York: Springer.

Pruyser, P. W. (1968). *A dynamic psychology of religion.* New York: Harper & Row.

Pruyser, P. W. (1987). Maintaining hope in adversity. *Bulletin of the Menninger Clinic, 51,* 463–474.

Russell, J. L. (1966). Time in Christian thought. In J. T. Fraser (Ed.), *The voices of time: A cooperative survey of man's views of time as expressed by the sciences and the humanities* (pp. 59–76). New York: George Braziller.

Thorson, J. A. (1998). Religion and anxiety: Which anxiety? Which religion? In H. G. Koenig (Ed.), *Handbook of religion and mental health* (pp. 147–160). San Diego: Academic Press.

Tracy, D. (1975). Eschatological perspectives on aging. *Pastoral Psychology, 24,* 119–134.

Weber, M. (1930). *The Protestant ethic and the spirit of capitalism* (T. Parsons, trans.). New York: Scribner.

Woodward, K. (1999). Introduction. In K. Woodward (Ed.), *Figuring age: Women, bodies, generations* (pp. ix–xxix). Bloomington: Indiana University Press.

Index

ROBERT C. ATCHLEY is Professor and Chair of the Department of Gerontology at Naropa University in Boulder, CO. His gerontology interests include adult development, spiritual development, long-term care, public policy, work and retirement, health change and disability, and family issues. He wrote the widely used introductory gerontology text, *Social Forces and Aging* and was the founding editor of the journal *Contemporary Gerontology*.

SUSAN H. McFADDEN is Professor and Chair of Psychology, University of Wisconsin Oshkosh. Along with Melvin Kimble, James Ellor, and James Seeber, she founded the Center on Aging, Spirituality, and Religion, St. Paul, MN and co-edited *Aging, Spirituality and Religion: A Handbook*. She has worked for many years to raise awareness of religion, spirituality, and aging in the American Society on Aging, the Gerontological Society of America, and the American Psychological Association.